S0-BCA-641

Critical Perspectives on Canadian Theatre in English
General Editor Ric Knowles

**PLAYWRIGHTS
CANADA PRESS**

416-703-0013 • orders@playwrightscanada.com • www.playwrightscanada.com

Environmental and Site-Specific Theatre

Critical Perspectives on Canadian Theatre in English

volume eight

Critical Perspectives on Canadian Theatre in English
volume eight

Environmental and Site-Specific Theatre

Edited by Andrew Houston

Playwrights Canada Press
Toronto • Canada

Environmental and Site-Specific Theatre © Copyright 2007 Andrew Houston
The authors assert moral rights.

Playwrights Canada Press
215 Spadina Avenue, Suite 230, Toronto, Ontario CANADA M5T 2C7
416-703-0013   fax 416-408-3402
orders@playwrightscanada.com • www.playwrightscanada.com

CAUTION: The essays in this book are fully protected under the copyright laws of Canada and all other countries of The Copyright Union. No part of this book, covered by the copyright hereon, may be reproduced or used in any form or by any means—graphic, electronic or mechanical—without the prior written permission of the authors, who have the right to grant or refuse permission at the time of the request. Any request for photocopying, recording, taping or information storage and retrieval systems of
any part of this book shall be directed in writing to Access Copyright,
1 Yonge St., Suite 800, Toronto, Ontario CANADA M5E 1E5 416-868-1620.

Financial support provided by the taxpayers of Canada and Ontario through the Canada Council for the Arts and the Department of Canadian Heritage through the Book Publishing Industry Development Programme, and the Ontario Arts Council.

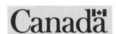 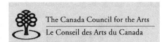

Cover image: Jin-me Yoon, between departure and arrival, 1996/1997. Partial installation view, Art Gallery of Ontario. Video projection, video montage on monitor, photographic mylar scroll, clocks with 3-D lettering, audio. Dimensions variable. Courtesy of the artist and Catriona Jeffries Gallery, Vancouver.
Production Editor/Cover Design: JLArt

Library and Archives Canada Cataloguing in Publication

Environmental and site-specific theatre / edited by Andrew Houston.

(Critical perspectives on Canadian theatre in English ; v. 8)
Includes bibliographical references.
ISBN 978-0-88754-806-2

1. Theater, Environmental--Canada. 2. Canadian drama--20th century--History and criticism. 3. Canadian drama--21st century--History and criticism.
I. Houston, Andrew, 1964- II. Series.

PN2304.2.E59 2007   792.0971   C2007-902790-3

First edition: May 2007
Printed and bound by Hignell Printing at Winnipeg, Canada.

To

Wendy, Oli, Sam,

and the home environment I too often

take for granted.

Table of Contents

General Editor's Preface

Critical Perspectives on Canadian Theatre in English sets out to make the best critical and scholarly work in the field readily available to teachers, students, and scholars of Canadian drama and theatre. In volumes organized by playwright, region, genre, theme, and cultural community, the series publishes the work of scholars and critics who have, since the so-called renaissance of Canadian theatre in the late 1960s and early 1970s, traced the coming-into-prominence of a vibrant theatrical community in English Canada.

Each volume in the series is edited and introduced by an expert in the field who has selected a representative sampling of the most important critical work on her or his subject since circa 1970, ordered chronologically according to the original dates of publication. Where appropriate, the volume editors have also commissioned new essays on their subjects. Each volume also provides a list of suggested further readings, and an introduction by the volume's editor.

It is my hope that this series, working together with complementary anthologies of plays published by Playwrights Canada Press, Talonbooks, and other Canadian drama publishers, will facilitate the teaching of Canadian drama and theatre in schools, colleges, and universities across the country for years to come. It is for this reason that the titles so far selected for the series—*Aboriginal Drama and Theatre, African-Canadian Theatre, Judith Thompson, Feminist Theatre and Performance, George F. Walker, Theatre in British Columbia, Queer Theatre, Environmental and Site Specific Theatre,* and *Space and the Geographies of Theatre*—are designed to work as companion volumes to a range of Canadian drama anthologies recently published or forthcoming from the country's major drama publishers that complement them: *Staging Coyote's Dream: An Anthology of First Nations Drama in English* (Playwrights Canada, 2003); the two volumes of *Testifyin': Contemporary African Canadian Drama* (Playwrights Canada, 2000, 2003); *Judith Thompson: Late 20ᵗʰ Century Plays* (Playwrights Canada, 2002); the various collections of plays by George F. Walker published by Talonbooks; *Playing the Pacific Province: An Anthology of British Columbia Plays, 1967-2000* (Playwrights Canada, 2001); and other projected volumes. I hope that with the combined availability of these anthologies and the volumes in this series, courses on a variety of aspects of Canadian drama and theatre will flourish in schools and universities within Canada and beyond its borders, and scholars new to the field will find accessible and comprehensive introductions to some of the field's most provocative and intriguing figures and issues.

Finally, the titles selected for *Critical Perspectives on Canadian Theatre in English* are designed to carve out both familiar and new areas of work. It is my intention that the series at once recognize the important critical heritage of scholarly work in the field and attempt to fill in its most significant gaps by highlighting important work from and about marginalized communities, work that has too often been neglected in courses on and criticism of Canadian drama and theatre. In its nationalist phase in the late 1960s and 70s, English-Canadian theatre criticism tended to neglect work by women, by First Nations peoples and people of colour, by Gay, Lesbian, Bi- or Transsexual artists, and by those working in politically, geographically, or aesthetically alternative spaces. While respecting, honouring, and representing important landmarks in Canadian postcolonial theatrical nationalism, *Critical Perspectives on Canadian Theatre in English* also sets out to serve as a corrective to its historical exclusions.

Ric Knowles

Acknowledgements

I want to thank Ric Knowles, the General Editor of the series, who has offered me a tremendous opportunity with this book, and who has extended to me a great deal of guidance and an extraordinary amount of patience. I also want to thank Wendy Philpott, who has been patient beyond comparison and supportive of this venture and others, no matter how difficult or absurd the demand upon our time together.

All of the essays and interviews included here are published with permission of the copyright holders. Chris Brookes' "Seize the Day: The Mummers' *Gros Mourn*," was first published in *Canadian Theatre Review* 37 (1983): 38–50; R. Murray Schafer's "*The Princess of the Stars*" in *Canadian Theatre Review* 47 (1986): 20–28; Nigel Hunt's "Hillar Liitoja: Chaos and Control" in *Canadian Theatre Review* 52 (1987): 45–49; David Burgess's "Schafer's *Patria Three*: The Cycle Continues" in *Canadian Theatre Review* 55 (1988): 34–42; Alan Filewod's "The Words are Too Important" in *Canadian Theatre Review* 61 (1989): 33–39; Natalie Rewa's "All News *Newhouse*" in *Canadian Theatre Review* 61 (1989): 40–42; Richard Plant's "Deconstruction of Pleasure: John Krizanc's *Tamara*, Richard Rose and the Necessary Angel Theatre Company" in *On-Stage and Off-Stage: English Canadian Drama and Discourse*, ed. Albert-Reiner Glaap and Rolf Althof (St. John's: Breakwater, 1996), 189–200; Rachael Van Fossen's "Writing for the Community Play Form" in *Canadian Theatre Review* 90 (1997): 10–14; Ric Knowles's "Environmental Theatre" in *The Theatre of Form and the Production of Meaning* (Toronto: ECW, 1999), 163–92; Kathryn Walter's "Lesbian National Parks & Services" in *PRIVATE Investigators: Undercover in Public Space*, ed. Kathryn Walter (Banff: Banff Centre Press, 1999), 45–46; Shawna Dempsey and Lorri Millan's "Field Reports from the Lesbian National Parks and Services" in *PRIVATE Investigators: Undercover in Public Space*, ed. Kathryn Walter (Banff: Banff Centre Press, 1999), 50–55; Shawna Dempsey and Lorri Millan's "Lesbian National Parks and Services and You!" in *PRIVATE Investigators: Undercover in Public Space*, ed. Kathryn Walter (Banff: Banff Centre Press, 1999), 48; Kyo Maclear's "Eyewitness Account" in *PRIVATE Investigators: Undercover in Public Space*, ed. Kathryn Walter (Banff: Banff Centre Press, 1999), 56–57; Hildegard Westerkamp's "The Local and Global 'Language' of Environmental Sound" in *Sonic Geography Imagined and Remembered*, ed. Ellen Waterman (Peterborough: Penumbra Press, 2002), 130–40; Sean Dixon's "Things I've Learned from Theatre SKAM," in *AWOL: Three Plays for Theatre SKAM* (Toronto: Coach House Books, 2002), 9–11; Jennifer Fisher's "Out and About: The Performance Art of Shawna Dempsey and Lorri Millan," (as "Shawna Dempsey and Lorri Millan: Performance Art Out and About") in *Caught in the Act: An Anthology of Performance*

Art by Canadian Women, ed. Tanya Mars and Johanna Householder (Toronto: YYZ-BOOKS, 2004), 189–97; Andrew Houston's "Deep-Mapping a Morning on 3A," in *Canadian Theatre Review* 121 (2005): 32–40; Andrew Templeton's "Sex, Cars and Shopping: Meditations on Social Disabilities," in *Canadian Theatre Review* 122 (2005): 45–49; Kathleen Irwin's "Arrivals and Departures: How Technology Redefines Site-related Performance" was presented at the Association for Canadian Theatre Research/Association de la recherche théâtrale au Canada in May, 2005, at the University of Western Ontario and is published here for the first time; bluemouth inc.'s "Please Dress Warmly and Wear Sensible Shoes" in *Canadian Theatre Review* 126 (2006): 16–22; Amiel Gladstone's "Beneath Bridges, Loading Docks and Fire Escapes: Theatre SKAM Tours *Billy Nothin'* and *Aerwacol*" in *Canadian Theatre Review* 126 (2006): 103–07; and Keren Zaiontz's "'This is not a conventional piece so all bets are off': Why bluemouth inc. Collective Delights in our Disorientation" was commissioned for this volume, and is published here for the first time.

Andrew Houston

Introduction. The *Thirdspace* of Environmental and Site-Specific Theatre

by Andrew Houston

> With faith and hard work you can bring all kinds of shit to life.
> You can step from a cookshack doorway onto a mountaintop just by saying the words and then seeming to see it.
> A human face is far more expressive than a lighting state.
> The occasional train is okay. Constant traffic noise is a bit of a grind, though.
> The back loading dock of Wonderbucks on Commercial Drive in Vancouver is a great place to do theatre. Especially when they let you open the loading dock and pile boxes in the exposed storage room in theatrical ways.
> Sean Dixon (11)

In every site-specific or environmental theatre project, the artist must spend a lot of time walking around experiencing the site; trying to gain some insight into its inhabitants, its workings, its reality, but also trying to imagine how it might possess a life not yet realized. Michel de Certeau is a useful guide for this kind of work. He thinks of walking as a sort of articulation; that is, the space offers itself as a language (the *langue*) and our wandering around it, our working it out, our imagining and even our fears and desires of what it might be, becomes a kind of articulation of this language (the *parole*). In comparing pedestrian processes to linguistic formations, de Certeau states that "[t]o walk is to lack a place. It is the indefinite process of being absent and in search of the proper" (103). The creation of site-specific and environmental theatre is akin to this act of enunciation, to be perpetually working between the absence of what we imagine the space to be and the material evidence of its proper and present uses. This is an act of artistic representation, but it is perhaps equally an act of social geography: a way of being-in-the-world and bringing to bear a social, political and historical consciousness upon our navigations through and experiences of lived space.

In *The Thirdspace: Journeys to Los Angeles and Other Real-and-Imagined Places*, geographer Edward Soja encourages us to think about space and the many concepts that compose, comprise and infuse it with meaning; encouraging a reconsideration of familiar terms such as space, place, territory, city, region, location, and environment, Soja's aim is not so much to discourage familiar ways of thinking about our environment but rather to encourage a process of questioning that may "expand the critical scope and critical sensibility of one's already established spatial or geographical imagination" (13). Soja's perspective is particularly important to this introduction to the work of environmental and site-specific theatre because similar to many of the practitioners, critical perspectives, and approaches revealed in the following pages, he understands the importance of the "spatial turn" in developing a more thorough understanding of the world. Without reducing the significance of the historical or the social, nor dimming the creative and critical imaginations that have developed around their practical and theoretical understanding, Soja's "third critical perspective, associated with an explicitly spatial imagination," has made an impact on the study of history and society in the same way that environmental and site-specific theatre approaches have broadened our perspective of spatial imagination in the theatre (14).

Soja's project begins with what he describes as an "ontological shift," or "a funda-mental change in the way we understand what the world must be like in order for us to obtain reliable knowledge of it" (14). He does this by conceiving of an "ontological trialectic" comprised of historicality, sociality, and spatiality. Soja's development of ontology to include the third dimension of spatiality is his attempt to develop a more three-dimensional understanding of being-in-the-world; or, as he states:

> The "making of geographies" is becoming as fundamental to under-standing our lives and our lifeworlds as the social production of our histories and societies. [...] Within this configuration, there are three interactive relationships that apply not only to ontology, but equally well to all other levels of knowledge formation: epistemology, theory building, empirical analysis, and praxis, the transformation of knowledge into action (14–15).

All of the environmental or site-specific practices examined in this volume can be seen to have developed from an attempt to cultivate praxis, a transformation of knowledge into action, and from this venturing forth, a position of being-in-the-world, as described by Soja. Perhaps the best examples of projects that materialize Soja's ontological trialectic are those that in various ways explicitly map the identity of a given community. Chris Brookes's "Seize the Day: The Mummers' *Gros Mourn*" and Rachael Van Fossen's "Writing for the Community Play Form" both describe the chal-lenges artists face in an attempt to inhabit the struggles, both internal and external, cross-cultural and based in socio-economic as well as historical difference, that are experienced in the very survival of a given community. The work of the Mummers Troupe is most often viewed as an example of collective creation in Canadian theatre history, and as Van Fossen's title suggests, her work is described in terms of how it ful-fills the Colway Trust community play model; yet both are included in this collection because each speaks so vividly about the environmental context of their praxis. Brookes's creation is entirely governed by the pressures of relocation felt in the community of Sally's Cove; the play offers the community a "handle" on how they may articulate their side in the dispute with the government, and Brookes is determined their work will not provide a catharsis of pent-up frustration, but instead focus the audience's energy, so that when they leave the performance they will be encouraged to win back their land from the national park. Every aspect of Van

Fossen's community play work in Saskatchewan is deeply embedded in the environment from which it emerges and in which it is performed. *Ka'ma'mo'pi cik/The Gathering* is as much about the resonant antagonism over unresolved aboriginal/colonial land disputes as it is about any form of coming together to heal differences; indeed, no performance about community in this part of Canada could happen without addressing this primary issue of the site. *A North Side Story (or two)* brings the antagonism over landownership into an urban context, addressing as it does the transformation of an inner city Regina neighbourhood, and the conflicts that ensue over cultural, generational, and socio-economic difference between neighbours.

A key insight into the use of Soja's trialectics of being as a frame of analysis comes from understanding that none of the elements of the trialectic have *a priori* privilege. That is, studying the historicality of a particular site, event, person or social group is not intrinsically any more insightful than studying its sociality or spatiality. Soja concludes, "The three terms and the complex interactions between them should be studied together as fundamental and intertwined knowledge sources, for this is what being-in-the-world is all about (15). This interdisciplinary focus is shared by all of the work discussed in this volume, but perhaps one of the best examples is found in the large-scale environmental pageantry of R. Murray Schafer's *The Princess of the Stars*, or the equally large-scale, carnivalesque *Patria Three*, as described by David Burgess in "Schafer's *Patria Three*: The Cycle Continues." R. Murray Schafer describes the pilgrimage of the audience to *The Princess of the Stars* the following way:

> And the audience? Instead of a somnolent evening in upholstery, digesting dinner or contemplating the one to follow, this work takes place before breakfast. No intermission to crash out to the bar and guzzle or slump back after a smoke. No women in pearls or slit skirts. It will be an effort to get up in the dark, drive 30 miles or more to arrive on a damp and chilly embankment, sit and wait for the ceremony to begin. And what ceremony? Dawn itself, the most neglected masterpiece of the modern world. To this we add a little adornment, trying all the time to move with the elements, aware that what can be done will be little enough in the face of it all. Here is a ceremony then, rather than a work of art. And like all true ceremonies, it cannot be adequately transported elsewhere. You can't poke it into a television screen and spin it around with anything like a quarter of a hope that something valuable might be achieved. You must feel it, let it take hold of you by all its means, only some of which have been humanly arranged. You must go there, go to the site, for it will not come to you. You must go there like a pilgrim on a deliberate journey in search of a unique experience which cannot be obtained by money or all the conveniences of modern civilization. Pilgrimage; it is an old idea; but when over five thousand people travel to a remote lake in the Rocky Mountains to see a performance of *The Princess of the Stars* it is evidently one for which there is a contemporary longing (qtd. in Schafer).

Schafer's work is famous for its ambitious scale and its ritualistic structure; in terms of its use of space, Ric Knowles's analysis ("Environmental Theatre") reminds us Schafer's *Patria Cycle* is notable for its liminal spaces: "each [setting] functions as a transition between realms, taking place at dusk, midnight, or dawn on shorelines, fairgrounds, and train stations." Schafer's interest in environmental theatre, as Knowles reports, is directly to do with creating possibilities for social actions that are not constrained by traditional theatre environments. Schafer believes that "one has three options with regard to the conventional theatre: to be sentimental about it, to be exploitative, or to leave it behind" (qtd. in Knowles). Moreover, as Burgess discovers in his interview with Schafer about *Patria Three: The Greatest Show*, his concern in this particular *Patria Cycle* is less about environmental staging and more about a social agenda, as he explains,

> *The Greatest Show* relates in particular to [...] my attempt to break down this horrible division between the professional and the amateur, the entertainer and the entertained, to find some way in which not only the actors, the musicians and the others involved in the performances, somehow in the middle between professionals and the amateurs, but also the entire audience (so called) is involved and participates (qtd. in Burgess).

Clearly Schafer's multidisciplinary performances are ritualistic in the way they manifest particular spatial and social relationships; however, as Knowles points out, concerning the third trialectical element of history, the *Patria Cycle* occupies dubious ground. Schafer's work has a tendency to obscure history in mythology and "flatten cultural difference" in a search for "the unity of all things material, spiritual, natural, and divine" (Knowles). Knowles gives Schafer full credit for innovative form, but takes him to task for some dubious, elitist content.

R. Murray Schafer possesses certain similarities to Hillar Liitoja, the founding Artistic Director of DNA Theatre, a Toronto-based company, the origins of which Nigel Hunt offers us a glimpse of in "Chaos and Control." Schafer and Liitoja have both been significantly influenced by the work of Ezra Pound (Schafer wrote a book on Pound [see Burgess] and Liitoja devoted his first nine productions to him) and both have a creative process governed by music. Liitoja's most significant, early theatrical influence is Richard Foreman, yet similar to Schafer, his scripts more resemble musical scores than plays. Liitoja was primarily attracted to the sensuality of Pound's poetry, and this experience seemed harmonious with his discoveries apprenticing with Foreman, who reinforced an instinctual approach to his work. Indeed, Liitoja's early work with DNA was an absolute affirmation of sensual impulse; as Hunt reports, on the nine productions devoted to Pound's writing, "the poems themselves would become events in a vital, sensual universe teeming with fragments of sight, sound, smell and touch" (Hunt). Hunt's article focuses primarily on *This is What Happens in Orangeville*, DNA's first highly successful production that clearly establishes Liitoja's environmental dramaturgy that at the time (1987) he considered to be a "frontal assault on our society's way of thinking in which reason is valued over instinct, and narrative over rhythm" (Hunt). Littoja's unique approach to theatrical environment is primarily focused on his interest in the audience-performer contract; in particular, he wants to subvert the audience's perception about their experience in the space; he wants nothing more than to fully stimulate the audience's senses, while delighting in their disorientation. As Hunt concludes:

> Whatever the individual reaction to Liitoja's work, it clearly provides an audience with an unusual theatrical opportunity to balance their decisions about where to sit, what to watch, and how to interpret the performance, with the compelling anti-logic of a world which defies the importance of these choices (qtd. in Hunt).

The trialectics of being in the theatrical environment of Hillar Liitoja would seem to be governed by a sensually-charged spatiality that disorients the perceptual capability of audiences to understand the performance in terms of sociality, and in this he is following a historicality that includes a lineage of radical poets, performers and sensualists.

Under the direction of Richard Rose, Necessary Angel's production of *Tamara* is environmental theatre that raises similar questions about the "social geography" created between audience and performer in Liitoja's early work with DNA Theatre. Richard Plant ("The Deconstruction of Pleasure: John Krizanc's *Tamara*, Richard Rose and the Necessary Angel Theatre Company") and Ric Knowles agree that while Rose and playwright John Krizanc's attempt to construct a "democratic theatre" where each audience member has free choice to follow each of the ten plots in the play, through stagings in various parts of the house, "to create his/her own work of art," so to speak; in practice, this impulse is deconstructed by how the form denies the audience completion of any artistic vision" (Plant). Indeed, the illusion of an environment of audience freedom is in fact a manipulated set of circumstances, a state of artistic "fascism," as Plant reminds us, "where choices are dependent upon the conventions set up by the production." Thus, while *Tamara* is challenging certain conventions of audience participation in the creation of theatre, it is simultaneously calling for a willing suspension of disbelief in a house, where the props, costumes, and staging attempt to re-create the events of the play in a manner that, as Plant suggests, is remarkably naturalistic. Knowles contributes that no matter how close the proximity of audience and performer in shared spaces throughout the house, the actors never acknowledge the audience's presence, let alone their participation, and so their role seems to be more defined as that of voyeur; which is likely closer to the social geography of fascism in Italy circa 1927 than Rose and Krizanc could have wished for. Moreover, when pushed in the direction of staging the confinement of characters with audience, as was the thematic intent in *Tamara,* perhaps the aesthetic ideals of environmental theatre are seen to be not too far off the experience of theatre hinted at in the early naturalistic manifestos of Emile Zola and August Strindberg, yet denied by the conventions of proscenium staging.

In *Newhouse,* Rose and dramaturge D.D. Kugler adapt Tirso de Molina's *Don Juan* (*The Trickster of Seville*) and Sophocles's *Oedipus Rex* into a multi-media, environmental exploration of the political structure of the Canadian government grappling with a public crisis presented by a plague that is obviously AIDS; as Kugler observes the environmental form used clearly provides an experience of the play's content:

> Thematically… we're looking for much more complex material that doesn't give simple answers, that in fact makes the complexity of real issues apparent.
>
> I think that spills over into the form. You really want to pull out of a proscenium context because it gives you a framed two-dimensional reality in a way. If you open the form out and get the audience inside the story structurally, they can see that the story spills over into their lives – that it affects them and they have an effect on it (qtd. in Plant).

In "The Words are Too Important," Alan Filewod concurs that *Newhouse* successfully removes the treatment of AIDS from the realm of personal relationships and the politics of medical treatment to the arena of public social policy, in large part due to the experience of its environmental staging in a hockey arena. In "All News *Newhouse*," Natalie Rewa comments on how the use of multiple stages, in part influenced by the allegorical arrangement of stages used to represent the body politic, and in part to simulate a certain multi-media experience of the public arena, make for an effective formal simulation of the play's content:

> The performance began with a simple presentation of opposites: at one end of the arena Newhouse's encounter with the woman at the Embassy ball in Washington; and, in the subsequent scene, at the other end, a reporter, appearing simultaneously in the flesh and on the screen, to inform the audience of the status of the crisis on Parliament Hill. […] This kind of rapid change of focus was sustained throughout the performance, but the need for the audience to re-gather round the stages where the Prime Minister was speaking lessened because they could readily watch the simultaneous broadcast.

To this, Knowles adds that the set was most clearly derived from the model of a medieval cathedral, in which early liturgical dramas were staged in a formation resembling the head of Christ (the apse for the priest), his outstretched arms (chapels on each side) representing the congregation or body/corpus of Christ, etc. He reports:

> The arena in which *Newhouse* was staged was mapped out with a platform at one end used by the prime minister (the head of government and the source of reasoned argument, as well as the play's Oedipus/ Christ figure as sacrificial victim), flanked by banks of television monitors and a small chapel: a "groin" platform at the opposite end, without screens, where Newhouse, the son of the minister of external affairs and the play's Don Juan and Trickster figure, seduced two of his victims; a central platform, also without screens, as the "heart" of the assembly, where action involving emotion took place; and two side platforms, the

"lungs," each divided lengthwise by a large screen and used as public areas, the media centre and embassy on one side, the bar and various other locations on the other.

As both Knowles and Rewa suggest, the audience play an active role in the completion of this staging of the public area as they must physically orient themselves in the "*platea*" or public spaces located around the various "*loci*" of power. The Prime Minister defines the *platea/loci* relationship strategically in that he only ever communicates to the audience through direct address; however, each audience member is free to establish his or her own spatial relationship to the Prime Minister, particularly because part of his communication is televised. The audience may be as close as they want to the staging of Newhouse's unprotected sex, for example, or they may choose to experience it from a distance, twice removed, as the effects of his actions are relayed via the press, who act as the chorus in the production, and are always televised and viewable from all around the site.

In this collection, *Newhouse* represents the best example of how environmental theatre may create an experience of Soja's trialectics of being. The many layers of historical and social resonance on the themes concerning the body politic, good governance in a time of public crisis, the private and public dimension of liberated sexuality, and so forth were all thoroughly made manifest in an arena; an environment that is as significant to Canadian identity through the sport of hockey as it is a recognized domain of political conventions, leadership campaigns, and the discourse connected to these events. This association of Canadian political history woven together with an environmental multi-media staging, replete with associations of moral lesson and the welfare of a community, make this production an exemplar of the kind of deeply felt and understood "lived space" or thirdspace that Soja envisioned in the development of the geographical imagination in his unique approach to social geography.

From Soja's thesis of the trialectics of being, he developed a second thesis, the trialectics of spatiality; this thesis was an expansion of the geographical imagination of the being-in-the-world, in order to address a series of troubling dualisms. Soja defines these dualisms the following way: "objectivity versus subjectivity, material versus mental, real versus imagined, things in space versus thoughts in space" (Soja 17). Further developing Henri Lefebvre's concept of *espace vécu*, or "lived space," Soja articulates an alternative mode of spatial inquiry that extends the scope of the geographical imagination beyond the confining dualism of what he describes as "firstspace" and "secondspace epistemologies" (17). Briefly, the firstspace, or perceived space, refers to the directly-experienced world of empirically measured and mappable phenomena; that is, the material space. The secondspace, or conceived space, in contrast to the firstspace, is more subjective and "imagined," and more concerned with images and representations of spatiality, with the thought processes that are presumed to shape both material human geographies and the development of a geographical imagination. Soja sums up this space in the following way: "Rather than being entirely fixed on materially perceivable spaces and geographies, it concentrates on and explores more cognitive, conceptual and symbolic worlds" (18).

If the firstspace is seen as providing the geographer's primary empirical data or texts, then the secondspace represents the geographer's ideational or ideological discourses; the ways a geographer thinks or writes about the data of the firstspace and about geography, in general. Moving beyond the firstspace/secondspace dualism, Soja suggests a thirdspace, or lived space, which is essentially a deconstruction of the dualism of the firstspace/secondspace; that is, a "both-and-also" space combining a "critical thirding-as-Othering" space of being and becoming (20). This concept, which is close to Michel Foucault's approach to "heterotopologies" (see Soja, *Thirdspace* 145–63), attempts to make practical and theoretical sense of the world, and thereby requires a continuous expansion of knowledge formation and a radical openness that enables us to see beyond what is presently known, to explore "other spaces" that are both similar to and significantly different from the real-and-imagined spaces we already recognize.

The trialectics of spatiality is comprised of three dimensions: the perceived, the conceived and the lived. According to Soja, the thirdspace as lived space is simultaneously:

> A distinctive way of looking at, interpreting, and acting to change the spatiality of human life (or, if you will, human geography today);
> An integral, if often neglected, part of the trialectics of spatiality, inherently no better or worse than firstspace or secondspace approaches to geographical knowledge;
> The most encompassing spatial perspective, comparable in scope to the richest forms of the historical and sociological imaginations;
> A strategic meeting place for fostering collective political action against all forms of human oppression;
> A starting point for new and different explorations that can move beyond the "third term" in a constant search for other spaces; and still more to come. (21–22)

The introduction of Soja's trialectics of spatiality coincides with the introduction of site-specific practitioners and commentary in this volume. To a degree the difference between environmental and site-specific, as spatially-engaged approaches to theatre creation and analysis, is primarily an issue of semantics. For example, Gay McAuley, an Australian researcher on the subject, uses the phrase "site-based performance" where I would say environmental theatre (McAuley 602). As a practitioner, I consider environmental theatre to be the placement of a particular text in a given environment, wherein the environment then begins to operate as an active agent in the process of developing the text in this particular place. My definition of site-specific theatre comes from Mike Pearson, an artist-researcher with whom I trained as a graduate student, and his definition is as follows:

> Site-specific performance is the latest occupation of a location where other occupations are still apparent and cognitively active. It is conceived for, and conditioned by, the particulars of such spaces: it then recontextualises them. It is inseparable from its site, the only context within which it is intelligible. (qtd. in McAuley 602)

Pearson uses the word performance as a way of liberating his practice from the historical and cultural baggage attached to the word "theatre" in Wales, the country where he lives and works. Moreover, the word performance opens up a conceptual understanding of the work, in fields such as performance studies, that has been slow to happen in theatre studies.[1] Considering the diversity of approach to site in the work of Shawna Dempsey and Lorri Millan, for example, as compared with bluemouth inc., perhaps the wisest way to frame the introduction of site-specific theatre in this volume is to say: insofar as environmental theatre concerns the placement of a text in a site, and site-specific theatre concerns the generation of a performance from a site, the apparent binary of these practices can be deconstructed. Environmental theatre, therefore, will become specific to the given site in which it is developed; while site-specific theatre may be meaningfully transferred from its site of origin to another site, provided there is integrity toward a relationship between the different sites incorporated into the work.

Shawna Dempsey and Lorri Millan's *Lesbian National Parks and Services* is the first site-specific performance to be examined in this volume, by Dempsey and Millan themselves ("Field Reports from the Lesbian National Parks and Services" and "Lesbian National Parks and Services and You!"); Kyo Maclear ("Eyewitness Account"); Kathryn Walter ("Lesbian National Parks & Services"); and Jennifer Fisher ("Out and About: The Performance Art of Shawna Dempsey and Lorri Millan"). Originally conceived for a residency at the Banff Centre for the Arts, the *Lesbian National Parks and Services* was part of a series of performances entitled "Private Investigations," with an aim of investigating tourism in the park, in hopes of uncovering some of its hidden costs and assumptions. Dempsey and Millan were curious about the extreme heterosexual bias in all of the advertising and marketing for visitors to Banff; and, as they were both accustomed to working with a costume as a resource for creation, they were both attracted to the attire of the park ranger. As a performance, the *Lesbian National Parks and Services* consisted of, as Fisher describes, Dempsey and Millan patrolling the park in uniform, "politely interacting in deadpan 'ranger speak,' earnestly giving confused shoppers directions, or edifying tourists about the lesbian geography of the flora and the fauna of Banff." In the costume of an authentic-looking park ranger, this work essentially provides the ground for a colli-sion of a perceived notion of "lesbian" as a deviant identity and "park ranger" as a helpful, protective facilitator of a park visitor's encounter with nature. The "Field Reports" and the book-length *Field Guide to North America* clearly demonstrate just how much thought Dempsey and Millan have put into this juxtaposition of identities, and the questions it poses for their "audience" about how nature is defined, about whether or not homosexuality is a part of the concept of nature, in a national park or otherwise, and about how certain stereotypes exist concerning popular culture's definition of who a lesbian is, and how she might look. In the performance of the *Lesbian National Parks and Services*, Dempsey and Millan have developed a thirdspace of being-in-the-world, offering a distinctive way of looking at, interpreting, and acting to change the social spatiality in Banff National Park and in the various locations to which this performance has toured. In addition to fulfilling Soja's first element of the thirdspace, this performance also fulfills the fourth; that is, it establishes a strategic meeting place for fostering collective political action against human oppression. Indeed, in the Field Reports and the various accounts of the Lesbian Ranger activity, it is important to understand the significance of Dempsey and Millan's face-to-face encounter with their audience; most often this encounter implies an ethical demand in the public to accommodate the Other of lesbian subjectivity; the ethical dimension of this experience is what Soja hoped to encourage in the thirdspace. Moreover, this ethical demand is felt profoundly because the audience, in the case of these performances in Banff National Park, were mostly unaware that they were participating in a performance. Finally, it's important to appreciate the tremendous humour and wit that accompanies Dempsey and Millan's attempts to clothe the sexualized lesbian body in the good-natured, knowledgeable and helpful discourse of the park ranger. Humour and sexuality are important elements in the way Dempsey and Millan transformed the social geography of Banff National Park.

Perhaps the greatest insight that can be gained from the praxis of site-specific theatre is the vital role the audience play in completing the event of each performance. Eugenio Barba has stated that "the theatre's raw material is not the actor, nor the space, nor the text, but the attention, the seeing, the hearing, the mind of the spectator. Theatre is the art of the spectator" (Barba 39). Indeed, site-specific theatre is the art of the spectator because, as I suggest in "Deep-Mapping a Morning on 3A," it is the job of the spectator to piece together the found and the fabricated in his or her journey through the site, and ultimately it is the result of the seeing, the hearing, the touch, the attention—indeed, the experience—of the spectator that ensures a living archive of the work of the otherwise ephemeral performance. The deep-mapping and archiving proposed as a possible outcome of *The Weyburn Project* is what Soja describes in the third element of the thirdspace; that is, the most encompassing spatial perspective, comparable in scope to the richest forms of the historical and sociological imaginations.

Hildegard Westerkamp's "The Local and Global 'Language' of Environmental Sound" pushes the role of spectatorship even further; we must learn to be sensitive as spectators to how we engage with a performance, but more so we must learn to be sensitive to how we tune into the world, as she states,

> a sound piece can be a *vehicle* for deeper understanding of acoustic environmental issues of perception, a *vehicle* for creating "more-than-meaning." Such work is not an end product but, ideally, a beginning from which to create new relationships to place and time for both composer and listener (qtd. in Westerkamp).

Westerkamp's approach to working site-specifically is to respect the relationship her work has to bigger frameworks, and ultimately to the world. Westerkamp's perspective epitomizes Soja's fifth element of the thirdspace, in that the starting point for a lived-space may be a vehicle for understanding more-than-meaning about the world.

Andrew Templeton's "Sex, Cars and Shopping: Meditations on Social Disabilities" examines the approaches used by Radix Theatre to animate various sites in our society that might be considered failed utopias: the sexualized body, the automobile, and a big box home furnishing store. Each performance cleverly opens up a space between the illusion of promise and the void of failure that often is the real experience of these sites, as they perpetuate a consumerist illusion of society. Templeton describes Radix's relationship to the locations they animate the following way: "For Radix, locations are not simple settings or thematic tools but are integral to decoding experience. Productions evolve directly out of the environment and they provide a vehicle for the audience to understand the environment in a new way." Templeton's description of Radix echoes Kathleen Irwin's account of *The Bus Project* in "Arrivals and Departures: How Technology Redefines Site-related Performance." Irwin describes a collaborative, media-based site-specific performance/installation that also animates a failed utopia of public transportation in our society. Combining an interactive video game terminal in the bus station with various modes of décor modification on the buses, *The Bus Project* explores notions of choice, chance, resilience, and transformation in the lives of those who frequent this mode of travel, and in the lives of those curious about the site and its inhabitants. Similar to the environments of social disability used by Radix, the bus station is a space perhaps best summed up by sociologist Marc Augé who has called such spaces of mass travel, exchange or transport "non-places." For Augé, a non-place is

> Where a dense network or means of transport which are also inhabited places is developing; where the habitué of supermarkets, slot machines and credit cards communicate wordlessly, through gestures, with an abstract, unmediated commerce; a world thus surrendered to solitary individuality, to the fleeting temporary, and ephemeral... (78)

As an address to the non-place of the bus station in downtown Regina, *The Bus Project* challenged practitioners and audience both to understand how technology might be used to establish a presence in an otherwise void-of-a-space, and thereby break down socio-economic, cultural, and disciplinary boundaries that stand in the way of making art of this nature available to under-accessed populations, and that prevent an inner city bus station from being a thirdspace, a lived space, through performance.

I will conclude this introduction by discussing a final grouping of approaches and perspectives on activating site through performance. Beginning with Sean Dixon's "Things I've Learned from Theatre SKAM," we are reminded of how when audience and practitioner alike leave purpose-built facilities to create theatre, a confrontation occurs with many engaging and affirming challenges. For example, in absence of realism and the proscenium arch, we may re-consider that "[t]heatre is not TV with coughing and line flubs" or that live music should come first—before lighting, before set, before canned music: "In our culture of the Xerox, of the Copy, the strength of theatre is in being, as much as possible, the Real McCoy." In "Beneath Bridges, Loading Docks and Fire Escapes: Theatre SKAM Tours *Billy Nothin'* and *Aerwacol*," Amiel Gladstone, Theatre SKAM's Artistic Director, shares the knowledge he has gained from the various pilgrimages his company has made, in search of sites and a community who will participate in an experience of refashioning theatrical convention, in the most unpredictable of places and predicaments. Gladstone describes what Soja would refer to as a shift from ontology to praxis, from materially concrete to the imaginary abstract and back again; Theatre SKAM's use of railway sidings, spaces under bridges, and so forth, is made more "real" by being simultaneously imagined through performance.

In "Please Dress Warmly and Wear Sensible Shoes," bluemouth inc. offer us a model of their collaborative process that at times assumes the form of a guide, at times a mode of speculation, and offers a good deal of revelation about the risk and investment in their approach to working collaboratively with each other and with the challenges posed by the sites they choose to animate. bluemouth inc.'s text is like a primer for the creation of Soja's thirdspace as lived space; an environment portrayed as

> multi-sided and contradictory, oppressive and liberating, passionate and routine, knowable and unknowable. It is a space of radical openness, a site of resistance and struggle, a space of multiplicitous representations, investigate-able through its binarized oppositions but also where there is always "other" spaces, heterotopologies, and paradoxical geographies to be explored. It can be mapped, but never captured in conventional cartographies; it can be creatively imagined but it obtains meaning only when practiced and fully *lived*. (Soja 28)

Keren Zaiontz further illuminates bluemouth inc.'s lived space in "'This is not a conventional piece so all bets are off': Why the bluemouth inc. Collective Delights in our Disorientation." In her examination of *American Standard* and *What the Thunder Saw* she applies Michel de Certeau's notion of tactics, placeless and improvisational "creative acts freely taken-up by spectators and performers alike," to our understanding of how the company has addressed displacement of these works, and in the process discovered the importance of cultivating a creative and critical "place to play" in an urban landscape pressurized by various special interests and civic agendas. In the way that bluemouth inc. create a thirdspace with their audience, it is possible to believe, that with faith, appropriate tactics, and hard work, it is possible to "bring all kinds of shit to life."

(2007)

Note

¹ For a broad discussion of the reasons for abandoning the word "theatre" for "performance", when addressing site-specific work, see Houston with Nanni; and Pearson and Shanks.

Works Cited

Augé, Marc. *Non-Places: Introduction to an Anthropology of Supermodernity.* Trans. John Howe. London: Verso, 1995.

Barba, Eugenio. *The Paper Canoe.* Trans. Richard Fowler. London: Routledge. 1995.

de Certeau, Michele. *The Practice of Everyday Life.* Trans. Steven Rendall. Berkeley: U of California P, 1984.

Dixon, Sean. "Things I've Learned from Theatre SKAM," *AWOL: Three Plays for Theatre SKAM.* Toronto: Coach House, 2002.

Houston, Andrew with Laura Nanni. "Heterotopian Creation: Beyond the Utopia of Theatres and Galleries." *Canadian Theatre Review* 126 (Spring 2006): 5–9.

McAuley, Gay. "Place in the Performance Experience." *Modern Drama* 46:4 (2003): 598–613.

Pearson, Mike and Michael Shanks. *Theatre / Archaeology.* London: Routledge, 2001.

Soja, Edward W. *Thirdspace: Journeys to Los Angeles and Other Real-and-Imagined Places.* Oxford: Blackwell, 1996.

Seize the Day:
The Mummers' *Gros Mourn*

by Chris Brookes

The use of theatre for social animation has never been as widely developed in this country as it has been in the Third World, and it's perhaps not surprising that contemporary experiments in this genre should have first occurred in Newfoundland, the province most closely analogous to a Third World entity within the Canadian confederation. During its 10-year life, the Mummers Troupe had the good fortune to be the leading edge of the political theatre movement in English Canada. Some observers claimed it was a spiritual descendent of the Canadian worker's theatre movement of the 1930s; it was certainly an inheritor of the Newfoundland worker's theatre tradition of the 1830s.

It was also one of the headliners of a peculiarly vibrant period for Newfoundland's indigenous cultural expression, and I think it is time to begin putting that period into perspective and to draw what useful lessons we can from it. The Great Newfoundland Artistic Revival of the 70s didn't happen because a bunch of people got together and decided it would be a Good Thing. It was triggered by the temper of the times.

The actual development of the Mummers Troupe was never as linear as it may appear in hindsight. It trod a meandering, often improvised but always determined path between a political philosophy on the one hand and the constant difficulty of keeping a small underfinanced theatre together during changing times, changing people, and varying commitments on the other. Sometimes we evolved rationally and carefully with our objectives in clear sight; other times, goaded by necessity, we just closed our eyes and jumped in spite of everything. Simply surviving as a political theatre within a province and a country awash with colonialism and entertainment-industry art dictated a constant crisis mentality which rarely permitted us the luxury of reflecting upon the finer points of theatrical evolution. What I have tried to do in *None of That Artsy-Fartsy Stuff* is retrace our tracks and perform a kind of structural analysis upon our more significant feats and foibles. I hope that the exercise contributes a useful perspective to the art of collective creation and popular theatre in Canada, and that our successes and failures, the lessons learned and ignored, can be of value to other artists working toward social change. Please steal any good ideas.

> So many things cry out to be done, all so urgently. The world rolls on.
> Time passes. Ten thousand years is too long. Seize the day.
> —Mao Tse-Tung

Sally's Cove, Monday July 30th:

This area is to be the site of the new Gros Morne National Park. Nine months ago the provincial news media carried coverage of local residents' dissatisfaction with the Park's proposed community relocation policy, but later reports made clear that changes in the policy had satisfied residents, and that opposition to the new park had ceased. But discussions we have had seem to prove this media image far from accurate. Most of the talk after our performances in this area has revolved around the park, with feelings often running pretty strong. Each community reacts differently; all seem confused.

In Sally's Cove, the audience had the most to say: most think the Park will destroy their community and they will be pushed out of their homes by a subtle but forcible relocation. They feel that outside help, particularly the news media, has deserted them. But there's a determination in these people. I am struck by a grim face which says quietly, "If they goes ahead and ruins our lives, then we got the right to spoil their dream too. If they drives me out they'll have to rename the place Charcoal Park, 'cause I'll put the torch to every tree in 'er before I goes."

We're told that the Park is to be officially opened in a few weeks—no one seems to know exactly when—with a federal-provincial signover ceremony in Rocky Harbour, 10 miles away.

There are five communities affected by the Park relocation policy: Sally's Cove, Belldowns Point, Bakers Brook, Green Point and Lobster Cove. The relocation policy itself includes a scale of compensation for families who move, and has been changed several times in the past year. Originally it required residents of the five villages to move immediately; now it is tempered to allow them to remain in some cases and pass on their land to one heir. Unfortunately most resident families seem to have several heirs who want to remain in the community, but no new houses may be built, and there are other restrictions. Basically, residents see the new policy as being the same as the old, but a little slower. In five to 10 years the result will be the same.

Sally's Cove is the focal point, and also the largest of the five communities. I get a curious feeling listening to these people talk about their fears. They seem desperate to talk, to have someone from "the outside" listen. Even we, young freaks from the city, are possible messengers.

Rocky Harbour, Thursday, August 2nd:

I've been thinking seriously about the possibility of staying in this area for a few weeks to create a documentary piece about the communities. If so we can't make a show directly about policies; we must take as focus the people, individuals, the things they tell us. The government's view is adequately publicized; our show will need to deal with the people's view of their future.

At lunch we decide to do it. We're due on the South Coast with *Newfoundland Night*, but this schedule can be postponed by three weeks. We itemize resources, note pads, tape recorders. (It may be important to remember precisely how people speak with us.) Any props and set requirements can be improvised from available materials in the area. We will talk predominantly with residents of the five affected communities and focus on Sally's Cove. (The people there have already offered the two-room schoolhouse for rehearsal space.)

Christopher Knight is afraid that our group is too diverse for any clear line of expression to emerge through the collective process, and opts for staying outside the project. The rest of us are eager. We discuss images that strike us as characteristic of this area: lobsterpots, contrasts, the optimism of government publications and the pessimism of the residents who read them. Andy suggests a final image for the piece: a champagne christening which breaks the communities instead of the bottle. We decide to leave such things hanging while we get out and talk to as many people as possible.

The official Park opening is rumoured to have been rescheduled for August 13th.

Sally's Cove, Sunday August 5th:

Collecting data in this place is saddening and frustrating. We all feel it. People here generally fear their community is doomed, and feel powerless to make their voices heard. They say that their opinions were never solicited by the officials, that their homes will be "signed away" by government bureaucrats, and that even the new Park relocation policy will simply be a "slow freeze-out," forcing them out over a period of a few years while making the government look good.

There's suspicion and distrust, no one is sure of what is happening, which families have already managed to move, how much money, how large a plum the government is offering to those who do move, etc. All the classic subtle workings of the archetypal resettlement policy. People are divided, nervous of confronting each other. "Is it true Phil is going to move?" "I heard they're going to close the school." Rumours abound. Why don't the government people realize what is going on? It all looks so clear in their office memos.

Last evening the company attended the regular Saturday night slide lecture for tourists at the Park Interpretation Centre in Rocky Harbour. An impeccably nice young biologist from the mainland showed impeccably nice colour slides and explained marshland plants. The mosquitoes were thick. No one asked him to explain the human fauna of the new Park whose roots cling as tenaciously to the same rocks. This morning he came to find us in the bus and presented a sample handful of baked apples to Christopher and Andy, who had never before tasted them. These Parks people are so nice. It would be easier if they looked like villains.

Conversation with a child from Green Point:

I: "Well, is your family moving out?"
He: "Yup."
I: "Are you glad?"
He: "Yup."
I: "Why?"
He: "Because when we moves, I gets a bike. Me father's gettin' me one."
I: "But wouldn't he buy you one anyway, if you were staying here?"
He: "No. 'Cause when we moves, see, the government gives us bits of money, and I gets a bike. We don't get no money if we stays."

Sally's Cove, Monday August 6th:

People here are kind to us. This is a small community (50 families) but noone seems to mind that we, young strangers, are inquiring about their affairs. It's probably presumptuous of us to expect people to talk and trust us. Why should they care about the creation of a play? Perhaps they feel that we can be their voice—I'm not sure. At any rate, the community has embraced us with gifts of fresh fish (West coast cod tastes different from East coast cod), homemade bread and beer, invitations to dinner. Everyone in the community seems interested, even the kids.

Coyley Endicott and his wife live close to the schoolhouse and are militant about their situation but think that we should have the answer to their problems. I try to explain that we're simply a group of actors, at best able to give Sally's Cove a reflection of itself. We can only re-express the questions—the people themselves must find their answers. They press us to finish the piece in time to perform it before the official park signover ceremony next Monday. My God, we can't make anything respectable in six days! Our last show required four months of work. Yet we have a responsibility to these people, the subjects of our creation. We can't simply use them in the name of art. If they are willing to take us into their homes and their confidences we can at least try to do what they ask. But can we make it in six days? Andy has the flu. I pray it doesn't spread to the rest of our company. We've spent all our time so far in research—first rehearsal is not in sight yet. With so little time we won't be able to get far enough with character studies to portray local individuals recognizably, and will have to rely on signs, nameplates instead.

Cow Head, Thursday August 7th:

I'm speedy—full of static sparks. The drive up here was beautiful; it's no wonder they want this scenery for a park. It is ironic that the people who live in the most beautiful parts of the coast are the ones to be relocated—those who chose to live closest to beauty. Example: Cow Head has been allowed to remain. It's a nice place, nothing special. Belldown's Point, however, a mile away, is slated for relocation. The reason? Belldown's has the most breathtaking sweep of white sand beach to be seen anywhere in Newfoundland.

A long gentle talk with the local minister: he feels deeply concerned about the changes the park will bring to this area, and doesn't see any easy answers. It was he who helped arrange the first public meeting between Sally's Cove and provincial politicians two years ago. Before that most Sally's Cove residents were unaware that their community was slated for resettlement. Although the federal and provincial bureaucrats signed the initial Park memorandum in 1969 providing for the resettlement of the five villages, no one apparently had thought to inform the residents. This kind of information lag isn't helped, I suspect, by the unavailability of newspapers on this coast.

Jane Hutchings is a retired nurse who has lived on this coast, and kept it healthy, for 20 years. She feeds us, stomach and spirit, while digging out a wealth of information on the Park which she has collected over the years. Reading it, I am constantly assailed by the dichotomies of most park literature which carefully explains how animals and birds are to be treated with care and respect and left undisturbed in their traditional habitats, but makes no mention of policies toward people.

It's enlightening to read biologists' reports which underline the importance of preserving, via the Park, a particular stand of virgin forest which is crucial to the survival of the Park's primary threatened species (and the official symbol of Gros Morne National Park): *lepus arcticus bangsi*—the Arctic Hare. Enlightening because this crucial piece of forest will not be included in the new Park. It belongs to the Bowater Pulp and Paper Company which is keeping it for future pulpwood cutting, thus ensuring the downfall of *lepus arcticus bangsi*. The official Park symbol assumes a curious touch of irony.

Jane agrees that big business rarely loses. The new Park's tourist attractions will line the pockets of motel-owners and ski-lift concessionaires, but for most people the story will be different. How is it that a giant paper company is permitted to hold on to an apparently vital piece of land while Dawson Roberts will be squeezed off his?

Sally's Cove Schoolhouse, Wednesday August 8th:

The first day of real work on the show itself, creative juices loosened up around five o'clock and we have some good images and directions to work with. There's still some research to be collected, and endless amounts of transcription to be typed from audio cassettes, but we've started putting it together. Things are clipping along so much more quickly than they did during last winter's creation of *Newfoundland Night*. I'm ironing the bugs out of this group-writing process, and can now see one of the undeniable virtues of collective creation playwriting: it's fast. For the immediate response required by this situation, it is ideal. A single playwright could never manage this pace alone.

The Sally's Cove kids, who've been hanging around the school all day watching us (see the actors eat their sandwich, see them type, see them drink coffee), ultimately prove invaluable. We have decided to use a mask in the final scene, but have no clay to model one. The kids triumphantly tell us of a natural clay deposit by Big Brook, only 100 yards away, and lead Christopher Knight up there to prove it. It's true! Now Christopher and the kids are fussing about in the back room with it.

We are becoming a spontaneous workshop for these kids. Half a dozen are involved with the mask work, another dozen are trooping down the road with Mary Walsh, videotaping everything in sight with our borrowed portapak camera. Oscar and Otto are our chief helpers, cannibalizing their fathers' junk piles to construct a giant lobsterpot for our set, and organizing their friends into work crews. I don't want to use the lobsterpot just for rustic background—it will be a human-size working model, symbolizing the relocation program: once residents allow themselves to be baited by the relocation monies, they will be trapped in the enclave of Rocky Harbour. And like the lobsters they used to fish for, they will never be able to return from whence they came.

In the local bar last night we found solitude impossible. Everyone wants to find out how our work is progressing, if we need help, have we heard the latest news: that the government is laying on a special free bus service next Monday to give all residents a free ride to the Park signover celebrations. "A big haw," Clarence says. We are feeling very close to the people here. Their hopes and fears are becoming ours. This would probably have happened in any case, but this kind of working process accelerates empathy. When I'm talking with someone here I'm trying to get inside his skin, to see things with his eyes, because I may be portraying him on Sunday night, speaking his words, using his inflections, believing his beliefs.

Donna came back from a day at Bakers Brook with a storybook scene from the Decker family. As one of their children was hustled off to bed, his elders reminded him: "…and don't forget to say your prayers: God Bless Mommy, God Bless Daddy, and God Damn the National Park." I make a note to remind myself to visit the Deckers next time I'm on this coast, and suddenly realize that next time Bakers Brook and the Deckers may not be there.

Today I heard men in the bar counting the days until Monday: "Well, boys, Sally's Cove got four days to live." Later, pausing in the tiny village graveyard trying to piece together the family bloodlines, I noticed the relatively short history of this community. The oldest stone still standing is JUCIAM CHIMERY, D.1848. He was a former pantry boy from a French fishing ship who deserted to hide out and make his home here. He took a wife REBECCA, D.1856. There are flowers at the foot of some small wooden grave markers. What will become of these stones when all the people have moved out? How will the nice young men of the Park Interpretation Centre reconcile a small graveyard with their National Wilderness Park?

I am in emergency working moods, wrapped in my caffeine tenseness like a ball of Christmas styrofoam, brittle and non-biodegradable. Time is the missing factor in this show's creation. We need time to walk the beaches and deserted fishing stages, to kick the lobsterpots and listen. Time to stop knowing the answers, time to stop chasing the rainbow and climbing the mountain, time to slide out the pores of our skins and let the fog finger our souls. We don't have much time, but neither do the people who live here.

Sally's Cove, Saturday August 11th:

A drain day. Interpersonal frictions blew most of the day, petty things we are all prey to. Well, what can anyone expect from six people living in a cramped school bus, throwing a show together in a week flat? I worry that the show may be like a campus revue. Is it worth all this for a bad show? Are we doing anything more than scratching the surface of this community's reality? Will the residents be offended by our version of their voices, their lives? Most important, will there be truth in what we do? At this point I can't hope to see this show objectively. There is so much still unfinished; we'll be lucky to have time for a complete run-through before tomorrow evening's performance.

I once saw a series of skits performed during a university student/faculty strike in Vancouver. The scenes about the strike were quite funny. The audience laughed a lot. But somehow when people walked out of the auditorium they knew the strike was over. They had lost. The performance had robbed their energy and sapped their will to continue, despite its heroic plotline. It had punctured their balloon with a stage catharsis, allowing the audience to feel that it no longer needed to achieve catharsis in the real struggle outside the theatre's doors. The play was well-intentioned but badly crafted, a pre-ejaculation. I do not want our show to be like that. A play which is designed to animate will not finish off its line of energy. It will pass the ball to the audience. The next scene, whatever it is to be, must be theirs.

Most of our lives we don't really listen to the words around us. Working like this, hanging on every word of a conversation, memorizing or taping, one begins to notice the poetry in the speech of ordinary people. Not poets cloistered in attic rooms, but lobster fishermen over a kitchen table: how magic is their choice of phrase? This play will at least have some beautiful lines. The whole myth of Art is autocratic nonsense— everyone, not just the artist, speaks with poetry, breathes with music. It is simply a matter of listening, not just in the art galleries and concert halls but out in the dust of the street. Shakespeare would have us believe that only noblemen speak in poetry, while the common people speak prose. Yet listen:

> **Coyley Endicott:** 'Tis not me home they're takin' away from me. I can get another one someplace else—good as this one, p'raps better. But 'tis everything else they're takin' away: me freedom.
>
> Look out there now—I got me few vegetables sot. Sot the Spring. I can catch me few fish for the Winter. I can pick me few berries. I can go up to Corner Brook. I used to go up twice a week and load the truck and bear 'er down and sell 'er out. And when I strikes, comin' down that arm, I can smell the fresh air. And that's true. I think you'll take notice o' that. There's a different air down here …

Sally's Cove, Sunday Evening August 12th:

We made it. And we couldn't have wished for a more enthusiastic audience: 200 people of all ages and sizes squeezed into the tiny schoolroom watching our vision of them. They heard their own words, those of their neighbours, their stories, their fears, their frustrations, their jokes and their rage. Many of the things people said to us strangers they would not have said as openly and candidly to their neighbours. It is similar, surely, with one's personal relationships—often deep truths can be shared more easily with strangers while they are still simple revelations unsullied by the leaden shoes of need. Like a child's colouring book, the shapes simply exist. Until the child tints each page with his own desire, makes it *his* colouring book. So it is that ours is an intimate show for this audience, and this has made for a rare sense of closeness. Perhaps the show realizes their identity as a community rather than as isolated individuals.

Do I imagine that there is a pride in all this talk, a pride that they and their community have been the fabric of a good piece of theatre? More to the point, I hope, is that they recognized a reflection of themselves, and saw some truth in it. Everyone is in high spirits, particularly our company of six. The community's response has even won over Christopher Knight's skepticism: he step-dances for the first time in his life.

Coyley, Eric, and some others sit together talking quietly and intensely. Later we hear that an *ad hoc* community meeting has been called for tomorrow morning.

Rocky Harbour, Monday August 13th:

Official Park Signing Day. The morning's meeting decided to protest the signing ceremony, scheduled for three p.m. in Rocky Harbour. We were asked to come along and perform the show (dubbed *Gros Mourn*) before the ceremony. I was cautious, fearing that we might become the focus, instead of the residents of the area; but Coyley put it to us: don't we empathize with them, share their concerns about the whole affair? Yes, of course. "Well then, you got to come. You fellas helped us by what ye done." He won't feel right about it if we're not included. As it developed later, the Park officials refused permission for a performance.

Most of the community turned out to dampen what was obviously planned by both governments to be a gala occasion: a multicoloured bandstand, bunting gaily flapping in the wind, a Canadian Forces Sea Cadet band from St. John's, refreshment tables, lots of speeches. The Sally's Cove protesters made a point of not taking the special government bus—they all drove here in their own cars.

The Minister of Indian Affairs and Northern Development, Jean Chrétien, is stopped as he tries to walk through the crowd of demonstrators. He is the federal minister responsible for National Parks and Sally's Cove is pinning its hopes on him. Many hope that Chrétien is simply unaware of the depth of their objections, and that by speaking with him they can convince him not to sign the Park agreement today. As they talk, I notice a curious phenomenon: our show has crystallized a terminology for many of the demonstrators. They use metaphors drawn from the play's imagery as they present their case. The play has clarified the Sally's Cove reality in a powerful way: it has given people a "handle" on it. Like any work of art, our show represents a way of seeing. And like any work of art, it is not neutral; it does not simply "uplift people." Which people does it uplift? Whom does it serve?

Chrétien says he is sorry, his planners tell him it must be done this way, because "It is the most striking piece of land we have in Eastern Canada." Tempers flare. Bud threatens: "If you goes ahead and signs it, I'd say there'll be 50 miles of park burned within a week!" Eric quiets him and tries to reason: "We're not asking you to give up your park. Just let us stay in our homes, give us a two-mile boundary around Sally's Cove, and give our children the freedom to build homes on our own land."

Chrétien is adamant and pushes through the crowd. I notice Milton cursing and breaking his picket sign over his knee again and again, until it is in tiny ragged pieces. He looks around helplessly. No one affected by it even knows the exact terms of the agreement which is to be signed. It has been kept secret and will only be made public after all the signatures are on.

Ed Maynard, the provincial member for this riding, arrives and is cornered by his Sally's Cove voters, but he demurs, saying it is not his responsibility. It is his signature which will go on the agreement as representative of the provincial government. In the background the implacable Sea Cadets thump out: "This Land is Your Land, This Land is My Land …"

The ceremony begins, by now an hour late. Most speeches hailing the popularity of the new park are squelched by the grim Sally's Cove contingent. As Chrétien and the provincial rep move to the table to sign the agreement, there is an agonized mass wail from Sally's Cove. The agreement is signed. The band loudly strikes up "O Canada." No-one cheers.

Sally's Cove, Thursday August 15th:

It is hard for us to leave this place. Last night was official goodbye time; we were treated to a big bash, with beer and songs and special sandwiches. There's a deep sadness in the air which everyone tries hard not to recognize. Our company is leaving for the South Coast, and those who live here avoid speaking of their future now.

The Sally's Cove people, our friends, asked us to perform *Gros Mourn* in other communities in the park area, and so we have spent the past two days playing St. Paul's, Cow Head and Rocky Harbour. We were accompanied to each performance by an escort group from Sally's Cove who helped us set up and talked with the audience after each show. Perhaps the play expresses a part of themselves which they normally find hard to explain to neighbouring communities. They sat amongst the audience of their peers, assessing responses.

Each of us in our own separate way has come to feel a part of this place. As artists we have actually done something useful. We have given birth to a work of theatre which is also a real and tangible tool for social action. We have clearly put our hands to the wheel.

Coyley came by the bus this morning with a copy of the *Western Star*. He was upset. I was too, after I'd read it. Their coverage of the demonstration is incredibly distorted, a real hatchet job. The front page headlines a photo of the demonstration: DEMONSTRATORS THREATS FAIL TO STOP PARK, and goes on to describe a "mob" of residents "organized by a travelling theatre group called The Mummers."

Great. The old red scare. Outside agitators stirring up the otherwise peaceful peasantry: We are described as having "made the picket signs," "organized the booing sessions," and having staged the "contrived demonstration" as a piece of street theatre with the residents of Sally's Cove as spear carriers. Sally's Covers are presented as avaricious real estate speculators, hanging onto their land as an "investment"! The writer quotes Donna Butt extensively: it turns out that they were old enemies from alternate-press days, and at the demonstration she apparently laid into the guy as a hack sellout to the establishment press. She thinks it may have got under his skin, but it's hard to believe such a vitriolic and biased piece of yellow journalism can be motivated just by personal vindictiveness. It not only smears the Mummers Troupe, but discredits the people of Sally's Cove and taints their whole cause with illegitimacy. A couple of pages further on we find the clincher: a big half-page article eulogizing the new park and its natural beauty. It's all taken from the official park office information releases, and it is by the same writer.

Coyley left to drive the 120 miles to Corner Brook and demand a retraction from the editor. It never appeared. A week later there was a flurry of letters from area residents decrying the original reportage and explaining their opposition to the relocation policy, but it's hard to offset the effect of front-page headlines with lucid letters on page four.

We played *Gros Mourn* briefly in St. John's to interested audiences and good reviews. If nothing else, this seemed to make people outside the immediate park area aware of the issue. We finished each performance by playing a tape recording of the Park signing ceremony as we slowly set fire to a row of smashed cardboard houses onstage. Later we toured the show to communities in the other three Atlantic provinces where three new National Parks were being instituted, and where similar relocation policies were being imposed. In one case, Kouchibouguac, the policy had already been implemented, and some residents had been forcibly moved.

Residents of all three other park areas who saw *Gros Mourn* found detailed similarities between the Gros Morne situation and their own, and confirmed the mutual interdependence of the four park schemes. Community opposition to a particular aspect of National Park policy in one province seemingly resulted in a corresponding change of that policy later in other provinces. All the separate communities were facing the same national policies, and our tour helped establish the need for information exchange between the different areas.

This led to the first People's Conference on National Parks in Halifax in December 1973. Delegates attended from all four of the in-progress Atlantic parks, including two delegates from Sally's Cove. Three weeks later the much-disputed Ship Harbour National Park in Nova Scotia was cancelled in favour of a series of provincial recreation areas which allow residents to remain in their homes. National Park policy went under official review.

For eight years the Gros Morne Park authorities stuck to their guns. Half of Sally's Cove was resettled. The remaining residents continued to fight. Now, nine years later the Park has said it is willing to negotiate enclave status for the broken community. Some of those who left under duress are talking of suing the government for damages. One of them is Coyley, quoted by newspaper and magazine articles: "I never intended to leave. I lived there eight years with the park, but it came down to either move and get my life straightened out or keep fighting, and there didn't seem much point in that anymore. If they turn it into an enclave now, I'm going to get a lawyer and push it right to the bitter end. They put us through hell, and 'twas no need of it!"

How did the Mummers Troupe come out of this experience? Well, we learned some practical lessons about technique, for one thing. We learned that a specific show built for a specific community can be valuable not only to the initial target audience, but to wider audiences. This of course is not universally so, and always a show's primary function and responsibility must be to serve the audience for which it was built. A show will be seen differently by outside audiences, and its relationship with them will necessarily be different. (i.e. as a vehicle of communication rather than animation.)

We certainly learned the importance of stage-managing the press. Thereafter we became much more careful about what company spokespeople said to the media.

Most importantly we learned to respect the dangers of parachuting into a community by ourselves. We are a theatre company. Theatre artists do not generally have the commitment to stay in a community for years if necessary, organizing and providing lead-in and follow-up to a project like *Gros Mourn*. Their job, the one that they do best, is to be off and doing again. The danger is that this can merely raise unfulfillable expectations if the community is left high and dry without the skills (organizational, not theatrical) to continue their fight. In the case of Sally's Cove, despite the dedication and determination of many residents, half of the community relocated over the next decade. This might not have happened had there been an organization on the spot with the ability to tackle the park bureaucracy and the long-term commitment to see it through. A play like *Gros Mourn* can be a useful and valuable step in a process, but it must not be the only step.

As a result, we resolved to go into future projects whenever possible in conjunction with a rural development association, union, or other local planning organization with the experience and expertise to follow through. Our shows, instead of becoming a one-shot shootout, could highlight a continuing development program, with a greater chance of ultimate success.

We examined the values of *Gros Mourn* as a community development tool. The University Extension service had a lot of experience using film in this way, and they were very helpful in making a comparative analysis. They noted that theatre is a much "hotter" medium than film or videotape, moving an audience more powerfully through involvement with live performers rather than with an unresponsive piece of celluloid. Theatre tailors its dynamics to its particular audience; film does not. Actors can answer questions; film cannot. Theatre is flesh and blood and belief and support; by comparison film is cold and mechanical. They are very different tools, both useful.

The kind of theatre we created with *Gros Mourn* doesn't always have to be political in an explicit way. In Newfoundland we find a people's expression seldom enough in either art or politics, and a play like this always has implicit value simply as indigenous theatre. The explicit aspects of *Gros Mourn* were not so much a result of the process (of involvement with a community) as they were a result of our being in Sally's Cove at a time of crisis. Had we created the play six months earlier, perhaps all the rest would have happened differently. We might not have catalyzed a demonstration. We might have catalyzed something better, something ultimately more effective. Why didn't we get there six months earlier? We didn't know about it. Why not? We didn't have the contacts. Yet.

After *Gros Mourn*, development organizations in Newfoundland began to take an interest in our work. As our experience grew over the next few years our work became more useful to those organizations and the Mummers Troupe established fruitful working relationships with many of them.

There was one more lesson we learned, by now a familiar one: that the collective "we" boiled down to Lynn and myself. In the Fall of 1973 Donna Butt went back to university; everyone else in the summer cast went up along to Toronto. Who could blame them? We had no money left. Lynn and I went back to Maddox Cove to discover that *Gros Mourn* had not endeared us to government officialdom. They were out for blood.

(1983)

The Princess of the Stars

by R. Murray Schafer

Introduction.

The Princess of the Stars is an environmental performance piece created for solo soprano or mezzo-soprano, two mixed quartets or choruses, four actors or sound poets, six dancers, flute, clarinet, trumpet, horn, trombone, tuba, four percussionists, and about 20 canoeists. It was designed for performance at dawn on an autumn morning. The work was performed last August on Two-Jack Lake, just outside the Banff townsite, in celebration of the National Park centennial. Its principal characters, costumed and masked, occupy the bows of the canoes from which they chant an unknown language constructed principally from various key words in a number of Amerindian dialects. The audience, seated on the shore of the lake, is informed of the action by a Presenter who also interprets some of the events. The musicians and singers are positioned around the perimeter of the lake whose irregular shoreline allows the canoes to enter from "off-stage." *The Princess of* the *Stars* was co-directed by its composer, R. Murray Schafer and Brian Macdonald, designed by Diana and Jerrard Smith, and stage-managed by Robert Pel, Janet Anderson, and Louise Currie.

1 / The legend.

Without man the world was born and without him it will end.

This is the story of the Princess of the Stars,
Daughter of the Sun-god and herself a goddess.
Her name is in the stars and you have seen it there.
Each night she looked down on earth,
Blessing it with kisses of light.

One night she heard a mournful cry coming up from the forest.
It was the Wolf, howling at the moon, his double.
The Princess leaned over the forest to see who was singing,
But in leaning down so far she fell from heaven.
Suddenly she appeared before Wolf in a great flash of light.
But Wolf, frightened to see the stars so close,
Lashed out at the Princess,
Wounding her.

She ran bleeding into the forest, leaving dew wherever she went,
Which was nearly everywhere, since she had no idea where to run.
By morning she found herself at the edge of a lake
And slipped into the water to bathe her wounds.
But there something caught her, dragging her down.
In vain she struggled:
In the end the waters closed over her.
You may see the stars of her crown at the tip of your paddle,
But the Princess you will not see.
The Three-Horned Enemy
Holds her captive at the bottom of the lake,
And the dawn mist is the sign of her struggling.

2 / The action.

All this has happened during the night. The story continues as the audience arrives at the lake in the darkness before dawn. In the distance we see a pinpoint of light moving slowly towards us from the opposite shore. At the same time the voice of the Princess is heard, singing an unaccompanied aria across the water. (The singer is a kilometer away.) Her haunting aria has something of the quality of a loon. Soon other voices from far and near begin to echo it as the light-point continues to move towards us. When it reaches the shore, dawn has broken enough for us to see an old man in a canoe, the Presenter. He tells us of the happenings during the night, then turns and calls across the water.

The action resumes. Wolf arrives to look for the Princess. He enlists the help of the Dawn Birds (dancers in canoes) who arrive to comb the water with their wings; but they are prevented from rescuing her by the Three-Horned Enemy, who is keeping her captive beneath the lake. A battle develops but is interrupted by the arrival of the Sun Disc (sunrise) who comes to demand what has happened to the stars. The Sun Disc drives the Three-Horned Enemy away, sets tasks for Wolf before he can release the Princess, and exhorts the Dawn Birds to cover the lake with ice and sing there no longer until Wolf succeeds.

The principal characters are either costumed and masked (as in the case of the Dawn Birds) or are enclosed in large moveable structures fastened to the gunwales of voyageur canoes depicting Wolf, the Three-Horned Enemy, and the Sun Disc. Since the characters in the canoes chant in an unknown language, the Presenter, a kind of earth spirit or medicine-man, acts as an interpreter between the observers and those performing the ritual.

The Princess of the Stars is designed for performance at dawn on an autumn morning. It forms the Prologue to the entire *Patria* series and introduces the central theme of the works to follow. From this lake, Wolf will go out in search of the Princess, seeking her forgiveness and compassion. If he can find her he will also find himself. Then she will at last return to the heavens and he, redeemed, will rise to inherit the moon. Wolf's wanderings will take him to many distant lands and he will visit many historical periods before he will return to find the Princess in the same natural environment he deserted at the close of the Prologue.

The unifying motive of the *Patria* works is Wolf's journeys though the many labyrinths of life in search of the spiritual power which can both release and transfigure him. He will travel under many names and assume many guises: impersonating a human as the displaced immigrant DP; as the Greek hero Theseus; as the dead Pharaoh seeking to be raised to heaven by the sun; or as the King in the "chymical marriage" or *heiros-gamos* of the alchemists. At times he may assume great pre-eminence; at other times he may be chased away as a fool, a criminal, or a "beast." As the labyrinthine nature of his wanderings intensifies, the Princess becomes personified for him in the figure of Ariadne, who helped Theseus escape the Cretan labyrinth in the well-known Greek myth. The thread-gift provided by Ariadne in the *Patria* series is the thread of music. Ariadne's gift is her haunting voice; this is what sustains and transforms Theseus-Wolf during his journeying.

Each of the *Patria* pieces is designed to exist on its own and many explore different theatrical settings and techniques, though all follow the theme of Wolf's search for his spirit in the guise of the Princess as it was introduced in *The Princess of the Stars*.

3 / The environment.

The environment of *The Princess of the Stars* is extremely important, not only for the effect it has on the audience but also for the ways it is intended to affect the performers. It relies entirely on what the Japanese call *shakei*, borrowed scenery; that is its entire decor. While the principal characters are on the surface of the water, the musicians and singers are positioned around the perimeter of the lake, which should be rural, showing as few signs of civilization as possible. The lake should be about half-a-kilometer wide and a kilometer long, with an irregular shoreline to allow the principal characters to enter in their canoes from "off-stage."

What distinguishes this from the traditional theatrical setting is that it is a living environment and therefore utterly changeable at any moment. The lighting alone is in a constant state of change and atmospheric disturbances can descend or retreat to affect a good deal more than the audience's state of mind and comfort. Having witnessed a good number of performances of *Princess*, I can say that it is a different theatre every time. Will there be a sunrise? Will there be dew on the ground or mist on the water? What if it is raining or windy? Wind in particular is the enemy of the production for not only can it make the canoes difficult or dangerous to navigate, but it can totally destroy the music: it may carry the sounds off in unintended directions so that the audience will miss much and the performers will miss vital cues. This latter eventuality is particularly unwanted since the work is structured to function largely without the direction of a conductor, the musicians listen and react to one another by ear rather than eye.

Thus the living environment enters and shapes the success or failure of *The Princess of the Stars* as much as or more than any human effort; and knowledge of this must touch the performers, filling them with a kind of humility in the face of the grander forces they encounter in the work's setting. But as we participate with these forces, allowing them to influence us in every way, is it not possible to believe that we as performers and audience are also influencing them as well? We disclaim belief that we can make the wind rest or the sun shine, though this is the principal motive of *Ra*, one of the later works in the *Patria* series, and neither is it remote from many ancient peoples, whose rituals were often conducted in the open environment. Then one danced to make the rains come or cease or to make the corn grow or the caribou appear. Yes, there must be something of that kind of faith in the minds of the participants as they approach a performance of *Princess*. I have seen beautiful performances in the Rocky Mountains when the sun stroked snow-capped mountains just at the moment of the Sun-Disc's entry, and I have seen haunting performances when the lake was enshrouded in thick mist. The production of this work will always be tinged with the excitement of a premiere. It will always be a theatre of "first nights only."

Though the text of *The Princess of the Stars* is original, the work is clearly related to Indian legends for, like them, it employs a story to account for various natural phenomena. There is dew on the grass because the Princess ran through the forest; and the mist on the water is the sign of her struggling to be free of the Three-Horned Enemy. The Dawn Birds appear at precisely the time the real dawn birds are waking up, and singers and instrumentalists around the lake coax them into song by imitating their calls. To know that one is affecting the environment in this way can fill one with awe. On more than one occasion loons or Canada geese flew across the lake in front of the bird-dancers mixing the real and the imitative to beautiful effect. The entire work is timed according to sunrise; for the real sun should synchronize with the arrival of the Sun Disc, who has received messages of the distress on earth from the birds who have awakened just before him. When at the conclusion the Presenter tells the Dawn Birds to leave the lake to be covered over with ice and snow, we know that this is precisely what will soon happen.

What is the effect of treating nature in this way? By mythologizing the fluctuations of nature we have intensified our own experience of it. We begin to flow with it rather than against it. We no longer spite it or shut it out as we do in covered theatres. This is our stage set and we have become one with it, breathing it, feeling it in all its mystery and majesty. Of course there will be problems, for nature is fickle. But, as Jung reminded us, she is never like humanity, never is she deceitful.

The Princess of the Stars is conceived for a situation. It should only be presented when the conditions are right. But since no producer can predict this and no union can enforce it, this is both its birthright and its stigma. Like the art of ancient times it is wedded to its time and place by indissoluble links which guarantee that no counterfeit experience could ever be a replacement for it.

4 / The tempo.

The tempo of a production of *The Princess of the Stars* is never fast. Even when Wolf and the Three-Horned Enemy engage in battle, they move at the pace of an armada rather than that of modern warfare. It should take the Presenter 15 minutes to come down the lake to the audience area at the beginning of the show; this prepares us for the tempo of the entire work. But something strange happens when nothing happens. The senses are sharpened with alertness, ready to print the decisive action when it occurs. There can be little doubt that primitive rituals are deliberately structured in this way. Long informationless interludes are punctuated by sudden events, which causes an adrenaline rush to the brain, making the experience memorable.

And so in the slowness of the breaking dawn we are alert to the smallest change. Perhaps the eyes wander to the hills and notice they have become lighter. Or we notice a ripple on the water as a breeze skims across it. Or we hear an animal scurrying for cover in the underbrush. (On one occasion an instrumentalist had an animal run between his feet while playing in the darkness.) In the slowness, tiny events become magnified; large events are haunting. I have seen small children transfixed as Wolf comes on the lake with head lowered and swinging from side to side in the long hunt before he arches his neck and lets forth a blood-freezing howl.

The music of *Princess* also participates in this slowness. Since sound travels at slightly more than 330 meters a second, it will take the music of a performer at the far end of the lake three seconds to reach the audience area and another three seconds for any echo to return. When we performed *Princess* at Two-Jack Lake in the Rocky Mountains, we gave the singers megaphones with which to focus the sound, bouncing it now off one mountain, then off another. The idea of employing megaphones in outdoor performances is certainly not new. There are diagrams of such instruments in the writings of Athanasius Kircher, and Sir Samuel Moreland published a brochure in 1672 describing a 21-foot horn he made by which the human voice could be projected up to a mile.

> If the lake is surrounded by mountains and forests, echoes become a special feature of the performance. The feedback of the echo will soon begin to modify the production which lengthens and lingers in breadth and resonance as performers lean how to turn this into advantageous cybernation. At Two-Jack Lake we were able to position the musicians so that their sound was funneled indirectly to the audience area, the auditor sometimes receiving the echo more prominently than the original sound. Indirect reception removes much of high-frequency sound, giving the tone a mysterious, remote quality—an effect, by the way, which was aimed at by Wagner, though in quite different circumstances.

5 / The ritual.

The comparison with Wagner is not inconsequential. Wagner wanted to hide his musicians in a pit, their appearance distracting from the drama. The result was the creation of a *mystischer Abgrund* (mystical abyss) which separated the audience from the action on stage, thus taking on many of the aspects of a ritual. In *The Princess of the Stars* the musicians are hidden from view by the trees; we do not know from where the sound will issue next; and the action is distanced from the audience by the lake, for only the Presenter comes close to shore.

But there are other features which draw *Princess* closer to ritual. When the Presenter speaks to us for the first time he tells us that before we may observe the "sacred actions" performed on the lake by "gods and animals," he must first prepare us. In a short dramaturgical incantation he turns us into trees in order that we may observe the events without interfering. In one sense this distances us from the action, and in another it implicates us as part of the natural decor of the production. We are reminded of the motto of the work: "Without man the world was created and without him it will end."

Language also contributes to the ritual effect of *The Princess of the Stars.* The gods and animals speak an unknown language or, to be more precise, a series of unknown languages, which the Presenter alone can interpret for us. Wolf chants an invented language incorporating some morphemic and phonetic elements of North-American Indian dialects. This lends it an ancestral dignity but has a practical significance as well since Amerindian languages not only have an abundance of long vowels but they contain few labials or other phonemes which do not carry well in the open air. Similar considerations also affected the choice of instruments: for instance, tests proved that log drums, so dull and muted when played indoors, took on an exciting resonance in their natural environment, particularly if they were placed over pits or gulleys, which acted as sound boxes. And so, log drums and tom-toms became Wolf's accompaniment instruments, four sets of them, played by drummers at four corners of the lake.

The singers' texts contain actual Amerindian words: "star, lake princess, wolf." These are not employed syntactically; they are colour words, chosen from a cross-section of languages, those of the eastern woodlands predominating. Another series of colour words is that forming the Sun Disc's welcoming music. Beginning with the ancient Japanese word for sun, "ohisama," sun words follow in a geographic curve around the world through the languages of Asia, Africa, and Europe. The Sun Disc himself speaks an invented language with a strong suggestion of Latin cognates. The Three-Horned Enemy's speech contrasts sharply with that of Wolf and the Sun Disc; neologisms, notable for their monosyllabic abruptness of compact vowels and waspish consonants, are given additional bite and distortion by means of a loud hailer implanted in the Enemy's costume. A further independent vocabulary is that of the Dawn Birds' chorus, this deriving partly from ornithologists' notebooks and partly from personal listening experience plus imagination.

Enough about the polyglottal nature of the work; it is an affair that will recur repeatedly throughout the *Patria* series, though not always with the same intention. The important thing to stress here is that when we come to witness a performance of *The Princess of the Stars* we are already at some remove from the action as suggested by the real and implied antiquity of the languages its characters speak.

All rituals are rooted in antiquity or must appear to be. If they have not been repeated uninterruptedly throughout the ages, archaic dress, conduct, and speech can assist in creating this impression. When we performed *The Princess of the Stars* on Two-Jack Lake, gaunt black-robed ushers conducted the audience from the road to their places at the edge of the lake. In a more complex handling of ritual, more elaborate preparation ceremonies, including the consecration of the site, may be desirable. Here, "holy nature" and the strange timing of the event seemed sufficient.

When the site is legendary its attraction is intensified. In his review of *Princess* the Banff poet Jon Whyte related a legend from Lake Miniwanka, which immediately adjoins the site of the production. In 1909 an Indian family was crossing the lake carelessly singing,

> Suddenly out of the water appeared the huge back of a fish many yards broad, only to disappear when out shot a beautifully shaped arm and hand, which clutched not in vain at one of the singers. Immediately a companion seized a knife and stabbed the arm through and through. The hand only clung the tighter to its victim and the surrounding waters were churned and lashed about as if the winds of heaven were left loose all at once (Whyte 16).

So there was a monster in the lake? And there was a woman possessed? Who can say she was not a princess. Of all the things said at performances of *The Princess of the Stars*, the most beautiful was that of a four-year-old child who murmured to her mother after all the characters had departed, "The animals were just pretend, weren't they, but the Princess was real."

We depart from the lake as the sun rises majestically above the mountain peaks bathing them in crimson and gold. Is this the same sun that left us yesterday, or is it the lord of the cosmos who has "set his commands for all to hear?" Perhaps for just a moment we feel what D.H. Lawrence intended in Apocalypse when he wrote:

> Don't let us imagine we see the sun as the old civilizations saw it. All we see is a scientific little luminary, dwindling to a ball of blazing gas. In the centuries before Ezekiel and John, the sun was still a magnificent reality, men drew forth from him strength and splendour, and gave him back homage and lustre and thanks. But in us, the connection is broken, the responsive centres are dead. Our sun is a quite different thing from the cosmic sun of the ancients, so much more trivial. We may see what we call the sun, but we have lost Helios forever, and the great orb of the Chaldeans still more. We have lost the cosmos, by coming out of responsive connection with it, and this is our chief tragedy. What is our

petty little love of nature—Nature!!—compared to the ancient magnificent living with the cosmos, and being honoured by the cosmos! ... (Lawrence 27).

6 / The pilgrimage.

For centuries our art has been produced for indoor environments. I will not dwell on the ways this has altered music, how it has conditioned the search for purity of expression and the suppression of all distractions, bringing about an intensification of acoustic image, hi-fidelity, amplification, and sound presence. Everything has been arranged to enhance these values. Musicians sit in a group on the opposite side of the building from the listeners, often disciplined by a conductor. They have set up unions to ensure that their working conditions are appropriate. Times of work and rest are dictated by contract. Light intensity must be sufficient; adequate warmth and controlled humidity for instruments must be guaranteed; proper sound amplification must be maintained. For this, a whole battery of non-musical specialists are engaged: stagehands, caretakers, lighting engineers, acousticians, recording engineers. Now the public needs to be informed of the undertaking, and to do this another fleet of experts is required: publicists, box office attendants, managers, promoters, printers, critics. All this apparatus is very costly to maintain. It will have to be paid for one way or another, and if the public cannot or will not do so, foundations and government agencies will be expected to come to the rescue, bringing new confederates onto the scene: boards of directors, accountants, planners, arts administrators, more managers, heiresses, royalty, etc.

The model I have given of the current musical or musical-theatrical undertaking was once very efficient, in fact such a paragon of efficiency that by the eighteenth century it actually served as the model for all future capitalistic enterprises. Here labouring professionals were harnessed and yoked under the leash of a foreman, promoted by expectant owners and backers before the first paying public in history. The commodification of art dates from this time and it extends today to all the auxiliary agencies who expect to make greater profits from it: publishers, broadcasters, recording companies, and performing rights societies. I do not allege that this model works efficiently all the time. In fact, as time goes on it works less and less effectively, or at least only works effectively when the cash flowing in from the public exceeds the cash flowing out for the services.

Now here is a work which, simply by moving outdoors, challenges us to breathe again. But disguised beneath its simple plot and musical textures are timely questions—big ones. When musicians play across a lake at a distance of half a kilometer or more, how are they conducted or supervised? Of what value then are conductors and managers? When everything is muted at long range (like the tinting of colours at a distance) how is presence to be obtained in the sound, or is this ideal to be abandoned? How do performers cope with unpredictable weather conditions, cold, dampness, or transporting themselves and their instruments over uneven terrain? Can we arrange a contract to remove the hazard of rain? And what about the managerial staff? We need boatmen not caretakers, trailblazers not electricians, naturalists not publicists.

And the audience? Instead of a somnolent evening in upholstery, digesting dinner or contemplating the one to follow, this work takes place before breakfast. No intermission to crash out to the bar and guzzle or slump back after a smoke. No women in pearls or slit skirts. It will be an effort to get up in the dark, drive 30 miles or more to arrive on a damp and chilly embankment, sit and wait for the ceremony to begin. And what ceremony? Dawn itself, the most neglected masterpiece of the modern world. To this we add a little adornment, trying all the time to move with the elements, aware that what can be done will be little enough in the face of it all. Here is a ceremony then, rather than a work of art. And like all true ceremonies, it cannot be adequately transported elsewhere. You can't poke it into a television screen and spin it around the world with anything like a quarter of a hope that something valuable might be achieved. You must feel it, let it take hold of you by all its means, only some of which have been humanly arranged. You must go there, go to the site, for it will not come to you. You must go there like a pilgrim on a deliberate journey in search of a unique experience which cannot be obtained by money or all the conveniences of modern civilization. Pilgrimage; it is an old idea; but when over five thousand people travel to a remote lake in the Rocky Mountains to see a performance of *The Princess of the Stars* it is evidently one for which there is a contemporary longing.

(1986)

Works Cited

Lawrence, D.H. *Apocalypse.* London: Penguin, 1974.

Whyte, Jon. "Princess of the Stars." *Crag and Canyon* (14–20 August 1985): 14–20.

Hillar Liitoja: Chaos and Control

by Nigel Hunt

Hillar Liitoja's theatre work, whether it is his settings of Ezra Pound's poetry, his staging of other people's texts, or the creation of his own, is at once a reaction against, and a celebration of, the fundamental incomprehensibility of the world. From his musical background and theatrical influences to his current techniques of creating his pieces (in which the traditionally separate tasks of writing and directing are usually blended together), Liitoja's challenging relationship between performance and audience can be seen as an effort to refocus the way we interact with the world.

Born in Toronto in 1954, Liitoja originally pursued a career as a concert pianist, studying with Anton Kuerti in Toronto and Pierre Sancan in Paris. In 1979, after losing faith in his own talent and future in music, he discovered two new interests: theatre and the poetry of Ezra Pound. Already in the early 1970s, while commuting to New York City for piano lessons, he had been impressed by such productions as Richard Schechner's staging of Sam Shepard's *The Tooth of Crime* and André Gregory's *Alice in Wonderland*, as well as the work of Polish experimentalist Tadeusz Kantor. Remembering the power of these experiences, Liitoja travelled to New York again in 1982 to see the final three performances of Richard Foreman's production of German playwright Botho Strauss's *3 Acts of Recognition*. In Liitoja's words, he was "blown away" by Foreman's innovative staging. Later, Liitoja worked as an apprentice/observer to Foreman for his European production of Kathy Acker's controversial opera *Birth of a Poet*. Impressed by Foreman's severe discipline, he learned not "to intellectualize but to absolutely trust my impulses and instincts and to go with them" without worrying about meaning. Another production that influenced Liitoja's decision to dedicate himself to theatre as his means of expression was Belgian director Jan Fabre's *The Power of Theatrical Madness*, which he saw several times in Europe. Liitoja comments on his reaction to Fabre's work: "I was bowled over. I couldn't function like I normally functioned. I walked the streets without knowing where I was going. I was stunned, bereft of normal perspectives and defences.... I didn't know how to cope, how to react, or what to think anymore." Most of Liitoja's subsequent work has attempted to recapture and share the way these theatrical experiences forced him to re-evaluate his perception of the world.

At the same time as Liitoja was discovering the power that theatre could hold over an audience, he came upon the poetry of Ezra Pound in a series of coincidences: after a recital, a diplomat's wife read him one of Pound's poems; he heard a tape on the radio of Pound reading his poetry and was impressed by the musicality of the poet's voice; while bored at a party he found a copy of one of Pound's books. He also was impressed by Pound's insight as an editor in his notes to T.S. Eliot on the facsimile of "The Wasteland." Liitoja decided to celebrate the powerful clarity of Pound's poetic images by setting them amidst his own theatrical events, believing that the vitality of Pound's writing could not be captured by traditional poetry readings but, instead, should be communicated in a context in which people are engaged in different activities. The literary qualities of Pound's poetry would neither be "acted out" nor just recited. Rather, the poems themselves would become events in a vital, sensual universe teeming with fragments of sight, sound, smell and touch.

Liitoja's combination of theatre and Pound has produced nine pieces so far: *Pound for Pound, Pound II (Pound!), Quarter-Pound, Half-Pound* (all in 1982), *Triptych* (1982 and 1983), *A Draft of XXX Cantos* (1984; for radio), *The Last Pound, Pound-O-Rama* (both 1985) and *Expound* (1986). The texts for all these shows are poems by Ezra Pound: *The Last Pound,* for example, uses all of "Hugh Selwyn Mauberley," and *Pound-O-Rama* has poems from *Moeurs contemporaines*. Liitoja constructs these pieces by first working one-on-one with individual performers; often he will ask them to pick their favourite Pound poems and prepare some sort of action inspired by the text, such as a scream, a dance, or an activity like cutting through wood with a saw. (Andrew Scorer, long active in Toronto's alternate theatre scene and a veteran of four of Liitoja's works, prepared a piece where he delivered the lines of a poem to a dummy and then stabbed it with a knife when he was finished. This action became part of *The Last Pound.*) Liitoja then will select the individual scenes that he likes and work on them intensively with the individual performer. Sometimes the scene arises from a combination of the performer's ideas and Liitoja's own conception. In *The Last Pound* Scorer also wanted to recite a poem while doing karate-style movements; Liitoja added to this his own image of chunks of raw liver being thrown at an actor: in the final show Scorer did both simultaneously. In these Pound pieces, as in all of his works, Liitoja ultimately decides what is or is not included but, according to Scorer, "there's actually more creative input from the actors than is usual in a play." After many weeks of individual rehearsals, Liitoja takes time out to "write the show" (as he calls it), creating a score on a long sheet of paper which determines when things occur. When read from left to right, the score, which lists cues for lighting, music, sound effects, and the various routines which the actors will perform, is really an elaborate time chart that keeps everything in sync with Liitoja's intentions but often out of sync with the audience's expectations. The final 10 days of rehearsal allow Liitoja to repeat the events which comprise the play so that he can adjust cues, volumes, and tempo. Although the final result may appear complex, with events happening in many different time cycles, the work for each individual is relatively simple. In this process, the director becomes an editor or conductor who arranges the raw material into an often musical structure. *The Last Pound,* for example, was based on the classical sonata form (presentation of two themes, transmutation, and final recapitulation).

In *Pound-O-Rama,* Liitoja's latest Pound piece to be seen in Toronto (*Expound* was created for Theatre Algoma in Sault Ste. Marie), the events included a woman hanging athletically from a ladder, a man in the audience reading quietly from a biography of Pound, a girl dressing and undressing (the repetition erasing the erotic possibilities of her nudity), a man sweeping the floor with a broom falling over and remaining still for several minutes, and a member of the audience who appeared to be mentally handicapped having a fit during a burst of loud symphonic music, subsequently being carried out of the theatre by two ushers (he was, in fact, part of the show). In this, as in all Liitoja's work, music, sounds, and action are repeated. The effect, which initially seems completely chaotic, eventually achieves a type of order or, at least, provides an indication that it is all very carefully choreographed. In *Pound-O-Rama*, for example, a woman blow-drying her hair went unnoticed as simply part of the general confusion until all other sounds gradually ceased, leaving only the noise of her activity alone on stage for a moment; then, just as slowly, the layers of events remounted, and her solo disappeared back into place. In fact, the whole show continually wound up and down in this manner, alternating between silence and slowness on the one hand, and noise and chaos on the other. The audience was interspersed throughout the performance space so that some were aware of things which others were not; all were aware that they were unaware of the complete activity, however; in such a situation, the audience is faced with the constant responsibility of choosing what to look at and listen to, and what to ignore. The piece demands that they continually refocus their attention and, in doing so, makes them aware of the active role of the perceiver in both live performance situations and in life.

Although the Pound pieces form the majority of Liitoja's work to date, he also has directed productions using other people's texts. In 1983, for example, under the banner of his newly-formed DNA Theatre, Liitoja directed Richard Foreman's 1974 play *(Pain(t)* at the aka Festival in Toronto. Liitoja's rehearsal process for this piece was fairly traditional inasmuch as all actors were present for all rehearsals, and most of the time was spent working on lines and scenes. Nevertheless, the company still found time under Liitoja's direction to develop their own vocabulary (based on musical terminology) to describe the different types of voices they would use within a line and their accompanying gestures. Scorer remembers his participation in the project as "a fantastic experience" with a "good sharing of input" among the cast.

Liitoja also directed *My Plants Came Alive and We Fell in Love*, "based" on a short story by Phillip Cairns, at the 1985 Rhubarb Festival. This piece featured Cairns reading a homoerotic text while peeling a mango and smearing it over his T-shirt; the beginning of a song by the Talking Heads was played repeatedly only to be cut off by a piercing scream; a woman talked nonstop to her hairdryer; a large punk rocker chased an actor out of the audience and around the theatre, claiming that she was really Kim Novak; a saxophone player, stripped to the waist and tied by a long rope to a gypsy fortune-teller, moved through the scene at the end. As with the Pound poems, the written text here became the inspiration or pretext for Liitoja's frightening and bizarre theatrical images. The audience was pushed to the limits (and in some cases beyond) by harsh, random and seemingly unconnected events occurring around the space in a wide mixture of styles. The punk appeared real and his violence did not look "acted," the text was a first-person description of a sexual encounter. But much of the rest of the action seemed crazy or absurd. The only unifying principle in this mad world of bizarre events was the audience—stranded as witnesses to something that cannot be understood, challenged to find a way to react to chaos.

The third type of work that Liitoja has done involves writing his own text. So far, the only example of this is his latest piece, *This Is What Happens in Orangeville*, which premiered at Toronto's Poor Alex Theatre in January 1987, was remounted at the Backspace of Theatre Passe Muraille last May, and toured to le Festival de théâtre des Amériques in Montreal in June, where it was cited by the festival jury for "experimentation in theatrical writing" and played to full houses. For this piece, inspired by the 1984 murder of two Orangeville children by a 14-year-old boy (Paul) and his subsequent confinement for insanity, Liitoja wrote dialogue for the psychiatrist and the boy prior to rehearsals, but only gave it to them bit by bit during the process. Stylistically naturalistic, this series of conversations forms the visual and structural core of the play. The psychiatrist, Dr. Saunders (Andrew Scorer), tries to determine Paul's (Peter Lynch) reasons for killing the two children only to discover that he has none. Paul explains that he wanted only to know what it would feel like to kill, and that he has no regrets over what he has done. The rest of the play, which surrounds these characters and the audience, features fragments from the people of Orangeville engaged in various activities. The boy's sister Malina (Shannonbrooke Murphy) bounces rubber balls and performs various movement exercises, explaining how she accidentally avoided being murdered by leaving school early on the day of the murders. Sam (Ed Fielding), Paul's father, mows the lawn, worries about his wife's dinner invitation to the neighbours, and bemoans the fact that his brain is "underenlarged." Milda (Sara Clenyg-Jones), Paul's mother, cooks omelettes and either drops them on the floor or serves them to any audience member quick enough to grab them; later she plays checkers with her husband. A sadistic piano teacher (Brian Shaw) forces his student (Kirsten Johnson) to write lines throughout the play such as "I will make better use of my time, and yours" and "I will improve my attitude towards playing the piano." (Throughout the run of the production, these pages of lines become a lobby display). Two so-called Automatons (Akascha Kerekes and Rosalia Martini) describe their quiet life in Orangeville and the horror of the murders. A man posing as an audience member (Rich Malouin) suddenly starts talking to a real audience member during the show, explaining that he is from Orangeville and rambling on about the strange statistical parallels which he has noticed lately between his town and Jupiter. A young girl (Liisa Repo-Martell) enters a few times throughout the play and freezes in tableau before, at the end, walking very slowly and completely naked through the playing space, holding a bunch of helium-filled balloons on a string. Two young "ladderboys" (Daniel Deller and Corin McFadden) first usher the audience into the theatre, shouting at them to sit where they like, to move as often as they wish, but not to sit in the armchair (reserved, as it turns out, for the psychiatrist); stripped to the waist, they spend the duration of the show screwing and unscrewing light bulbs, timing the absence of the psychiatrist between his scenes, sharing this information with individual members of the audience, and taking flash photos of the audience. An Ominous Presence (B Bob) also orders the audience around on occasion. Even Liitoja himself becomes part of the show, collecting stray rubber balls, trying out various places to sit, or enjoying an omelette. Throughout, oppressive symphonic music (Brückner, etc) builds to repeated crescendos as if mocking the lack of linear progression on stage. The play ends its two hours with the balloon girl's slow parade, a message on Liitoja's answering machine from someone in Orangeville declining to talk about the incident repeating over and over, and a tape of a psychiatrist talking to Liitoja about the effect of child murders on society. Light from the string of bare light bulbs on stage, the house lights and the cameras' flashes alternate on and off. Gradually all of the performers exit and the audience is left in the dark, then thrown into the light.

The effect of this carefully choreographed chaos is a blurring of the normal distinction between Paul's plausibly insane behaviour and the stylized, disassociated actions of everyone else. Of course, Liitoja stacks the deck towards the creation of such relativity by showing us Paul's cool explanation for his deeds, not the grisly murders themselves. But the impression persists, as the play informs us, that "people are freaks and bizarre miracles." Quebec theatre critic Paul Lefebvre found himself "deeply touched by this play and the theatricality of it." In his programme notes for the Festival of the America's production, he suggests that the play "is not an attempt to elucidate what really happened in November, 1984. Instead it offers the audience a random presentation of fragments of various levels of speech and images, indisputable, real fragments, that destroy the very idea of realism, replacing it magnificently with that of reality." Amongst Liitoja's choices of reality some fragments are more interesting than others: for example, the hostile manner of the ladderboys' demands and commands to the audience seem amateurish and overdone; and the nudity of the young girl is more exploitive of women than suggestive of innocence, forcing the audience into complicity with the director if they remain, making us wonder if he really is asking us to leave. Such portions detract from the powerful juxtaposition of Liitoja's clearer images by muddying the sensual experience with concerns about production technique and ethics.

While Liitoja's text for the boy and the psychiatrist and the lines for Malina were all written ahead of time, like the Pound pieces, the rest of the play evolved with one-on-one rehearsals (one-on-two in the case of Paul and Dr. Saunders), then with the creation of a score and, finally, intensive repetitions and adjustments with the entire cast. For some segments Liitoja knew exactly what he wanted and insisted that the performers produce "photocopies" of their actions. In other cases, he let the performers decide what to do within certain parameters. Scorer explains that his scenes with Lynch were unblocked; he was free to do as he wished, even in performance, as long as the scene where he binds Paul's hand was done exactly as Liitoja decreed. At other times Liitoja's work concentrates on the exact position of the performer's body movements and delivery of lines. Always, the work is oriented towards how things look, how they coordinate with other activities, and how they develop the overall relation to the audience. There is no attention to psychological motivation or character exploration. According to Scorer, Liitoja "works best with actors who work more with intuition and less with method." Liitoja finds his actors by going to our theatres where he recruits from both the cast and audience. His *Orangeville* group is young: the average age is about 25, with six of them under 20.

The juxtaposition of freedom and discipline in the rehearsal process is reflected in the contrast of chaos and control in the shows. Sky Gilbert, artistic director of Toronto's Buddies in Bad Times theatre, and one of Liitoja's first and most persistent supporters, sees in Liitoja's work a parallel to sadomasochism: "It's highly sexual," he explains, "it's based on the rules and the code of conduct of S&M. Dominance, submission and power. It's what makes his work offensive to some people.... It's so dangerously close, it opens up our impulses ... it makes us horny because we all really want to dominate or be dominated in our lives ... people are always in the closet about their need for dominance and power." Gilbert sees this S&M relationship as highly theatrical and healthy since it allows such impulses to be satisfied vicariously. Gilbert concludes: "There is something sick about his work, but that's a compliment." For Gilbert, the often abrasive aesthetics of Liitoja's pieces is necessary to achieve his frontal assault on our society's way of thinking in which reason is valued over instinct, and narrative over rhythm.

Whatever the individual reaction to Liitoja's work, it clearly provides an audience with an unusual theatrical opportunity to balance their decisions about where to sit, what to watch, and how to interpret the performance, with the compelling anti-logic of a world which defies the importance of these choices. Liitoja, who has confessed that "it's the arts councils that are forcing me to articulate my work," primarily intends his pieces to occasion stupefaction: "I love to see the audience figuring things out—in vain! I love these people being stimulated, their minds trying to figure out what is going on with their senses.... We're stuck in outmoded ways of perception; it's nice to have things jolted and revaluated." Whether Pound's poetry or the Orangeville child murder case, the "subject" is primarily a pretext for Liitoja's presentation of the mad and maddening world which surrounds us. While his work requires that the mind actively try to order and understand the array of events with which it is presented, ultimately the work remains non-intellectual since the mind is subverted to the senses. Finally it adheres only to Liitoja's fundamental motivation, his basic belief that "there's got to be an absolute beauty in what is unknowable, incomprehensible.

(1987)

Schafer's *Patria Three*:
The Cycle Continues

by David Burgess

> *Ladies and Gentlemen, Patria Music/Theatre Projects and the Peterborough Festival of the Arts are proud to present:* Patria Three: The Greatest Show, *a feast for the ears, the nose, the eyes and the stomach. Here, you will experience a world of truth and error, delight and terror, of the real and the unreal, the ideal and the surreal. Pieces collected from far and near, a collection so astounding no one will grasp it all in a single visit. In a moment, you may wander at will through this haunting spectacle of thrills and illusions and you will be amazed at what here may be found (and lost). But have no fear, for I, Sam Galuppi, am your guarantee that the show will run as good clean fun.*
>
> — R. Murray Schafer (31)

The boldness of the speaker sets the tone for *Patria Three: The Greatest Show* by R. Murray Schafer. This is no mere play, or even an opera, no run-of-the-mill piece of music theatre; this is an event with a capital 'E'. Schafer the composer, environmentalist, teacher, dramatist, is working on the scale of a county fair, and the strutting Ringmaster character sets it all in motion.

Hundreds of performers and costumed crew members fill Peterborough's Crary Park. They sing, dance, tell fortunes, read poems, play instruments, run games of chance, and act in restricted shows in the four theatres. As many as a thousand visitors can watch, listen, smell, taste and feel their way through the grounds. Diversions, intrigues, freaks of nature, chills, thrills, laughs and a web of Greek myth are offered to one and all, in exchange, that is, for a coupon.

An elaborate workshop of *Patria Three: The Greatest Show* was mounted in August, 1987, running for just two performances. This was preparation for what will be a more or less full-scale production of the show in August this year at the same outdoor Peterborough site. Once again the local Peterborough Festival of the Arts, with the support of Trent University will team with Patria Music/Theatre Projects to co-produce. This will continue the unique and ambitious artistic collaboration of the founders of the Patria, composer/writer R. Murray Schafer, director Thom Sokoloski, and designers Diana and Jerrard Smith. They have ambitions to stage the entire body of the composer's *Patria* cycle, a series of interrelated environmental music/theatre pieces.

The Greatest Show takes its name and much of its performance and design vocabulary from the travelling circuses, carnivals, and chautauquas that, in the days before mass communications, were so important to the cultural lives of the smaller towns and cities of this country. The work begins and ends with all audience attention directed toward the stage in the central "Odditorium." But after the introduction of the main rivals, the forces of Black and White Magic, and the beginning of the "plot" dealing with the mythic Ariadne, the show breaks with the conventions of theatrical narrative. The audience, armed with a map in the program, then stroll the grounds, individuals picking up information as they go. A fortune teller will read tarot cards, singers will serenade with a ballad, or the carnie at a game will entice with his spiel, but all of these seemingly unrelated pieces weave together to create a theatre world of Schafer's imagination. While the visitors move about as they choose, partly "making their own play," the performers are moving through the area in timed, set patterns which director Sokoloski likens to "football manoeuvres."

The design style borrows heavily from the small-town fair, circa the 1930s. Visual allusion is also made to the music hall, medicine shows, alchemy, and Greek myth. The Smiths say they drew much of their inspiration from photographs of old Conklin touring shows, but also looked to old movies and other sources. The alchemical and mythic aspects of *The Greatest Show* are initially incongruous, given the dominant imagery, but as the designers point out, these are preoccupations of Schafer which strongly link this piece to the others in his cycle. Furthermore, the myth is the source of a story that is built up through the separate events.

R. Murray Schafer's preoccupations and his many occupations make him unique in Canadian arts. Born in Sarnia, Ontario, in 1933, he began studies in music at University of Toronto, although he was "ejected" in his first year. He travelled in Europe in the fifties, compiling a book of interviews of British composers and writing another called *Ezra Pound and Music*. In the sixties he built a reputation as a composer of symphonic and choral works, and began research into "soundscape" and music education. In November, 1987 he received the first $50,000 Glenn Gould Prize in recognition of his achievements.

In 1965 CBC television broadcast the premiere of Schafer's first music/theatre work, the bilingual opera *Loving*. Soon after, partly through dismay with opera-producing structures, and partly as a result of a broader dissatisfaction with existing mixed-media and interdisciplinary forms, Schafer began to formulate a new approach to performance. He criticized the way in which theatre production stressed text, dance focused on choreography, and opera emphasized music, even though elements of the arts overlapped. He concluded that the traditional approaches in these fields, though interdisciplinary, entailed a hierarchy, making them "rank-order creations." He sought a new way of combining music, acting, dance, poetry, and visual art, which he termed "theatre of confluence." In 1979 he wrote:

> The works of the future will be distinguished from rank-order creations
> by being conceived on all levels simultaneously. All the parameters of

these new works must be elaborated on coevally. It matters little whether this is accomplished singly or collectively.

If this sounds like Wagner's call for *Gesamptkunstwerk,* Schafer readily acknowledges the similarity. It is not only the desire for integration which links Schafer to the German Ringmaster. The scope of his endeavour is also Wagnerian.

After *Loving,* Schafer composed a huge work entitled *Patria One: The Characteristics Man.* This portrays D.P., a mute immigrant (not unlike Caspar Hauser) who struggles to assemble an identity against the onslaught of the mass media. Primarily because of the improbability of finding a production for a work that required so many performers and such a large budget, Schafer shelved the piece for a time. In the seventies however he returned to the music/theatre, taking up the earlier work and beginning a cycle of linked pieces, which he calls "Patria" from the Greek for land, the root of "patriotism."

Patria Two: Requiem for a Party Girl was the first part of the cycle to be performed, in a workshop at the Stratford Festival's Third Stage in 1972. In 1981 his *Prologue: The Princess of the* Stars was produced at Heart Lake, north of Toronto. This was the first of Schafer's experiments with outdoor staging, and the first collaboration with Jerrard and Diana Smith. The piece is a "dawn ritual" that takes place on a flotilla of canoes on the water, while the audience watches from the shore. The Smiths also worked on the Banff Centre revival in 1985. In 1983, the Smiths designed costumes and sets for *Patria Six: Ra* produced by Comus Music Theatre at the Ontario Science Centre [see *CTR* 47]. This is a ten-hour all-night ritual where the audience members "play" robed initiates in an Egyptian priesthood. The 1983 production and a subsequent production at the Holland Festival in 1985 were both directed by Thom Sokoloski. The experience of *Ra* led Schafer, Sokoloski, and the Smiths to form Patria Music/Theatre Projects.

In November of 1987, the Canadian Opera Company mounted a less than satisfying production of *Patria One: The Characteristics Man,* directed by the Shaw Festival's Christopher Newton. This production's problems seem to have reaffirmed the commitment to long-term collaboration by the members of the Patria team. They speak of the value of knowing all the pieces well, and the way work on one has fed the work on others. Directors, designers and writers have sometimes evolved a long-term collaboration in Canadian theatre on an ad hoc basis, but one would be hard-pressed to find a comparison to the long-range collaboration planned by this artistic team.

The foursome will continue their partnership with a fall, 1988 production of *Patria Four: The Black Theatre of Hermes Trismegistos,* slated for Liege, Belgium, and *Patria Five: The Crown of Ariadne,* tentatively scheduled for production in Halifax and Montreal in 1990. Currently they are mounting the full production of *Patria Three: The Greatest Show* to run this August, with plans to repeat the show in 1989.

Ideally they envision a permanent base where eventually the entire cycle, which now includes seven full-length works, will be mounted together in a festival. Peterborough has been extremely hospitable to *The Greatest Show* so far, and the possibility exists that it may evolve into Schafer's Bayreuth. In Canada, where ambition is so often muted, and where festivals have usually celebrated dead foreign artists, this seems audacious. But then again, R. Murray Schafer does not lack audacity, and his team-mates share his vision. Whether they create a new Bayreuth festival or not, their accomplishments so far have defied the odds, and they have shown remarkable energy and ingenuity in finding solutions to the problems posed by existing producing structures.

...

The Text: Schafer on *The Greatest Show*

Burgess: How does *The Greatest Show* differ from a museum re-creation of a small town fair?

Schafer: The only difference between this and a real small town fair of the old days is that many of the acts and what I call "editing units" or scenes in the work are, one would discover, related. As you stroll around in your perfectly free way, assimilating a bit of this and a bit of that, you will discover that something you've heard an actor say in one corner of the fair relates in a very substantial way to something that is being carried on in another corner. So it is really quite an intricate network of interactions. I don't think that prevents the ordinary public from appreciating the work. We have found that although the work has those sophisticated intentions for those people who want to seek them, there is still appeal for the person who wants to enjoy the work in an uncomplicated way.

Burgess: Would you agree that *The Greatest Show* is more overtly "populist" than the other pieces presented so far in the *Patria* cycle? If you do agree, is this thrust going to become more evident in the productions to come?

Schafer: Well, I think it's more populist in the sense that it is a fair and at a fair an entire community can be found. So, it's not elitist in any sense. Although, as I have said, the work is every bit as complex as any of the others, still the appearance of it is that it is not a complex work.

One of the intentions, too, with *The Greatest* Show was to involve an entire community, not only as audience, but also as performers. Seventy-five per cent of the cast of about one hundred and fifty in *The Greatest Show* comes from Peterborough. They are local performers and they bring a kind of enthusiasm that is difficult to really match if you bring in professional entertainers from the outside. Twenty-five per cent of the cast is, let us say, professional, whose purpose it is to give the community performers a bit of a boost: to make their work a little tighter, cleaner, sharper. But it is a community project and I think all that evidence suggests that it is populist.

I don't think this necessarily suggests an exclusive direction of the *Patria* cycle because the work which follows it is *The Black Theatre of Hermes Trismegistos*. Hermes Trismegistos was an alchemist and this is a very mystical work about alchemy, designed to be produced in a deserted mine at midnight to a fairly exclusive group of people.

Burgess: How do the content and, especially, the form of *The Greatest Show* further your stated environmentalist agenda?

Schafer: I'm not sure that *The Greatest Show* relates in particular to the environmentalist agenda. It does relate to the social one: my attempt to break down this horrible division between the professional and the amateur, the entertainer and the entertained, to find some way in which not only the actors, the musicians and the others involved in the performances, somehow in the middle between professionals and the amateurs, but also the entire audience (so called) is involved and participates. The strange thing about going to a fair or a carnival is that the moment you put on a mask or lose your wallet while you're upside down on a sky-ride, or win a prize and are forced to carry around a blue balloon for the rest of the evening, you have become an actor. There is a great deal of that in *The Greatest Show*. The public is encouraged to participate in the work and to some extent become actors. There are even some restricted shows that require you to win a ticket to get in. To win one you have to play games, do various required things, if you want to get into those shows. You can't buy your way in. It is part of an attempt to create a new kind of art-society, if you will.

The environmentalist works are rather different. There are some of them, particularly *Princess of the Stars*, not only because it is created for performance outside, around a lake at dawn, but also because some of the characters come from the environment. The "dawn birds," the "Sun," are actual characters in the work. By personalizing nature and attaching significant legends to nature, people are drawn to appreciate it. A mountain is no longer just some old mountain that you dig up for the minerals, it is a particular mountain with a particular story, and you have to think twice before you go and chop into it.

Burgess: Do you hope for a permanent site for *The Greatest Show*, and for that matter, for the entire *Patria* cycle?

Schafer: No. Well, yes and no. I think that *The Greatest Show* could become a repertory piece. I would like to see that happen. I think *The Princess of the Stars* could become a repertory piece. I think that those works could be done at particular places, *Princess of the Stars* perhaps in the Rocky Mountains, *The Greatest Show* perhaps in Peterborough. They could be repeated continuously and become characteristic of those places.

What we need in Canada is more of those kinds of spectacles. We suffer from neophilia, from the idea that we have to grab hold of the whole world. We've got to do everything here. This is of course, what our friends at Stratford, Shaw, the CBC and the Canadian Opera Company are imbued with: that mission to bring the entire world to our doorstep. And, as a result, they don't do anything particularly well.

What to me would be more important would be to have a real home for these works. They would evolve by being performed regularly there. Also, some of these works could not be performed anywhere else; they require a site in Canada. They are intensely nationalist works in that sense.

They would create a counter-stream to the prevailing notion that all art should be immediately accessible throughout the entire world. They would create another idea, which is really a much more ancient one, which is that of the pilgrimage to a specific place to see or hear something that is not accessible anywhere else. You cannot see it on television, you never will be able to see it on television. So, if you want to experience it you have to actually go to the site. I think that works such as *The Greatest Show*, *Princess of the Stars*, perhaps even *Ra*, are works of that sort. But since they use so many different settings, some outdoors, some indoors, they could never be harnessed together and performed at one particular place.

Burgess: What was the reaction of the audience at the workshop in Peterborough? What did you learn from them?

Schafer: Well, my reaction was that the audience was totally involved in the work in the way I hoped they would be. The audience was very mixed, too, because the park in which the show was held is used for different things in the course of the summer: rock concerts, concerts of ethnic music, and other things of that sort. So, I wouldn't say that they came with any colossal expectations of attending the latest piece of avant-garde Schaferiana …. In fact, most of them would never have heard of Schafer. *The Greatest Show* even jokes about this, you know: that they don't know or don't care who the author is and there he is, trying to take credit for the work but the performers are just scoffing at him.

That also suggests the way in which a work like *The Greatest Show* would slip back into anonymity, how it would no longer be the intellectual property of one creative individual but would gradually become a community property. As the acts are gradually transformed by the performers... The things that work in them they'll keep, the things that don't they'll change. They'll find new lines, new music, to communicate better.

• • •

The Staging: A Three-Dimensional Illusion

Thom Sokoloski has directed R. Murray Schafer's *Ra*, and *The Greatest Show*, which he will direct again this summer. In the fall he will direct Schafer's *The Black Theatre of Hermes Trismegistos* at the Festival of Liege, Belgium and there are plans for him to direct *The Crown of Ariadne* in 1990. He was artistic director of Theatre Autumn Leaf and a co-founder of Toronto's Theatre Centre.

Burgess: How did you first come into contact with R. Murray Schafer?

Sokoloski: That happened in 1982. I had just been speaking with Billy Bridgman—she was running Comus Music Theatre. I had seen a review of Schafer's *Princess of the Stars* in *NOW* magazine, and said, "Wow, this is great. Who is this person doing this? Nobody else I know is doing this kind of stuff …" So, I talked to Billy and she said that it was R. Murray Schafer and she let me read through his *Characteristics Man* and the *Requiem for a Party Girl* and *Princess*. I noticed that in the introductions to each of these pieces he talked a great deal about Reinhardt, Meyerhold, Vahktangov, and dashes of Artaud and the Russian constructivists, who I really admire. So then we arranged a meeting, Murray and I, and we started talking. We talked about *Ra* and then I got involved. I think we connected pretty fast, right away, when we first met. I was young and he knew that, but at the same time, I was doing okay in Toronto at that time …

Burgess: How and when did directing *Ra* evolve into forming Patria Music/Theatre Projects?

Sokoloski: That took a lot. We had done *Ra* and it really went over well, it won a Dora for innovation, but, at the same time, it had gotten a bit carried away. It became almost too much, almost something elite. It wasn't necessarily a way in which I thought things should go, in terms of the way it was produced by Comus. Nor was Murray happy with those aspects. Then we were invited to Holland and we took control of it—Comus helped, but not a lot. We found we managed better artistically when it was just the group of us, Murray, Jerrard, Diana and myself. After Holland, in 1986, we thought of putting something together that we wouldn't necessarily produce work with, but would be a kind of a starting point that we could use to apply for monies and start creating things. So it gave us a kind of base. I think Murray wanted that for a while—to have his own company called Patria. I mean, not that we do anything monumental on our own—what we do is basically co-production. But at least when we go to Belgium this fall it ends up being a Patria Music/Theatre co-production and that name gets spread around.

Burgess: Can you describe the collaboration process that you and Murray follow when you have an upcoming show?

Sokoloski: Well, first we read the script and then I interrogate him on what he really wants, because Murray certainly sees it. For example, there's a part in Ra where the audience has been initiated into the "priesthood"—they've learned certain chants and so on. They come in this procession into a cathedral, and for me it was important that at this point things had somehow changed. I didn't know exactly how or what things had changed so I just questioned Murray about what he would sense if he were the audience walking into this place. Many times he would be the audience. I would go ahead and stage it, and he would "play" the audience, and see if he experienced what we had discussed.

Burgess: How do you incorporate the music into your preparations?

Sokoloski: It's important right from the beginning, because it's in the music where I'll find the ambience. Sometimes, if the music hasn't been recorded, I'll sit down with Murray and he'll be at the piano and he'll play it for me. And we'll talk about how it connects things thematically. Then I'll begin to use those sounds, sometimes in voices, or for the mood. You have to really stick with it because as a director, if you're not using the sounds, the suspense or the crescendos or the diminuendos appropriately the piece will just slide away from you.

Burgess: What are the directorial problems posed by *The Greatest Show*, compared to a more traditional play or opera?

Sokoloski: Initially I saw the problems of simple organization, co-ordination more than anything. Murray's work has a very strong element of structure to it which has to be formalized and created. He proposes it, but he doesn't propose the workings of it. That's one thing that fascinates me about it: developing the work and creating the beehive of everyone doing his or her part within the context of the whole activity.

First of all, the main thing you realize is that you are dealing with a fairground piece, a piece that takes over an area of land and sets itself up. You have booths and tents and main stages, and roving elements. So, as a director, you really can't look at it straight on, as you'd do on a stage. I can never stand somewhere on high and look down on it. What you end up doing is creating a ground plan, almost football manoeuvres or invasion manoeuvres, that are all diagrammed on paper and everything is timed. Certain acts move from place to place, until you begin to get these geometric patterns. At some points groups will run into each other and there will be conflict between the characters.

The other thing is that I couldn't direct something this big alone. So what I've done is subcontract, you could say, with three associate directors. They're almost like a second unit on a film. I direct the main stage events, and confer with them while they go off and work on smaller sections. Then, at one point, after they've worked at assembling many of the parts the overall staging happens and I take a bullhorn and direct the whole thing. And you do need a bullhorn. It's just too big, you'd lose your voice.

Burgess: Ideally, what would the audience experience at *The Greatest Show*?

Sokoloski: The audience is kind of inside, walking through this illusion, and I try to give it authenticity, a kind of authentic illusion. What we're trying to create this year is the feeling that once you are in those fairgrounds, the illusion is sustained, you can't see the makings. Everything that is making it is also part of the illusion. When you go to the circus, you see people who are putting up the tents and stuff but they're not separate, they aren't props people or tech people, they belong to that world. And you might see them later on in the show as a clown or something. So, ideally, the audience would enter the illusion three-dimensionally.

• • •

The Design: Looking Right from Two Feet Away

Jerrard and Diana Smith are long-time collaborators of R. Murray Schafer and are co-founders of Patria Music/Theatre Projects. Diana designed costumes and Jerrard designed masks and/or sets for *Ra*, *Princess of the Stars, and The Greatest Show*. Jerrard also designed Robert Desrosiers' *Blue Snake* for the National Ballet and made the masks for Linda Griffiths' *Jessica*.

Burgess: How did your association with R. Murray Schafer begin?

Diana: Well, as so many things do, almost by accident. In 1981 Murray, along with New Music Concerts, was planning to mount *Princess* at Heart Lake near Brampton. And he wanted large structures on canoes—the piece takes place on these canoes. He thought that what he wanted was a maskmaker rather than a propsmaker because in effect they were huge masks. He called up the Ontario College of Art and asked if they knew anybody, and it so happened that the person he spoke to did, and that turned out to be Jerrard. In the meantime I was still a student at the college, I graduated that year. My studio [at OCA] filled up with strange masks and I kind of got dragged into making birds' wings and wolf coverings and everything else. We've been working with Murray ever since.

Burgess: Why form Patria Music/Theatre Projects?

Jerrard: The idea is that Murray likes to keep people together once it's been proven that they work as a team. We worked successfully together with Thom on *Ra*, twice: both here and in Holland, and the idea was that if we could keep this core group of people together to develop Murray's work there would be a consistency that would carry through the works. Patria is just a loose organization. There is no rigid structure really. We are incorporated, we're non-profit, but that's about as far as it goes. We don't have an administrative staff or anything like that. We can apply for grants although so far we can't apply for private donations because we haven't received our charitable number yet. So, we are on the ground floor right now.

Burgess: Can you describe your method of work with Murray?

Diana: Working with Murray is very collaborative. He doesn't appear suddenly with a finished, set-in-stone project.

Burgess: It seems you'd have the opportunity to begin working on a *Patria* piece at an earlier stage in its development than is typical in Canadian theatre.

Diana: Definitely. I'd say we are very lucky that way, and I think Thom would agree with us. We can be in touch with a piece from very early on in its development. Murray has often incorporated ideas that have come out of our discussions into the finished works.

Jerrard: We'll sit down and Thom and Murray will give us ideas for the designs and we'll suggest ideas on how things might be staged. I mean, it's not like we do the designs and Thom does the staging (although of course eventually that's his domain) but in our process of working together we can discuss back and forth.

Burgess: How did *The Greatest Show* end up in Peterborough?

Jerrard: After we did *Princess of the Stars* in Banff the Inter-Arts Department decided they would like to do *The Greatest Show*. They hired us to do the initial design work, but subsequently they ran into financial difficulties and had to cancel the program. Well, that was great in a way, because at least we got the design work done. The next step was to look around for another organization or production facility. So we thought of approaching a small town. I guess it was Thom who thought of Peterborough because he had some connection with Artspace.

So, we talked to Artspace, Arbor Theatre, the Theatre Guild, Peterborough Symphony, Magic Circus Theatre, Trent University, of course, and a few associated interested individuals. In late 1986 we had a meeting and the participants expressed an interest in following up the idea of doing the show. We, that is, Patria, got some money through grants from arts councils and foundations for a workshop. So we approached Peterborough and said "We have $30,000, that's a start …. Can you add to that?" They said yes, and raised about another $30,000, so we had about $65,000 for a full-scale workshop.

Burgess: What problems does *The Greatest Show* pose to you as designers?

Diana: We face design problems on many different levels because everything has to work more like a movie set than a stage set, really because it's being seen from all sides and from everywhere. So, it has to have the overall look that's right: people have to look right in groups, whether it's six people on the stage or four people behind you. They also have to stand up to the intimacy of face-to-face contact with the audience. So you can't get away with stage tricks as far as decorating costumes. They have to also work as clothes, with the same requirements as a film close-up. The same goes for props. They have to look right from two feet away, and they must work properly, but then they also must convey something to an audience from a stage over, say, fifty feet away.

Jerrard: We have a lot of work to do because we not only have to design the sets and costumes but also the backstage areas, the front of house, the stages, the whole thing: the theatre itself. But, then again, because we are not limited by an existing format, a physical plant, we have the advantage of setting it up exactly as we want, as the piece requires.

(1988)

Works Cited

Schafer, R. Murray. "Theatre of Confluence (Note in Advance of Action)." *Open Letter* 4th ser. 4–5 (1979): 30–48.

The Words Are Too Important

by Alan Filewod

Necessary Angel's *Newhouse* is a significant departure from the norm of political theatre in Canada. Its treatment of AIDS removes the issue from the politics of personal relationships and medical treatment and places it in the arena of public social policy. The text projects a near-future society in which an unnamed sexual plague has reached epidemic proportions. The controversy becomes the focus of an election campaign in which the audience assumes the role of the mass electorate. The performance strategy of the play recaptures the public voice of classic tragedy, in which private scenes take place in public spaces. The audience's experience of the tragedy is mediated by the constant presence of the mass media, who follow the leaders in scrums and televise the scenes onto the banks of monitors that surround the playing space. The essentially medieval configuration of the space allows the audience to move from platform to platform, and brings the action to the floor as actors cross the arena.

The text of *Newhouse* draws upon two classic sources. Sophocles' *Oedipus* provides its political debate between the prime minister who is determined to find a just social policy, only to discover his own tragic contradiction, and his Creon-like Minister of External Affairs who crosses the floor to bring down the government. Tirso de Molina's *Don Juan* (also known as *The Trickster of Seville*) provides the basis for a questioning of sexual behaviour in an age when sex means death. *CTR* editor Alan Filewod spoke to director Richard Rose and dramaturge D.D. Kugler about the play.

CTR: Could you talk about how *Newhouse* was conceived?

Richard Rose: Well, it went through a lot of generations and versions. I've always been interested in the Don Juan story, in trying this sort of modern update, and I had the opportunity to do this thing at the California Institute of the Arts. I used students there to improvise on the Don Juan story, a mixture of Moliere's *Don Juan* and Odin von Horvath's *Don Juan*, reset in Los Angeles. This was about three or four years ago. The AIDS issue was there to cope with and the students all improvised and assembled the show—kind of like we did with *Mein*—but the content wasn't very thick or very deep so I didn't really like what was going on with it, I didn't know what to do. It was about a guy who came to Los Angeles, who climbed up the social ladder using his sexual magnetism. I guess it was about the power of sex that politicians have, using sex as a political tool. But at the same time while I was doing that in Los Angeles, Rock Hudson had just sort of spilled, and there was a surge of information about AIDS, especially in Los Angeles. It started to emanate all over North America but it was as if Rock's greatest role was to do that, to send up this massive weight of information—that someone real could have it, someone famous could have it.

The experience of AIDS when I was in Los Angeles and subsequently when I came back to Toronto was a kind of hysterical panic, an obsession with it. All these new things were coming out, the press was pumping out tons of information but nobody knew the answers. The research kept changing every day. So I realized it was very difficult to do a story of Don Juan, given today's sexually transmitted diseases and the stakes of sexual freedom. We did a version which we workshopped in 1987, which had a little bit of the *Oedipus* story in it but it wasn't very prominent. The conceptual idea was to take place on the streets of Toronto and you'd follow the Don Juan figure as he went through this journey. That's all the Don Juan story really is—one big journey from country to country, from bedroom to bedroom.

The adaptation at that point emphasized von Horvath's version. It was a Don Juan that came back from the war, it was a guy who had changed... Don Juan had changed his response. It did combine a bit of the Molina Don Juan: the rake who is advocating sexual freedom, thinking that's out of the 60s and 70s about sexual freedom, and then suddenly he's faced with this disease and is possibly a carrier and is being investigated by the health authorities. That works to a point but von Horvath's Don Juan's very inactive, in fact he is being acted upon; it's one man and 25 female characters and they all act upon him and eventually he becomes the person he was before. He didn't want to be a Don Juan but he eventually falls back into that trap. There was a little bit of *Oedipus*. *Oedipus* was meant to happen on TV so this Don Juan figure would run into a political story which didn't seem to directly affect his life but was one more crisis in the government. We just took snatches of *Oedipus*, it was kind of thin, at that time.

D.D. Kugler: In effect, the Don Juan story which appears in *Newhouse* now is only the first third of the one that appeared in the workshop at that time. So the final two parts of the Don Juan workshop are available for a sequel to *Newhouse*.

Rose: The Don Juan finally gets diseased, and as he comes back from the war, he has this traumatic experience, he wants to be a changed man, he doesn't want to be a sexual rake any more. He wants to return to his love of many years ago and redeem himself and marry her and become normal but he can't find her. She's disappeared. That society moves him more towards decadence and he eventually just gets sucked into it. And although the workshop Newhouse was quite different, he became more and more an involved politician. But out of that workshop version we felt lots of dissatisfaction with the script and after taking some more time off to think about it we decided there was a need for more Oedipus.

We wanted to do this thing where the audience would wear headsets and the actors would broadcast to them on an FM frequency from a small radio station. They would just follow the Don Juan figure and see the Oedipus stuff on TV and then get bused to various areas of the city for changing scenes and stuff like that. We couldn't do that. I wanted to get more theatrical because it got very TV-like, very film-like, and we relied a lot on those techniques, and so did the language and the style of the theatrical presentation. It was built on that concept—really intimate, you hear the character right in your ear, and very visual. We couldn't do that, we couldn't afford it. I decided to move to a more theatrical presentation, expand the Oedipus story, give it equal weight. It seemed I got more and more interested in the political aspects.

CTR: And what attracted you to *Oedipus* in the first place?

Rose: Well, in California, I do remember, there was a whole series of political reactions. A senator came down with AIDS, quite an old senator. He got it from a blood transfusion from an operation and he wanted to start building quarantines. He was already, like, 79, he was going to die soon, okay, and he was really pissed off that he had got this disease from a blood transfusion, so he wanted to start building quarantines. In the election at the time, there were the Lyndon Larouches of the world with their hysterical politics. It seemed to me that the issue had to have political ramifications and that some day at some point someone would use it as a political weapon and over that course of time as politics began to go through this shift, it moved from policy to personality. You elect your politicians based on their personality or personal lives, not on their policies, and their personal lives become subject to political tactics.

I was very interested in how the personal becomes at the same time a really easy tool—how sexual disease could be used as a political tool to bring down a government. I wanted to deal with a prime minister, with the head of government trying to work with reason and compassion, trying to cope with something approaching epidemic levels trying to beat back hysteria, trying to get people to become responsible for all the things Canadians are good for—peace, order, good government, reason, responsibility, conducting themselves in a safe sex manner. And yet he's attacked on one side by the evangelists, making it quite personal, turning it into a political attack, beginning to maim people, beginning to research into peoples' lives, trying to link people into chains, making accusations and casting aspersions on their character and their political ability to lead. When I decided to make it a prime minister I wanted to suggest the possibility that everybody could have it, which is certainly common now but at the time I was writing I was still seeing it within the gay community, it was some kind of gay disease. So I wanted to pit the fragility of democracy against an epidemic and show how easily that could be transformed and how people would come to make such rash decisions out of fear and how fear could be a strong political tool for anybody who wanted to impose quarantine measures. I figured that if it does reach those levels I don't doubt they'll impose quarantine. There's a Minister of Health in Ontario who says he would have no problem in imposing quarantines in view of public safety. Bluntly said it. It passed by in the papers.

CTR: That was an issue, they did it in the prisons in fact.

Rose: They just impose it quite quickly and there won't be any problems. Look at the War Measures Act. It came in because there was great fear all around. We in Canada always lay down to that. And pitted against that—this was the last part of the play to really develop while we were in rehearsal—was the Newhouse story which was to pit the opposite argument against safety and responsibility. Or against what the evangelist was arguing, which was that this was an act of nature, we were simply following nature's course. We tried to pit the evangelist in such a way that he wasn't one of the Jimmy Swaggarts of the world.

CTR: Is that why you portrayed the evangelist as a paraplegic?

Rose: Actually it was Lou Gehrig's disease because with Lou Gehrig's disease there is no feeling. It's not painful, it's just that your body loses feeling. Sexuality wasn't important to him but thinking would be. Like Steven Hawking, all he can do is think.

Kugler: He owes more to Steven Hawking than anyone else. If you look at Steven Hawking's preface you'll find a lot of his dialogue.

CTR: The choice worked—he was a very chilling figure.

Rose: In a way there's no fear factor—a disabled person is not a threat. But a prime minister who is full-bodied, vital, has a sexuality, male, is a threat. You can almost trust the other person because he doesn't seem to have any ego. Very fragile. At the same time … he'll never get it, there's no way he can unless someone injects him. The body isn't important to him. But the Prime Minister has desires, he's acted upon his desires and suddenly he's hit by fate. And on the opposite side is the Newhouse/Don Juan figure who—this was the more difficult part—argues still for sexual freedom.

Kugler: Almost sexual irresponsibility, which is the nature of desire.

Rose: The difficult thing was always making him honest, to avoid the Don Juan as manipulator, liar, a rake, a cheater, a rapist—to get away from all that to a Don Juan who is more of a seducer but completely honest. The intent was to unleash desire on other people through his language. He confronts them saying, "if you want it then you should act on it."

In a sense there are four different debates going on, four points of view. The Prime Minister is the enemy of Don Juan because he's saying "be responsible, be reasonable, act with conscience."

Kugler: He's the most reasonable, the most human argument to Don Juan, whereas the servant is the most extreme.

Rose: We wanted to avoid as much as possible coming down with a moral statement. Give each force equal weight. Give the evangelist reasonable arguments, arguments we could buy or accept. Even in the back of my mind, I think, gee, maybe it's overpopulation, it's nature's way of responding … doesn't this happen to *deer?* Don't the wolves kill off the deer to balance the population?

The evangelist's argument is in a way an environmentalist argument: we're acting against nature. We live by sacred laws—thou shalt not covet thy neighbour's wife—

which have existed much longer than the sexual revolution—although there have been many sexual revolutions. These laws are there to protect our health.

The Prime Minister's argument is an easier one to present. Agree to act reasonably and responsibly. We'll all wear condoms … You look at those kids, they ain't gonna wear condoms.

CTR: The issue was made more complex by the social projection. You show us a society where women are relegated to the background, a society that has reverted to Victorian formality in social manners, in dress, in a range of values beyond sexuality.

Rose: The costuming choice we were faced with was: would fashion become more sexual in light of a sexual plague, or become less so? We returned to a conservative look—wrapping yourself up, protecting yourself, the wearing of gloves. A sense that there are toxins everywhere, a denial of the flesh, an attempt on the part of fashion to deny the body. People protecting themselves from sexual tension in the air because that would only arouse interest, arouse desire and you know where that would lead— someone would die eventually.

CTR: By setting the Don Juan story in the midst of an election campaign, you connected the debate on sexual freedom to larger political issues on Canadian-American relations. Was that deliberate?

Rose: We put America as the state leading the quarantine because we always seem to follow in their footsteps, much as I hate to say that—it seems our policies echo their actions. There was a brief time in the Trudeau era when it seemed to go against that but we've certainly lost that. It's like the whole thing with drugs now—that was what Reagan was doing a year ago, and now we're doing it, and everyone's talking about the drug problem in the country, a war on drugs. It's a carbon copy of what they were doing. There is no originality, no sense of identity. And this tremendous pressure, economic and cultural—as soon as they act, we're influenced. AIDS is much more prevalent there than here, maybe not per capita, I'm not sure of that, but it's certainly very present in New York.

Being in New York doing *Tamara* was also a great influence on us. I remember the parties. There'd be no sexuality in the room. People just shut it down. People were dying everywhere that summer. The casting director would go every week to memorial services. It was rife in the theatre community, and in the city as a whole. At the same time there were all these wild parties and sex clubs where nobody touched.

CTR: One of the strongest aspects of the play is the progression from the issue of disease to political relationships. You showed how sexual conservatism can grow into political conservatism as well. Beginning with Newhouse's seduction of the congressman's daughter immediately put the issue in the political arena.

Kugler: That was taken directly from Tirso de Molina's *Don Juan*. He's in exile and seduces the daughter of someone powerful. It's there in the structure of the source.

Rose: In *Don Juan* the king helps his chamberlain, Don Juan's father, cover up for Don Juan. We changed that orientation to the pressure of guilt by association. The father is acting to save his own political career because it would be a tool used against him. The fact that he is able to cross the floor once the election happens protects his own image.

And this thing of his son sleeping with the daughter of a Kennedy becomes terribly difficult—those are secrets one has to hide. There are always relationships between personal life and political behaviour. The reverse is true of the Prime Minister—his political beliefs affect how he conducts his personal life to the abuse of his personal life. There is a time when you don't want to know and you shouldn't know. The idea of volunteer testing … the desire to know and trying to figure it out and dig out the secret—that is Oedipus. Publicly he has to live by his beliefs, and his wife is saying, "I don't want to know, I don't care."

CTR: What direction will the next part take?

Rose: I want to stay true to the *Oedipus* story.

Kugler: This is just one part of the *Oedipus* trilogy.

Rose: There is an Antigone figure that re-emerges and *Oedipus at Colonus* … As the plague population grows, there's civil war between the plague people and the non-plague population. Separation in communities. So I want to follow that line where the Prime Minister goes into exile and quarantine—some kind of Colonus.

And there's the Don Juan who goes into a kind of exile and escapes to re-emerge and sneaks back into society with a new name—Newman. He becomes a sexual terrorist. He becomes involved with politics and enters the government. He reveals that they're using the plague to make money.

Kugler: They're buying into the blood banks, all the suppliers …

Rose: He starts sleeping with everyone he can possibly sleep with. And it's a new society, with secret sex clubs. He sleeps with everyone he possibly can and does an exposé of everyone he's slept with. A sexual terrorist. Wives, husbands … he does it to everybody he possibly can, using his tool, which is his sexual magnetism.

CTR: Why is AIDS never mentioned as such? It seems to work as a metaphor, an intensified version of the disease we know.

Rose: We didn't want to get bogged down in the realistic details of the disease: This could happen / this couldn't happen. We're not really interested in the specific details or the transmission of that disease or the nature of the disease as it's known now or next week.

Kugler: The details are changing all the time. All we know about it is that we don't know about it, and because we don't know about it, that's ignorance, and because we have ignorance we have fear, and that's essentially what we wanted to deal with.

CTR: It works because instead of responding on a level of fact, we respond on the level of social policy. The audience was engaged. It seemed to matter to them.

Rose: Our own sexual lives were at stake, how we conduct ourselves. Everybody's thinking, is it an act of nature? These thoughts are running through our minds. Do I fear it with this person, do I not fear it with this person, or do I just say fuck it, I'll do what I did ten years ago and just sleep with this person if I want to.

Kugler: For everyone, all the answers are true depending on the moment. It's very hard to establish a rationale for yourself and live by it. Very few people can do that.

CTR: Were you able to assess how the audience responded to the show?

Kugler: My sense was that the play wasn't liked by the theatre community and wasn't liked by the gay community. That was my sense, but I don't know if it was true or not. It wasn't prophylactic. It wasn't a how-to show dealing with the nuts and bolts issues. We didn't want it to be informational about a specific disease. An actor friend of mine said, "I wish you had someone who is actually suffering from the disease in it"—and he's gay, he works as a buddy with people with AIDS. There's probably a whole lot of agenda with that. He wants to see his story. It wasn't a disease that's the issue but the political and social effects the disease has.

CTR: Why did you choose to mount the show in a hockey rink?

Kugler: It was the only place big enough.

Rose: The only place available on our terms. For all the difficulties it turned out to be one of the most interesting and easiest places to set up in, because they already have a lot of power and facilities. Sound was difficult until we put up those curtains. Plus it was freezing cold. We expected it to be warmer in April.

To get that sense of the audience in the middle, the set was originally to be modeled on the human body, the government being the head. Money intervened. One of my desires was to have the floor sloping, sculpted in such a way as to have rises and curves like a body. The middle dais was meant to be the heart, where critical action takes place. But unfortunately we couldn't do that. We meant to use the body as a kind of cage—all those actions taking place inside the body. We cut that in week two of rehearsal because we knew we couldn't afford it.

We wanted to get that sense of coming to a public event which was a government issue, gathering at the foot of the steps of parliament, that sense of the audience— participation isn't really the right word—but being *inside* the play.

Kugler: Totally present but totally excluded.

CTR: In a way that exclusion replicated the political process in which people are engaged but effectively disempowered. That was reinforced by the use of video. Watching the TV crews reporting the action and then watching the images on TV constructed us as passive observers caught up in the middle of great events.

Rose: That surprised me. I was surprised by the concentration when we flipped on the video monitors.

Kugler: You found yourself believing the image more than the event that happens in front of you. You'd look at the event and end up watching the video because it was way more real than the event that you could reach out and touch. That was totally fortuitous. We never anticipated anything like that.

CTR: The hockey rink was also an accessible space that required a different response. People are used to public gatherings in rinks.

Rose: Someone said it was like going to a party, a rock'n'roll dance party, like going to see a band at a rink.

Kugler: Lots of times I heard people say, "I didn't like it." I asked them, "Did you move around, try to follow it?" No. The show may not work if you follow it but *I know* it won't work if you don't.

CTR: It was fascinating to watch the crowd surge in a general wave of movement whenever the action moved.

Kugler: Like the creation of a beast. The body politic.

Rose: They were meant to be like the veins. The design was supposed to have things through the space, like arteries. We sort of did that, bringing the action to the floor. We needed more height to make it work—arteries, pathways, interconnections. We would have put Washington way off, not in the body but high above, feeding the body versus Ottawa inside the body.

The designer said he'd like to see it on a proscenium stage. He said they miss the play too much; we should put it back on the stage so they can hear the words. The words are too important.

(1989)

All News Newhouse

by Natalie Rewa

The launching of a CBC all-news television channel in July confirms the contemporary need for a substitute for first-hand knowledge. On-the-spot reporting reassures us that we can get on with our lives because someone will draw our attention to anything that goes amiss. "News" also creates the illusion that the battle, the court judgement, or the manifesto is simultaneous with the audience's viewing. Moreover, with such dissemination of information and image, commentary is implicit.

This fascination with news reporting has had an effect in the theatre and, at the same time, access to video equipment has encouraged theatre practitioners to use video in performance. While this technique may be rationalized in particular ways in particular instances, it also poses significant questions about the relationship of the audience to a not entirely live performance. Several productions in recent seasons, adapting a function of television news, have made video a method of an omniscient narration.

In Carbone 14's production of *Marat/Sade*, for instance, live video was used during the performance to extend Weiss's metaphor of the audience as visitors *cum* voyeurs at an asylum. Locked in large observation "cages" to protect them from the inmate-performers, the audience could watch a simultaneous broadcast of the action on banks of television monitors. The arrangement of the screens resembled an institutional surveillance system. In contrast, Canadian Stage's production of *Donut City* incorporated simulations of the evening news report and an afternoon soap opera as reiterative techniques. As part of a store window display within the environmental set, the television broadcasts made the audience part of the streetscape, but at the same time isolated them from the experiences of the "street kids," as when the routine televised report of the murder of a prostitute showed the downtown site where the victim was found—a location within the set. The soap opera on the TV depicted a young prostitute who escaped the harshness of the street to become a glamorous and expensive call girl, in quasi-middle class surroundings: a sharp contrast with the "actuality" in the live performance, and with implications about media as well as morality.

Necessary Angel's *Newhouse*, an adaptation of Sophocles' *Oedipus* and Tirso de Molina's *The Trickster of Seville*, also used video as a composite narrator. Initially perceived as a way of verifying the live performance, in terms of its physical visibility, the video soon assumed the authority of on-the-spot news reporting. Supplemented by computerized bulletin boards, which projected "tabloid" headlines like the ones in

Toronto subways and banks, the videos constituted a telling image of our information-drenched environment. But the video and news bulletins, dominating as they were, pertained to only half the play; the other half was marked by an obvious lack of media coverage. Significantly the blanketed half was the part of the plot concerned with the immensely important and deliberately concealed sexual exploits of Newhouse, while the televised half was the political conflict between the Prime Minister and his opponents. To accompany this we had the live manifestation of a chorus of journalists equipped with tape recorders and video cameras, who pursued the Prime Minister for the televised news coverage that the audience then saw on the screens.

Rose and Kugler's source for the Prime Minister is Sophocles' Oedipus. Their other source has yielded Newhouse, modeled on Don Juan. Newhouse is the hedonistic seducer, careless of a public policy against unsanctioned sexual activity. The role of the King of Castile, who restores moral order in the wake of Don Juan's recklessness, has been given to the Prime Minister, who attempts to define an acceptable position regarding public health. Significantly, Don Juan's father, a faithful servant of the King, has been recast as the cynically pragmatic Minister for External Affairs who desperately diverts media attention from his son's exploits.

The use of video corresponds to the kind of theatricality inherent in the sources. The scale of the Greek amphitheatre where *Oedipus* would have been first performed for thousands of spectators was monumental. The almost constant presence of Oedipus on stage and the declamation of Sophocles' rhetoric was essential for audience understanding of the relationship between Oedipus and the Thebans. In *Newhouse* simultaneous video broadcast of the live performance served to replicate the focus on the central figure. As the object of news bulletins, the Prime Minister assumed a role similar to that of an Oedipus set against the *skenae* of the amphitheatre. (The focus of the camera excluded the need for even minimal reference to any illusory décor.) The Prime Minister was not only a physical presence, as in *Oedipus*, but also a contemporary image, looking out to the hypothetical audience of millions (represented by a real audience of a hundred or so) from a bank of television monitors. The personal trust invested in an elected individual was reciprocated in a pseudo-personal way through the intimacy of the television technique. The Prime Minister spoke sincerely to the cameras as if to an individual; the audience, on the other hand, had to accept the reporter as their collective spokesperson and the perspective chosen by the camera operator.

In contrast to the sparse visual imagery and static presentation in *Oedipus*, Tirso's *Trickster* invited the spectators to imagine Don Juan in a variety of settings: a noblewoman's bedroom, a seashore, and a country wedding. Originally performed in the open-air courtyard theatres of Spain, Tirso's vivid description of locations within the dialogue made elaborate scenery unnecessary. The diversity of Don Juan's seductions in terms of scene and action was tempered by the fixity (moral and physical) in the references to the king. This distinction in the verbal imagery is maintained in Rose and Kugler's adaptation. In their plot, the Minister for External Affairs' evasion of a media scandal is registered by an environmental presentation of Newhouse's marauding, rather than one recorded by the cameras. The rapid shifts between playing locations—bedrooms, bars, backyards and backrooms—contrasted with the use of television reportage (and manipulation) in the other half of the play. The presentation of Newhouse's seductions allowed for a division of attention between the woman and Newhouse and a certain freedom of choice for the audience as to which it would observe most closely. As it watched the Prime Minister the audience was addressed directly; as it watched Newhouse, the audience remained unacknowledged and unobserved.

This relation between the stage and audience was made possible by the use of multiple stages around the periphery of the hockey arena. The performance began with a simple presentation of opposites: at one end of the arena Newhouse's encounter with the woman at the Embassy ball in Washington; and, in the subsequent scene, at the other end, a reporter, appearing simultaneously in the flesh and on the screen, to inform the audience of the status of the crisis on Parliament Hill. After this brief "news bulletin," attention was redirected to the Embassy in Washington. This kind of rapid change of focus was sustained throughout the performance, but the need for the audience to re-gather round the stages where the Prime Minister was speaking was lessened because they could readily watch the simultaneous broadcast. Quite deliberately there was too little time for the spectators, suffering from a deliberately imposed "information overload," to digest the implications of any one scene.

Also significant was the configuration of the stages and the use of different kinds of video monitors to denote different kinds of information. At one end of the arena a large platform was the site of the rational aspects of human endeavour—government. An impressive superstructure of scaffolding went almost up to the building's supporting girders and a false proscenium was created by the columns of television sets that flanked this stage. The platform itself extended beyond this false proscenium, creating an apron, and this was connected to the auditorium by stairs the width of the playing area, a setting somewhat reminiscent of a Greek amphitheatre. Next to this platform was a smaller acting area, designated, primarily by lights, as the chapel. The proximity of these two areas was meant to suggest the relationship between politics and religion in appealing to reason and curbing human desire.

Along the sides of the arena were two long platform stages: on the one side the platform served as a media centre, where the Prime Minister was interviewed, as the offices of the Embassy in Washington, and as the bed of the woman whom Newhouse seduced on her wedding night. Facing this stage area, along the length of the other side of the arena, was a platform that served as Commander Gordon's house and as a hospital at one end, and as a bar and as a hotel room at the other. Each of these lateral platforms was divided by a large screen and other smaller screens. The media centre had a stack of monitors, the bar had only one 24" screen and the doctor's office in the hospital had a small monitor.

Situated between the lateral platforms was a multi-level platform with a large ramp, which in production became known as the "heart dais." There were no television monitors on it and emotional scenes took place there: the Prime Minister's confrontation with his wife as he considers the possibility of his contact with the disease, and Chambers' appeal to Newhouse to heed the warning about safe sex.

The fifth platform, opposite the site of government, was also without television monitors. Here were presented two of Newhouse's seductions.

According to Graeme Thomson, the designer, the arrangement of platforms was meant to represent, allegorically, the parts of the body politic. At opposite ends were the seats of intellect and desire, the central dais was the heart, along the lengths of the arena were the lungs, and the four entrances to the arena were meant to correspond to the limbs. Thomson considers this configuration a pun on the presence of media in contemporary society. During the performance the spectators were aware of the tension of opposites represented by the two main stages, but the conception of the total design was not made explicit.

The attention to video in the performance was particularly interesting when one considers what the initial plans for the productions entailed. Dorian Clark, who was involved with the workshop version of 1987, points out that the multi-focal approach, using media, was always intended. Initially *Newhouse* was to be an outdoors extravaganza with several stages located in downtown Toronto, to which the audience, equipped with earphones, would travel. A second idea was to use a single outdoor location with the cityscape as a backdrop. For practical reasons the production was moved inside.

These early plans confirm that Rose always meant to distinguish between what the audience merely saw and what actually commanded their attention. Thus, Thomson's design for the arena emphasized the facility with which the audience could see the performance without coming closer to the live action. The interest in Newhouse's seemingly unbridled sexuality was constantly being "interrupted" by political bulletins. The audience was encouraged to check whether or not a scene was being broadcast simultaneously. The authority of the media was used carefully in this performance, but the reliance on media coverage to narrate an understanding of the world tended to overshadow the significance of the live performance.

(1989)

The Deconstruction of Pleasure:
John Krizanc's *Tamara*, Richard Rose
and the Necessary Angel Theatre Company

by Richard Plant

As an introduction to the work of Necessary Angel, [1] this article provides brief commentary on several stage productions and culminates in a reading of *Tamara* with reference to some of its performances. My point about *Tamara* is that the naturalistic elements of its stage production urge audience members to construct the most pleasurable experience possible from the illusionistic performance circumstances. Simultaneously through its deconstructive mode, the metatheatrical semiosis prompts the audience to interrogate the nature of that construction of pleasure. Those Necessary Angel productions which I mention as context for *Tamara* can be seen to urge, to some degree, a similar consideration of the "truth" of pleasure—both the pleasure derived from mimetic illusionary stage performance and from ethically questionable behaviour in daily life.

Consistently among the most exciting work for the stage in Canada over the past decade or so (1978–1989) has been that of Richard Rose and the Toronto-based Necessary Angel Theatre Company founded in 1978. Their seasons have been high-lighted by innovative stagings in a variety of styles and venues, environmental to proscenium, and have included riveting productions of challenging plays, such as *Jacques and his Master* (1986) by the Czech author Milan Kundera or *The Castle* (1987) and *The Possibilities* (1989), these latter two by British playwright Howard Barker.

Many of their shows have been generated from within the company itself, as for example, was *Mein* (1983, remounted 1985), a collectively created, expressionistic handling of the inner world, the "fears, desires and impulses" (Mietkiewicz) experienced by "I", a young business executive on the way to the top. Marked by wittily choreographed movement, the play fragmented "I" into five performers (three men, two women, all in dark grey business suits) who presented the ironic iconography of his/her triumph over another applicant for a job, "I"'s subsequent promotion in which the displaced boss committed suicide, and then "I"'s fall from grace. Available to the audience throughout the imagistic, allusive *Mein* was an ironic, theatricalized experience of the "struggle" *(Kampf)* obliquely suggested in the puns of the title. The pleasure found by the materialistic, corporate mentality in "success," that is, dominating and possessing (mein/mine), was seen to be undercut by the pain of those oppressed and the shallowness of the "lifestyle" gains.

In 1989 Necessary Angel staged an adaptation by noted author Michael Ondaatje, dramaturge D.D. Kugler and Richard Rose of Ondaatje's novel *Coming Through Slaughter*, centred around a search for the tormented jazz musician Buddy Bolden who has disappeared. The Silver Dollar, one of Toronto's low-end bars, was an appropriately atmospheric site prompting the audience to enter an illusion of New Orleans jazz life. And clearly some audience members were transported, as Robert Crew's review might signal:

> The audience is plunged straight away into steamy New Orleans in about 1906. On the small stage, a glistening, nearly nude woman is performing the Oyster Dance. The malleable mollusk starts on the forehead and slips slowly past some interesting slopes and valleys before ending its journey around about the knee. Phew! (Crew)

But the illusion was often strained, sometimes by limitations in the production, for instance the terrible sightlines experienced by some of the audience. At other times, the presentational mode was foregrounded by strategic theatrical devices, as for instance when the actor playing the tormented Bolden moved into his other role of the rational Narrator and recited passages clearly identifiable as part of the novel, while the performers enacted them in various presentational modes. One of the effects of this conscious theatricalism was that the audience's attention was directed out of the naturalistic illusion toward the metaphorical resonances of the performance—questions about pleasure, pain, loss, madness, creativity, identity.

Just before *Coming Through Slaughter*, the production of Rose's own play *Newhouse*, (April 19–30, 1989; also created with D.D. Kugler) in a Toronto hockey arena allowed audience members to walk about a cityscape formed in the shape of a body[2] by a number of "stages" on the arena's perimeter and at its centre. The fast-moving action they followed was an ingenious interweaving of an imagined Canadian sociopolitical reality, *Oedipus Tyrannus* and Tirso de Molina's *The Trickster of Seville*, with material from Moliere's *Don Juan*, Seneca's *Oedipus* and Diderot's *Rameau's Nephew*. Described as a "speculation about possible, but avoidable, future events," (Rose) the play centres on two people, a Canadian Prime Minister (Oedipus) and Newhouse (Don Juan), the son of the Minister of Foreign Affairs. The Prime Minister's liberal-minded attempt to deal with a national epidemic of a sexually-transmitted disease leads him into conflict with conservatives and fundamentalists, and to the discovery that he has the fatal illness himself from an undisclosed extra-marital affair years before. In a climate where promiscuous sexual activity should be deemed a criminal offence (some of the Prime Minister's opponents want legislation to that effect), Newhouse's profound allure and insatiable sexual appetite lead to clandestine affairs whose volatile implications—he has contracted the disease also—threaten the government and raise weighty issues for everyone: "Is he an irredeemable menace knowingly infecting others with a deadly disease? Or is he the last vestige of devil-may-care spontaneity in an increasingly paranoid and suffocated society?" (Wagner).

The performance was shaped by dramatic tension between, on one side, the "timelessness" of the mythic echoes of *Don Juan*, *Oedipus* and the other works, as well as the allegorical, quasi-medieval world of multiple staging. On the other side was juxtaposed the immediate reality of the audience, the theatrical actuality of the individual playing spaces, and the references to everyday Canadian society, politics and personalities (for example, the actor playing the Prime Minister looked like Brian Mulroney). Within this diachronic/synchronic tension other conceptual frames were at work. As Richard Rose has said: "The audience members are voyeurs in the intimate scenes (the 'private', hidden political dealings, sexual and domestic affairs) and in the *Oedipus* story they become part of the public" (Rose). In performance, this public world existed amidst the audience, for example in news scrums where media figures with microphones and television recording equipment interviewed the politicians. As designer Graeme Thomson commented before the show: "...the piece will really be moving through the crowd a lot. At various times, when the Prime Minister and Minister of Foreign Affairs are being hounded by the press from all quarters, the audience will be forced to scatter" (Wagner).

These images of a "you are there" reality gained part of their public identity, their authority, from being "broadcast" throughout the performance space on screens, which ranged from ordinary televisions to large videotrons. (The "private" moments were not caught on camera.) The result was the creation of not only different sizes but different layers of reality: the theatrical illusion of the private world established a dialectic with the authenticated or documented public reality, and expanded into self-reflexive scenes where the audience could see itself on the screens watching the events being recorded (Rewa 40–42). These reverberant images were poised to operate in a fashion dramaturge D.D. Kugler has explained:

> Thematically...we're looking for much more complex material that doesn't give simple answers, that in fact makes the complexity of real issues apparent. I think that spills over into the form. You really want to pull out of a proscenium context because it gives you a framed, two-dimensional reality in a way. If you open the form out and get the audience inside the story structurally, they can see that that story spills over into their lives–that it affects them and they have an effect on it. (Wagner)

The artists may have been overly optimistic in their vision of the interactivity of *Newhouse*, particularly the audience's power to impact on the "story," since the production offered no openings in its mimetic narrative for audience intervention. The performance made clear that the production was aimed at exploring serious issues:

> ...how fear and ignorance are used as tools to manipulate social policy and political structure...alternative views of the public and private person...the ruthless pursuit of knowledge [and its implicit] arrogance that assumes all knowledge is attainable. (Kaplan 49)

However, the predominant impression, as Natalie Rewa argues (Rewa 40–42), appears to have been that of audience excitement generated by the novelty of the decentralized, multi-matrixed staging. This is certainly not an inconsequential artistic achievement in its challenge to proscenium theatre, but clearly not all the artists envisioned.

As successful as works such as *Mein* and *Newhouse* have been, the most fruitful collaboration for Necessary Angel has been that between Richard Rose and his high school friend, the playwright John Krizanc, also a founder of the Company. In addition to *Tamara*, to which I shall return shortly, they have worked together on Krizanc's *Prague*, which was a runner-up for both the Chalmer's Best New Canadian Play Award and a Dora Mavor Moore Award in 1984. *Prague* also earned the 1987 Governor General's Award for drama. In it, the director of a Prague theatre, motivated by guilt over betraying his father to authorities years earlier, endangers his company and family in an attempt to stage his own subversive play. *Prague* is intellectually and emotionally rich, a "critique of fascism" (Krizanc, qtd. in Knowles 28) with wit, and complexity in the manner of Tom Stoppard's works, such as *Professional Foul*. Unlike *Tamara* and other of the Necessary Angel plays, *Prague* takes metatheatrical advantage of a proscenium stage but deconstructs the illusions of that theatrical idiom at the same time as it examines the nature and function of art in an oppressive state. The subject is one on which Krizanc has commented outside of his plays:

> It's wrong for writers to be heroic. Ours is not an age of heroes. Every hero, or moralist, creates more and more victims, and totalitarianism can eat up as many people as want to throw themselves at the wall. (qtd. in Knowles 30)

Krizanc has expressed concern about the responsibility of artists, as well as the costs involved in "heroic" action:

> I was intrigued by Vaclav Havel and Pavel Kahout and the other Czech writers who were standing up against Communist totalitarianism. I really admire those writers…. I was saddened because the dissident movement had been so successfully crushed, but I also have to question the consequences of those actions, of the stands that were taken. For example, Pavel Landovsky, who signed the Charter of 77, is now in Vienna and he's been told not to return. But as a result of that action, his first wife lost her job, the son from that marriage was kept out of university, and the daughter was not allowed to graduate. Her apartment isn't heated, so she has a hacking cough and goes around like Camille. You think, so he's a better man for this because signing the Charter was the right thing to do. But what is the human cost? How many people have to fall in order for there to be goodness? (Jansen 34)

One of the links which has joined Rose and Krizanc has been their mutual interest in creating theatre which is interactive in ways that traditional theatre is not and in which the experience of the form is inherently that of the play's socio-political and ethical concerns. Their highest profile work has been *Tamara*, the unheralded, unassuming hit—loosely referred to as "environmental" or "promenade" theatre—of Toronto's "Onstage Festival" in 1981. Since then, *Tamara* has had "successful" productions in Los Angeles, Mexico City and New York, and is being considered for performances in other countries.[3] In Los Angeles, where it won numerous awards, the production developed a cult following of "Lifers," those who came back five times or more. Overall, *Tamara* International has grossed somewhere in the vicinity of $10,000,000 (including the sale of T-shirts and other memorabilia), an unheard of sum for a Canadian play from the small theatres.[4] The script has been printed by a major publishing house and, tangentially, there has even been a *Tamara* novel released in the United States, although John Krizanc has not allowed his name to be connected with it. An irony of all this is that the more "successful" *Tamara* has become at the box office, and the larger the production has grown, the less successful it seems to have been in achieving what its author and director have expressed as their serious intentions.

The action of the play occurs on January 10 and 11, 1927 in Il Vittoriale degli Italiani, the country home of Gabriele D'Annunzio, on the occasion of a visit by Tamara de Lempicka, the captivating artist from Poland who was portrait painter to many prominent individuals at the time. D'Annunzio has been carrying on a passionate correspondence with Tamara, and has invited her to paint his portrait. But, as the other eight members of his household know, he is attempting to add Tamara to his long list of lovers which already includes Eleanora Duse and Isadora Duncan (Krizanc 29). In the play as in history, D'Annunzio is the world-famous, nationalist Italian poet and hero whom Il Duce keeps out of political circulation and in a life of cocaine and sexual indulgence under a "protective" house arrest at Il Vittoriale. But Krizanc's D'Annunzio is the antithesis of the figure Isadora Duncan describes from personal experience:

> Perhaps one of the most wonderful personalities of our time is Gabriel D'Annunzio, and yet he is small and, except when his face lights up, can hardly be called beautiful. But when he talks to one he loves, he is transformed to the likeness of Phoebus Apollo himself.... When D'Annunzio loves a woman, he lifts her spirit from this earth to the divine region where Beatrice moves and shines. In turn he transforms each woman to a part of the divine essence, he carries her aloft until she believes herself really with Beatrice, of whom Dante has sung immortal strophes.

> Only one woman [Duse] in the life of the poet withstood this test... and so before her D'Annunzio could only fall on his knees in adoration, which was the unique and beatific experience of his life. (Duncan 5–6)

Also at Il Vittoriale are Gian Francesco de Spiga, an "inebriated composer, dilettante"; Dante Fenzo, a valet and ex-gondolier; Mario Pagnutti, a "mysterious new chauffeur"; Luisa Baccara, a former concert pianist; Carlotta Barra, a young dancer; Aelis Mazoyer, head housekeeper and D'Annunzio's confidante; Emilia Pavese, a "light-fingered" maid; and Aldo Finzi, a Fascist Captain stationed by Mussolini to guard D'Annunzio.[5]

Like D'Annunzio, whose liberty and artistic creativity have been compromised, the members of the household are each seeking freedom from forces oppressing them, but ironically each person has fixed on an ideological goal which denies freedom and overwhelms his or her integrity and creative potential. Krizanc's view is clear in this regard: "What I hate is people who let truth become subservient to political ideology. I think it has to be a personal truth" (qtd. in Jansen 34). De Spiga, who is not above passing off another composer's work as his own, has become a secret member of Mussolini's Fascist Party, believing that in this way he can protect art and his music. He is in love with Luisa, who gave up her art to become D'Annunzio's mistress, but she is now rejected and broken. Carlotta, a religious, racist fanatic (the Italian equivalent of a member of the Aryan Youth movement), seeks D'Annunzio's letter of recommendation to dance for Diaghalev; Aelis has sexual designs on Carlotta. Emilia comes from embittered poverty and will do whatever is necessary to rise in the world: steal, sleep with Finzi or with Mario. Dante is blindly in love with Emilia and has secretly had a child with her. Finzi, in love with Luisa, is surviving as best a Jew can at the time by joining the Fascisti. Mario, whose father is the Fascist Duke of Milano, is secretly a communist attempting to convince D'Annunzio to turn in that direction, but who will kill D'Annunzio as a last resort if he refuses. Tamara believes, or appears to believe, in art for art's sake.

When audience members arrive at Il Vittoriale (in Toronto a Victorian mansion; in Los Angeles the Hollywood American Legion; in New York the Seventh Regiment Armory), they are issued passports and greeted by Dante. Capitano Finzi stamps the passports and explains that they must be carried at all times, that anyone not able to produce his or her papers when asked will be deported. The audience, in Toronto a total of about 40, in Los Angeles about 125, and in New York approximately 160, then congregates in the "Atrium" where de Spiga is playing the piano (in New York champagne was served). Various members of the cast carry on a dialogue which introduces the characters and explains the house rules: in essence, each audience member is a guest at Il Vittoriale and is expected to act as a guest. Each person can follow whatever member of D'Annunzio's household he or she chooses throughout the evening, but no one is to go through a closed door nor follow any performer who shuts a door behind him/her. At the Intermezzo, everyone will be invited to enjoy refreshments and share information.

By the end of the evening, the audience has been close witness to dark political and sexual intrigue. Some spectators have seen Tamara reject D'Annunzio and humiliate him by calling him syphilitic. Everyone has seen D'Annunzio at the end of the play raving about his past glory in Fiume and snorting cocaine poured on the floor and a dead body. That body is Mario's, whose communist identity has been revealed and who has been shot accidentally by Finzi in a struggle with Emilia. (Not everyone has seen that, nor anything else except D'Annunzio's raving.) De Spiga has triumphantly crushed Finzi by announcing untruthfully that Luisa was always de

Spiga's, but he is subsequently crushed himself on learning from Tamara that Luisa has committed suicide. Tamara, after revealing Luisa's body to de Spiga, leaves the house calling everyone (including the audience) "Fascistes." (Tamara speaks French throughout much of the play.) Emilia refuses to leave Il Vittoriale, so Dante flees by himself to find their daughter. Carlotta had departed earlier with a letter from D'Annunzio, without knowing that it explained he had written only because he owed her father money. Despite careful plotting, everyone's plans have been brought to ruin by accident, human error or unforeseen awareness on someone else's part. The ending can be seen as chaos and devastation for the characters in the play.

For the audience, there is a parallel experience to the characters' chaos. The performance itself might be described as the enacting of ten plots, each centered on a person in the house, which intersect with one or another at various times in the evening. Because of the nature of the performance (noises off, actors visible in hallways and so forth), audience members will constantly be aware that action is going on simultaneously in other parts of the house—and, able to follow only one character, will be aware that they cannot see it all. Moreover, each plot is incomplete itself because it depends in part on the actions of characters in other lines of the narrative. The overall experience fosters in the audience a sense of being unable to comprehend exactly what is happening, a sense of fragmentation and confusion. Intermission provides a kind of relief: sharing experience allows the pieces of the puzzle gathered by one person to join with those picked up by others resulting in a greater sense of what has occurred. But ultimately audience members are foiled in their Aristotelian detective work. Narratively, there are just too many loose ends, too many events unexperienced, unexplained to get a sense of the whole.[6]

Published reaction to *Tamara* in performance has been generally favourable, at times ecstatic, if not very perceptive, as John Krizanc's "the incomprehension of the reviewers drove me crazy (qtd. in Jansen 36)" would indicate. In Toronto reviewers called it a "surprise hit," commented that it was "brilliantly staged" and described the experience in terms of watching like "a fly on the wall." They spoke of the vicarious thrill of taking part in romance and intrigue, and of the joy in trying to put the pieces together. Many acknowledged the aforementioned sense of chaos and fragmentation; some treated that as a flaw. In Los Angeles, published commentary was much as in Toronto, but in addition, expressed interest in what stars were involved, both on stage and in the house. Attention was drawn to the catering by Ma Maison, and to the paintings by Tamara De Lempicka (Jack Nicholson, among others is a collector) adorning the walls (until they were withdrawn for safety reasons). There were references to the $500,000 budget (in contrast to $28,000 in Toronto which swelled to $40,000 before the six months were finished), to the fact that Karen Black could fill the house at $75 a seat, and eventually to the cult of "Lifers." Mexico had a special interest: Tamara had lived there, somewhat ingloriously, in her later years, replicating her earlier paintings. Published commentary spoke of the Mexican who invested in the production, of the $117,000 spent to buy the house in which it was played, and of the nationally famous soap opera stars who filled the lead roles. Reviewers described the piece as novel and passionate, and very enjoyable. New York, where an elegant buffet of Il Vittoriale-style food, champagne and even a "Tamara Cocktail" was part of the evening, was not greatly different, albeit larger in all respects, and on occasion somewhat jaded:

> Come to think of it, "Tamara" rather resembles one of those misguided sightseeing tours at the end of which nothing is more welcome than the waiting bus. (The armory amenities include plenty of well-distributed settees.).... Beyond the novelty and the refreshments, perhaps it appeals to the Peeping Tom instincts of an age when supermarket tabloids and slick gossip magazines have made a major industry out of publicizing other people's scandals. (Beaufort 22)

The overall impact might be indicated by the subsequent opening in New York of other "promenade" theatre events.

As time goes by and scholars have a chance to study the performance in light of the published and unpublished scripts, as well as printed criticism and other resources, this response is changing. Richard Paul Knowles, in his usual perceptive fashion, points out how the play and its language deal with the failure of the artist to take a stand (Knowles 27–33). In his "Foreword" to the published edition, Alberto Manguel offers an insightful analysis touching on several of the points mentioned here. But in short, the performance response seems to have centered on the novelty of the staging, the "good-natured decadence" (Gussow 24) of the food and drink, and the fun of piecing it all together. It has generally dismissed the play's serious intentions and profound disquiet. [7] As John Krizanc says, "if you go for the sex you miss the climax" (Krizanc 38).

In retrospect, this is understandable. The experience of the play can be seen to depend on two counteracting impulses. On one side are the results of John Krizanc's and Richard Rose's attempt to construct a "democratic theatre" that allows the individual in the audience freedom to make choices, to create his/her own work of art: "I thought the best way to write a critique of Fascism was to give people more democratic freedom than they've ever had in the theatre…. For the audience, the intermezzo is important because it's about freedom of information, which you don't have in a Fascist state (qtd. in Jansen 34)." Yet the performance mode simultaneously deconstructs the move toward apparent freedom, denying the audience completion of any artistic vision. The spectator creates his/her art within what is at root a manipulated set of circumstances, a state of artistic "fascism" where the choices are dependent upon the conventions set up by the production. At the same time *Tamara* is breaking with traditional theatre, the performance mode calls for an illusionary art, the "willing suspension of disbelief" by the audience, in a realistic (I might argue naturalistic) theatre where the house, props, costumes and the characters are aimed at re-creating the place, people and events of January 10 and 11, 1927. This illusionist form invokes our perception of the illusion in "Aristotelian" terms of a beginning, middle and end, a narrative linear plot, and a resolution of issues—an invocation of closure. Ironically, the choices available to the audience all end in the same state of chaos and incompleteness. On the other side is the non-illusionary world, the world of theatrical event, deliberate artifice or falseness. The audience is constantly made aware that these are actors in front of them; the spectators bump into other spectators; they consciously walk about a house they do not know; they consciously (self-consciously?) stand in a room watching representations of life at Il Vittoriale. The theatrical mode is foregrounded urging them to be critical or detached about what they are experiencing, and ultimately to think about it.

And what might they think about? Signs communicate entrapment, sterility, over-indulgence and selling-out. Just as D'Annunzio has sold out to his own rhetoric, Fascism and lust, and just as the other people in his house have sold out to their respective ideologies, so the audience has sold out to the novelty of the artifice, its form, the promotion, voyeurism and the pleasure of "good-natured decadence." The tendency to seek the "illusionary"—that is in both the usual "misleading impression" sense and the theatrical realism sense of the word—world of pleasure has kept them from fully taking part in the serious discoveries to be made. As John Krizanc points out: *"Tamara* is the only play I have been to where people actually talk about the play (at intermission). But on the other hand, *Tamara* is destroyed by the sum of its parts, because the subtleties of the play, its implications, are overwhelmed by the experience" (qtd. in Jansen 34)."

Tamara serves as an example of the work of Necessary Angel, chiefly that shaped by Richard Rose and John Krizanc or D.D. Kugler, which has been concerned with creating performances where the audience—and often characters in the performance—seemingly have their cake and eat it too. The various Necessary Angel productions have challenged the limitations of realistic theatre—there are lots of people who get pleasure from this critical action—while often treating the audience to the pleasures of theatrical illusion. At the same time, this metatheatrical mode has been the performative envelope for questioning the pleasure-oriented moral, ethical and political values of a middle-class, English Canadian audience.

(1996)

Notes

[1] Favourable conditions rarely exist for even short-term maintenance of a theatre company in Canada. Nonetheless, several artists, including founders Richard Rose (Artistic Director) and John Krizanc (Resident Author), have worked extensively with Necessary Angel: performers Tanja Jacobs, Elizabeth Hanna, Mark Christmann, Bruce Vavrina and Denis Forest; designers Dorian Clark (also a founding member) and Graeme Thomson; stage managers Sarah Stanley and Cheryl Landy (also an Assistant Director).

[2] Designer Graeme Thomson explained the design as follows: "Because the show deals with the body in a number of contexts—the physical body, the body politic

and so on—an overhead view of the arena would show a stick figure of a human form with a number of raised platforms. The head is the seat of government, the church and the press sit on a shoulder, the bedroom is placed in the groin. The physical set as well as the props will be scaffolding, to suggest the skeletal nature of the body" (Jon Kaplan, in *Now*, April 13–19, 1989, 49). It is unfortunate that the conditions of performance, one of which was an inadequate source of funding, did not allow an overhead camera shot of the playing space. I would be very surprised to learn that many of the audience were aware of this significant three-dimensional metaphor.

[3] *Tamara* opened in Toronto on May 8, 1981; it was remounted at Dundurn Castle in Hamilton, Ontario in November 1981. The productions in Los Angeles (script revised), which opened in July 1984, and in New York (script revised again), which opened in November 1987, were still running in October 1989. The production in Mexico opened in November 1986.

[4] One of the ironies of *Tamara*'s history is that out of the gross income, John Krizanc has earned only approximately $24,000 (as of the date of the writing of this article). He has been advised that to claim the $60,000 he is entitled to would likely cost about $40,000 in legal fees.

[5] These characterizations are taken from the cast list published with the text of the play.

[6] The publication of *Tamara* allows readers the opportunity to deal with the narrative in a linear fashion tying loose ends together. To some extent this linear experience is available to audience members who return, (as did the "Lifers" in Los Angeles) many times. But linearity is denied in a single attendance at performance.

[7] Typical examples: Martin Hunter reviewing the play in publication referred to the production as a "gimmick" in *Toronto Star*, July 1, 1989; Mel Gussow in the *New York Times*, December 3, 1987: "There are references to politics and also to art of the period, but 'Tamara' is not to be taken too seriously. It is basically a clever diverting whodunit."

Works Cited

Beaufort, John. "If you don't warm to the play, maybe you'll like the buffet." *The Christian Science Monitor* (21 December 1987): 22.

Crew, Robert. "Engrossing play features fine lead performer." *Toronto Star* (8 June 1989): C1.

Duncan, Isadora. *My Life*, New York: Liveright, 1955.

Gussow, Mel. "The Stage: 'Tamara.'" *New York Times* (3 December 1987): sec. 3, 24.

Jansen, Ann. "Interview John Krizanc." *Books in Canada* (March 1988): 34.

Kaplan, Jon. "Dramaturge Kugler redesigns the body." *No* (13–19 April 1989): 49.

Knowles, Richard Paul. "'The Truth Must Out': The Political Plays of John Krizanc." *Canadian Drama/L'Art dramatique canadien* 13.1 (1987): 28.

Krizanc, John. *Tamara.* Toronto: Stoddart, 1989.

Krizanc, John. "Innocents Abroad." *Saturday Night* (November 1984): 34–38.

Mietkiewicz, Henry. "Mind-boggling *Mein* still fascinates." *Toronto Star* (22 February 1985).

Rewa, Natalie. "All News Newhouse." *Canadian Theatre Review* 61 1989): 40–42.

Rose, Richard. "Director's Notes," Programme for *Newhouse.* Toronto, 1989.

Wagner, Vit. "Drama packs arena with sex, plague and politics." *Toronto Star* (14 April 1989: D5.

Writing for the Community Play Form

by Rachael Van Fossen

People only slightly familiar with the community play art form often wrongly assume that these plays are written collectively with the community, or are "written by committee," with the playwright acting more or less as an expert recorder, scripting material into dialogue and scenes as directed by the community people, or even critiquing work that the community people have themselves written for the play. I readily admit there is room in the community play art form for a process involving local people in the actual writing of the play. That process, however, is different from my own, and certainly different from the plays of the Colway Theatre Trust, on whose work the Canadian community plays are based.

When someone asks me how I set out to write a community play, I use nebulous words like trying to capture the "spirit" or "essence" of the community. I talk about the work being rooted in thorough research, both primary and archival, over an extended period of time in the community. Then I talk about the audience: it's vitally important, I believe, that a community play is written with the audience of the community in mind. The community must see, and recognize itself, in the play—and in the production. A community play of this kind cannot therefore be written for a tourist audience or a professional theatre-going audience. These audiences will come anyway; when they leave with a feeling that they were part of something extraordinary, it's because they were invited to participate in the community's expression of itself. The play, although written by me, belongs mostly to the community, and their sense of ownership will have been my greatest accomplishment.

So, how do you find this "essence" of community? Almost invariably, I know when I've found it the first time I hear someone say, "Oh, the play can't be about that. You can't talk about that in the play." If the play were being written by the steering committee, I would have to follow those instructions. If community people were responsible for making decisions about content, either the play would never be written because nobody would ever agree, or it would be written and represent only a very small portion of the area's demographic, whose interests are the same. When I encounter conflicting or contradictory viewpoints (as you will invariably, in any community) I make these the conflicts of the play, and attempt—as best I can—to present these different perspectives objectively and in as non-judgmental a way as possible. In Fort Qu'Appelle, during the research phase for the Calling Lakes Community Play, a town councillor told us the play could not be about land and land ownership, because "it's too controversial, with all these native land claims going on." In the end the central metaphor of the play became—guess what—the land. The play did not deal specifically with contemporary land claims negotiations and settlements, but the Tribal Council was pleased to see the signing of Treaty Four was the big turning point ending the play's first act. (You can bet that any time someone doesn't want to talk about a particular issue, there are always a few who do.)

It is difficult to talk about the writing of community plays as a thing separate from their production. It is impossible to talk about the writing of the play without talking about the community involved. Although the productions are text-based, they are nonetheless similar to, for instance, Theatre Passe Muraille's collective creations in the 1970s because the plays are not created for publication; nor is there any intention that they will be produced again, either in or outside of their community. Indeed the thrill that community play audiences experience is thanks largely to the feeling of having taken part in a very important, very large and celebratory one-time event, an event that involves local people in the public telling of their own stories. The text should not really exist apart from the production, and cannot be interpreted by a director without referring back to the community. The production aesthetic should be as closely related to the community as is the content of the play, and the two are inextricably inter-dependent.

The best known of the Saskatchewan community play projects was also the first: *Ka'ma'mo'pi cik/The Gathering* was first produced in 1992 in Fort Qu'Appelle. Co-written and co-directed by Darrel Wildcat and me, *The Gathering* dealt with very separate and seemingly distinct versions of history, as seen through the selective eyes of mostly white, mostly European immigrants and their descendants who still live in the area, and through the watchful and quite rightly revisionist eyes of the area's First Nations and Métis peoples, whose histories remained, at that time, little known among the general population. The device we used for bringing these histories together in a conflict-driven narrative was to invest the separateness of the two communities in the characters of the Cree trickster Wesakeychuk, and a character modeled on the Renaissance fool and other European clown figures. Wesakeychuk and the Fool struggle throughout more than a century of history to tell "their" version of events, and struggle for possession of The Mudball: a physical prop as embodiment of the concept of the land, and questions of land "ownership".

It is a common assumption that community plays are always historical plays. It is also true that most have indeed dealt with historical material. In 1995 Common Weal co-produced, with a neighbourhood steering committee, the first urban community play in Canada. The play that resulted was *A North Side Story (or two)*. The neighbourhood was (still is) North Central Regina, known colloquially as Moccasin Flats, The Rez, or, these days, The Hood. During research for this inner city project, it became clear early on that the script needed to deal more directly with pressing contemporary issues. Yet the re-telling of history from an aboriginal perspective was no less important than the inner city, and as a result *A North Side Story (or two)* included a series of flashback scenes as lived by one of the contemporary characters on a journey of discovery: Marie's "road trip through time" allows the audience to relate present circumstances of the neighbourhood to a historical context. In simplistic terms the sequence might be titled: "This is How We Got to Where We Are Today."

Similar to *The Spirit of Shivaree* (Eramosa Community Play, 1990), the jumping off point of the North Central play was a contemporary conflict: in this case neighbourhood homeowners, neighbourhood youth, and neighbourhood prostitutes vying for control of the streets and, more importantly, control of their lives. In *A North Side Story (or two)* it is the contemporary characters who drive the drama forward. The youth and the hookers hang out on the street. They are much maligned by other residents, the homeowners, who fear for their safety and their property values, and are imagining horrible atrocities going on at the infamous party house next door. A crime is committed. The wrong kid is identified as the perpetrator. In the unraveling of the stories a character who is both one of the youths and one of the prostitutes literally saves the day, but dies in a fire at the party house.

The stories of the North Central play are largely fictional, but derive from the real life of the neighbourhood. Many of the characters were based directly, or indirectly, on people whom I met during the research for the play and the development of the project. "Party houses" are a ubiquitous symbol of rampant fear in the neighbourhood among long-time homeowners who are residents. Street prostitution has become more and more evident as poverty increases. Many young people are involved in working the streets, and Aboriginal people are over-represented. House fires are common in this part of the city where slum lords are the norm, and proper smoke alarms, although required by law, are rarely installed. Children do perish in these house fires. The situation begs the question: who is responsible for their deaths? With no easy answers or solutions, a challenge to the audience is made explicitly: the play ends on a line whispered in unison by the full cast of community people. They hiss, "What are you going to do about it?" The final chorus of the song "Life is a Gamble" picks up:

> Life is a gamble, you're given your cards
> You're given your cards and you get what you get
> But you can decide what you want to do
> Your life is your own and the struggle yours too
> You can decide what you want to do, what you want to do,
> what you want to do.

Singing, the cast and crew leave the stage where they have just taken their bows, and cross into the promenade area, shaking hands with the audience, and, when the singing has done, they engage people in conversation about the experience of the play.

In 1992, in *The Gathering*, an eerily beautiful soprano solo introduced the finale. Billy Morton wrote the lyrics, which captured the more hopeful, perhaps more fanciful spirit of the project in the Qu'Appelle Valley:

> One voice calling across the ages
> Joined by another they speak of the past
> Soon the voices of thousands gather.

Leaving the quarrel, together at last
Just like a harmony chorus sounding
Through past and present and time yet to come
We must remember that all things living
Are equal in every way under the sun
Close the circle, the play is done.

The different thematic and stylistic choices in these two plays, one rural and the other urban, are in a sense exemplified by their different endings. *The Gathering's* more gentle story-telling served to avoid further alienating an already divided population. The intention and over-riding principle of the Calling Lakes Community Play in Fort Qu'Apelle was to bring people together, people who have rarely had an opportunity to meet. Many Fort Qu'Appelle residents have lived in or near the town their entire lives without ever having set foot on a reserve, although there are several within a 10 to 20 minute drive, and reserve residents are regularly in the town to conduct business and shop. The community play project did bring people together, and the fairytale ending of hands joined in a circle was an appropriate ending for that play, at that time. For a brief moment, a glimpse of harmony...of utopia...of what is possible.

To be sure, racism still thrives in Fort Qu'Appelle. But *The Gathering* gave people permission to be ignorant of each other, and managed, for many, to bridge the gulf. The urban project demanded a somewhat harder edge, and a harsher voice. The steering committee had given the project a focus on youth, and an important goal was to involve as many young people as possible in the project's development and production. The script dealt with issues relevant to youth in the neighbourhood, and involved high school students and recent dropouts in the research process. A good number of teenagers continue to revise the script throughout even the rehearsal period, correcting outdated street slang. The line "Olds is just tryin' to be a tough guy," became "Olds's jus tryna be solid." Using the term "dude", I discovered, is a fast way to date the playwright as a child of the seventies. A great night out is a "slammin' party," which also has connotations of recreational drug use, especially T's (Talwyn) and R's (Ritalin). The word "cool" lives on, but a person does need to practice saying it just right.

With more older people involved in the Calling Lakes project, the use of language was a different issue all together. Where the North Central steering committee chastised me for language far too tame for the inner city (I remember at one meeting someone telling me: "Shit isn't even a swear word in North Central, for fuck's sake!"), one member of the Calling Lakes steering committee in 1992 was offended by the word "fart." Issues of censorship and self-censorship are no less problematic in community plays than in the conventional professional theatre, and probably more.

Darrel and I also made conscious choices to use anachronistic language in some of the historical scenes in *The Gathering*. To do so lightened the load considerably for non-professional actors, and provided some cheap laughs along the way. Hence the comment from Hudson Bay trader Harmon to the free trader LaRocque, "I heard since the transfer you were stuck out in the boonies," or from Sky Woman about a mixed marriage, "If I wanted a hairy man I would make him bearskin pyjamas."

In 1994 Don McEwen was contracted to design the sets for *A North Side Story (or two)*, and we held ongoing telephone meetings even as the script was still being developed, concerned mostly with finding images and production values more appropriate to an inner city setting than the earthy tones and textures Ruth Howard and volunteers had lovingly crafted to blend with the Qu'Appelle Valley for *The Gathering*. As a bit of serendipity, the big-top tent we rented for *A North Side Story (or two)* was available only in dimensions much longer than they were wide. Stages along the sides of the tent became sidewalks. The audience in the promenade stood, literally and figuratively, in the street. For the 1992 play in the Valley the promenade area was a square, emphasizing the importance in the play of the Four Directions, such an important part of the Cree creation story.

In 1995 Don was keen to incorporate slides and video projection as integral to the inner city, youth-oriented aesthetic we were after. Of these projections, I remain most fond of a segment near the end of the play: during a scene change to the charred remnants of the party house, one of the actors conducts "streeter" interviews with audience members in the promenade, about issues of the neighbourhood dealt with in the performance. The live interviews were simultaneously projected, larger than life, on a screen at one end of the tent. The technology worked beautifully here, serving the community play's function of implicating the audience in the action of the play in an innovative and effective way. In production, the aesthetic style of *A North Side Story (or two)* to a large degree maintained, in spite of its multimedia aspects, the rough-hewn, home-made, found-materials "feel" that is associated with these large-scale plays. I love this about community plays: the ability to explore more than one option, and incorporate different styles in the same production.

The plays are, nonetheless, highly theatrical, and the element of surprise plays an important role. In *A North Side Story (or two)*, historical flashback scenes incorporating large images of, for instance, a buffalo stampede, or a satirized Lieutenant Governor Dewdney, often burst into the promenade sandwiched between highly realistic contemporary scenes taking place on the stages. It is possible to blend elements of pageantry with documentary, such as the 16-foot puppet of Queen Victoria who presides over the signing of *Treaty Four* in *The Gathering*, for which much of the scene's dialogue was adapted directly from historical documentation.

This question of documentary provides an interesting point of comparison between the urban and rural projects. Besides the obvious exception of the mythical roles, most of the characters in *The Gathering* were real historical figures brought to our attention by community researchers. (Notable among the other exceptions are the characters from the Cree civilization scene that opens the play.) Thanks to some very diligent amateur historians, we were even able to base historical women's roles on real people. Elizabeth Hall really did immigrate to the Valley from Eramosa, Ontario, and was known for her work providing medicine and relief supplies during hard times. The scene of domestics in Act Two is edited from verbatim accounts of three women from the Standing Buffalo reserve talking about their grandmothers, who worked off the reserve cleaning houses and taking care of the white women's children while their own were away at residential school. These women played their grandmothers in the 1992 production.

It is important in a community play to have substantial, interesting parts for women. On average, about twice as many women volunteer to be actors as men. The women's stories are extremely difficult to find when working largely from archival material, most of which has been documented by and about men. Even Elizabeth Hall's life was only scantily recorded compared to, for instance, the Hudson Bay clerk MacDonald, the Anglican lay minister Assinibonian Charles Pratt, or the famous chiefs Starblanket and Piapot. The difficulty is doubled or trebled when looking for recorded accounts of Aboriginal women.

A mostly contemporary play was freeing in this way. Although the play did deal with history, only Dewdney among the historical characters was drawn as being a real person. The focus of the play allowed for characters to be entirely fictionalized (although, as mentioned earlier, many were inspired by, or were amalgamations, of people I had met during the process). History tended to be treated more imagistically, and related more explicitly to the contemporary. An example of this is the brief image of actors dressed as Ku Klux Klansmen, in front of a video image of a burning cross, and chanting "Get them out! Get them out!" The incident is real enough: an actual cross burning took place in the 1920s, on the very site of the play itself, in opposition to the influx of Chinese immigrants to the neighbourhood. But the image and the chant alone were sufficient to make a statement: a community meeting scene about the prostitution issue precedes the KKK scene, and the only point on which people can agree is "Get them the hell out of my neighbourhood." Immediately following the KKK, a prostitute character confronts these concerned residents, and has her say. After all, she lives in the neighbourhood too.

Even long-time residents involved in the North Central project were more interested in examining the contemporary life of the community than getting caught up in accurate presentation of real historical figures. But the inclusion of real people from the past was extremely important in *The Gathering*: for both Aboriginal and non-aboriginal participants these characters emphasized a sense of pride in and recognition of their heritage. In *A North Side Story (or two)* people seemed to have more fun recognizing parts of themselves and others (their neighbours) within the fiction of the play. Everyone in the neighbourhood knows someone like the crabby old white couple Ed and Evelyn, whose misfortune is to have slum housing and party houses continue to deteriorate next door to their own immaculately maintained property. The local woman playing Evelyn identified strongly with her character, whose husband wants to sell the house and move to Kamloops to get away from the fast-changing neighbourhood. To Evelyn, their house in North Central is home, and she secretly sabotages his efforts by vandalizing their own property whenever potential buyers are to due to come.

The Gathering and *A North Side Story (or two)* do share some common historical content, although dramatically the history was used in different ways. Both plays had scenes dealing with the days, not so very far removed, of all-powerful Indian agents, and passes required by the government for Indian people to leave their reserve land. These laws originated with fears of Indian uprisings in the days of the Riel-led rebellions, but remained on the bureaucratic books until changes to the Indian Act in the 1950s. I learned from Verne Bellegarde, a member of the Steering and Research Committees in Fort Qu'Appelle, that in 1953 the Indian agent on his reserve still demanded a cut of the proceeds, in the form of a side of beef, before he would grant a permit to an Indian family to sell their livestock.

In *The Gathering*, "Future Dreamtime" was used to bring white homesteaders into the action earlier than a strictly chronological structure would have allowed. Without this device, the majority of white people in the cast, and especially the women, would have had little to do until after the treaty signing which ends Act One. We also concocted fantasy scenes such as the women's song "How Come They Didn't Ask Us" as crucial opportunities to bring together the racially diverse cast. Without these scenes, the cast of native and non-native would have spent the majority of the rehearsal period with little or no interaction, given the play's structure of telling the histories separately. These examples are but a small sampling of the ways in which the concerns of the community can have a direct impact on the structure of the play.

Do I get tired of suppressing my own "writer's voice," in the interests of serving the community? We had more we wanted to say about that place, much of which was unsuitable to a community play.

Writing a community play can be a daunting and often frustrating responsibility. There is a delicate balancing act between needs and opinions expressed within the community, and the creative sensibilities of the playwright or playwrights. I manage to walk that tightrope, and I keep going back to it, because the rewards are so great. People trust me with their stories, and that trust is, in itself, a very great gift. Armed with those stories and, alongside those wonderful and interesting people, I get to create powerful theatre with a real connection to its audience, the community. Theatre like that is worth doing, even when people you've come to like and respect want you to cut all the farting out of the play. Which, by the way, we didn't do.

(1997)

Environmental Theatre

by Ric Knowles

> The bifurcation of space must be ended. The final exchange between
> performers and audience is the exchange of space.
> —Richard Schechner, *Environmental Theater* (xxvi)

In Canada, what collective creation has been to naturalistic drama, environmental theatre is to the modernist tradition: if, in its pushing and questioning of process and its insistence on particular kinds of authenticity, much Canadian collective creation can be seen as post-naturalist, then much Canadian environmental theatre can be seen as post-modernist. [1] Not surprisingly, the history and range of environmental theatre in Canada are as proportionately small, relative to the rich tradition of collective and collaborative work, as the body of modernist writing for the Canadian theatre is small in relation to the dominance of naturalistic forms on Canadian stages.

There has nevertheless been a significant body of work produced environmentally in Canada since the late 1960s and early 1970s, work that treats the politics of theatrical space in ways that are analogous, in the context of modernist forms of focus, optics, and power, to the ways in which collective and collaborative work, and the contexts of rehearsal techniques, theatrical organization, and the construction of characterization and narrative, treats the politics of process. In terms of dramaturgical structure, what collective and collaborative work performs in the temporal dimension environmental theatre effects spatially.

Richard Schechner, who coined the phrase "environmental theatre" and first theorized it in the late 1960s and early 1970s, traces its contemporary roots in the West to modernist developments in music and the visual arts, notably through composer John Cage, Dada, and a number of avant-garde visual artists, mostly American. [2] Schechner, together with Michael Kirby, also draws heavily in his accounts of environmental theatre, particularly his own work, on Oriental, African, and other "primitive" forms of ritual and performance in much the same way that modernist artists in other forms ransacked rhythms, images, and techniques from cultures that they constructed as Other. In spite of its attempts to multiply focus and democratize theatrical space, environmental theatre as it developed and was theorized in the United States in the 1960s was post-modern primarily in the historical sense that it grew out of a modernist aesthetic, and it shared with the modernist project, as outlined in chapter 2 [of Knowles's *The Theatre of Form and the Production of Meaning* —ed.], a tendency to cannibalize other forms and traditions, to objectify women (who tend to appear in the literature as "girls" and on the stage as subservient and "usually at some stage of undress" [Sandford xxii]), and to focus on ahistorical, formalist, and self-referential patterns and structures in which the individual human subject is either mechanized or treated as the individual/ universalist object of asocial varieties of mid-century American psychotherapy (see Schechner, *Environmental Theater* 193–226). The first strand of Canadian environmental theatre discussed in this chapter, represented by the work of R. Murray Schafer and Hillar Liitoja, grows directly out of these 1960s experiments in the United States and shares many of their most characteristic features.

But environmental theatre in Canada has also, in a different and distinct manifestation, been post-modern in an explicitly political way that has more to do with Linda Hutcheon's articulation of "the politics of postmodernism" than with the depoliticized excesses of post-modernism as it has come to be understood through writers/prophets such as Baudrillard, Lyotard, and many American theorists. Ever since Schechner coined the term, environmental theatre, at least in the stated intentions of its creators and theorists, has articulated—if not always achieved—an explicitly political agenda problematically disposed toward its modernist predecessors. This is particularly true in its politicization of space and democratization of focus, its insistence on the engagement or implication of audiences within the dramatic frame (or its explosion of that frame outward), and its deployment of socially transformative modes such as ritual, shamanism, or magic.[3] In his reintroduction to the 1994 edition of *Environmental Theater*, Schechner argues that,

> In a word, environments ecological or theatrical can be imagined not only as spaces but as active players in complex systems of transformation. Neither ecological nor performance environments are passive. They are interactants in events organically taking place throughout vivified spaces. A performance environment is a "position" in the political sense, a "body of knowledge" in the scholarly sense, a "real place" in the theatrical sense. Thus, to stage a performance "environmentally" means more than simply to move it off of the proscenium or out of the arena. An environmental performance is one in which *all the elements or parts* making up the performance are recognized as alive. To "be alive" is to change, develop, transform; to have needs and desires; even, potentially, to acquire, express, and use consciousness. (x)

It is its post-Brechtian concern with consciousness, its implications for the construction of social space within and beyond the theatre, and its more or less explicit concern with the operations of power in society that have made environmental theatre congenial to many contemporary Canadian theatre workers, including those, such as Richard Rose and John Krizanc, discussed in the second half of this chapter, who have for the most part abandoned such things as audience participation and audience-performer contact (see Nelson 92–93).

* * *

March 1993. Once the audience had assembled in the rectangular and empty industrial space on George Street in Toronto's east end, occupied at the time by Buddies in Bad Times Theatre, the small platform stage at one end of the room picked itself up and began to move with apparent hesitation into the centre of the room. It paused there for a moment before continuing on to the wall at the opposite end of the space, forcing spectators to scramble out of the way. The stage rested for a moment before once again lifting its skirts and continuing its perambulations about the room, so that in the end not a single spectator was left stationary. Once everyone had been forced to move at least once, the stage settled for the moment in the centre of the room, and eight cast members—six of them naked and smeared with mud—emerged from a trapdoor in its centre and began to dance around the platform, enticing, cajoling, and otherwise confronting the audience. Eventually, the platform broke up into constituent parts, and the entire space was shared among actors, spectators, shifting platforms, lighting effects, and sound sources. As reviewer H.J. Kirchhoff said, "you keep moving," but "when you move…you find yourself in a spotlight, with naked people next to you or in front of you, doing things engaging, vulgar, and/or amusing. You move, and find yourself involved with something else." I had my portrait done, in crayon, by a naked woman seated next to me. Later I found myself face-to-groin with a cast member urinating into a glass. "[Y]ou keep moving.[4]

As this description of Pow Pow Unbound's 1993 production of *Stage* suggests, the roots of at least some environmental theatre in Canada remain firmly in the participatory/ confrontational 1960s tradition as represented by Richard Schechner and The Performance Group's infamous *Dionysus in 69*. And those roots are firmly within the tradition of the modernist avant-garde.

It is not incidental that the two most dedicated practitioners of (and polemicists for) environmental theatre in Canada, R. Murray Schafer and Hillar Liitoja, were trained as musicians and began their careers with a fascination for the work of the archetypal modernist poet (and fascist propagandist) Ezra Pound. Although his early interests were, not insignificantly, in painting and sports (Colgrass 33), Schafer is first and best known as a composer and educator, having won the first international Glenn Gould prize for outstanding contribution to music, having published widely on music education and soundscape theories (including the widely read and much translated *The Tuning of the World*), and having had his music performed internationally. Schafer's first work was *Ezra Pound and Music*, the compilation and editing of Pound's writings on music after Schafer met the American imagist poet in Venice in the late 1950s and debated with him "about poetry and music and, very likely, politics," according to Robert Everett-Green ("Polemics"). In an article based on an interview with Schafer in Toronto in 1991, Everett-Green also quotes the composer's opinions on (European) quality and (Canadian) vulgarity, multiculturalism, assimilation, and nationalisms,[5] opinions that would not sound out of character coming from the post-war Pound, whom Everett-Green describes as Schafer's "one time poetic mentor" ("Polemics").

Perhaps more to the point, Schafer's artistic influences and interests are entirely compatible with those of Pound, together with other modernists with whom Schafer has been linked or has linked himself, such as Berg, Schoenberg, Webern, and Stravinsky; Joyce, Lawrence, Eliot, Cocteau, and d'Annunzio; Kandinsky, Klee, Buckminster Fuller, the Bauhaus, the Dadaists, the Italian Futurists, and the Russian constructivists; as well as theatrical practitioners and theorists such as Reinhardt, Meyerhold, Vahktangov, Artaud, and, both notably and frequently, in the wide-ranging interdisciplinary aspirations of Schafer's "theatre of confluence," Wagner. [6] Several of these artists, not incidentally, have been linked in their philosophies, or their subsequent deployment by others, with the European extreme right. I have no wish to suggest that Schafer's political opinions are in any way allied with neoconservative extremism. It is, however, worth considering his major work, *Patria* (which Schafer translates as, "homeland" but which might more accurately, and more disturbingly, in light of his brand of nationalism, be read as "fatherland" [7]), in the context of his explicitly elitist, anti-republican, and antidemocratic political views, which are embedded to some extent in the deep structure of his work.

In his book *"Patria" and the Theatre of Confluence* and elsewhere, Schafer frequently inveighs against a contemporary society in which "Heroic myths are not popular ... because there is no room in them for mediocrity." He laments the ways in which "republicanism [has] dwarfed everyone" (197), and he suggests that "an unwritten article in the republic's constitution is the right to remain ignorant" (198). He laments, then, a time in which "the victims"—by which he means the uneducated, the physically, mentally, or emotionally handicapped, and immigrants [8] —"are treated as invalids, requiring crutches and social workers rather than the inspiration of heroes" (198).

The "artist," however, clearly is "not a social worker" for Schafer, who frequently and at some length articulates his feeling of alienation from an unappreciative and mundane (Canadian) society and who prefers to align himself with what he sees as an artistic and intellectual elite for whom hermetic and other mystical texts remain meaningful, as they have been for the "highest" civilizations:

> Such texts do not originate in low civilizations. They occur in the highest. A few individuals—at first a very few—sidestep society to regard it in a totally different manner, from a trans-mundane perspective, accessible perhaps only to the physically inactive. Such were the gnostic philosophers; such were the alchemists to whom they are related. And by a comparative gradient so far unexplored, we see resemblances between these individuals, hermetically sealed off from the masses, and certain modern artists:
>
> Joyce, Kafka, Beckett. We see it also in the arrogance of d'Annunzio, the spinsterish voice of Eliot, the fustian politics of Pound, everywhere

where figures of maximal intelligence have been isolated or have sought isolation from the public arenas of social life. (141)

Not surprisingly, then, Schafer's work for the theatre for the most part eschews any form of participation that empowers the audience or involves it in the process of creation, "lest theatre should fall victim to collective or herdesque whine" ("Theatre of Confluence" 38). Schafer is interested, finally, not in participation but in presentation, not in process but in product—"the fact of art," as he says, or "arti-fact" (46). He thus argues that "There is no reason why an audience, prepared to be an audience, should expect to be anything but an audience":

> The assumption that the audience knows best what it wants is question-
> able. The blurring of the distinctions between the giving and receiving
> of art can be tragic. In the West everywhere one notices this frightful
> descent into homogeneity, blurring distractions, obliterating the idio-
> syncratic, dragging the leaders down and the led up onto some middle
> ground of fulcrumed banality. Both communism and democracy are
> systems dedicated to smoothing out differences between men [sic]. Of
> course, you *can* make a congenital dunce into a prime minister but this
> is no guarantee of improvement in the state. Those who are prepared to
> pass the responsibilities of the artist to the audience will merely be
> rewarded in the same way as the liberals who first prepared the revolu-
> tion of democracy: their heads were the first to fall when mass-man [sic]
> took over. (37)

Schafer's "theatre of confluence," moreover, is explicitly articulated throughout *"Patria" and the Theatre of Confluence* as being multidisciplinary, not out of any interest in the pluralistic problematizing of each artistic discourse or in any multi-faceted or democratizing multiplication of perspectives. On the contrary, it is defined and defended as an art form "conceived on all levels simultaneously [and] elaborated coevally" ("Theatre of Confluence" 46), "a kind of theatre in which all the arts may meet, court and make love" in the service of achieving a transcendental unity (31)— a "counterpoint between the senses" (34)—that is greater than that available to any one art form on its own.

Schafer's work, then, distances itself from some of the most characteristic—and politically interventionist—features of the environmental theatre movement in the United States in the 1960s. Nevertheless, his musical and sound compositions—particularly his theoretical work, *The Tuning of the World*—seem to be comparable to, or compatible with, those of one of the 1960s gurus of environmental theatre, John Cage. Schafer is also like Cage, Schechner, and others in paying tribute to, drawing on, and arguably appropriating non-Western languages and forms of ritual and expression—as well as the rituals, legends, and languages of North American Native peoples, Greek mythology, and the Catholic Mass—in a kind of condescendingly Rousseauesque primitivism and faith in what he calls "the recovery of-the sacred" ("Theatre of Confluence II" 7–10). [9] Interestingly, many of "Darko Suvin's critiques of the "liberal sentimentality" of what Suvin calls the "Rousseauist approach" of the

1960s Happenings movement apply closely to Schafer's work (287). Suvin points out that political, economic, and ideological analysis in Happenings was eschewed in favour of "pseudo-biological values" for historical faith that "a return to supposed fundamentals outside civilization will illume present-day life" (287). In Schafer, as in Happenings, this substitution of "pseudo-biological values" for historical ones arguably results in "a Eucharist without a Real Presence, a dumb Symposium" (287). [10]

As in many modernist works, and as in the "interculturalist" work of theatre practitioners and theorists such as Peter Brook, Ariane Mnouchkine, and Eugenio Barba, the deployment of Native, Egyptian, Japanese, Greek, or other forms tends in Schafer's work to be done somewhat indiscriminately, flattening cultural differences in a search for "the unity of all things material, spiritual, natural, and divine" (Schafer, "Theatre of Confluence II" 5), a search that is completely congruent with his expressed distaste for multiculturalism and other pluralistic policies and practices (Everett-Green, "Polemics"). As for Brook, Barba, and the visual artists of the modernist period who turned to African and "*japoniste*" raw materials for inspiration, the forms, traditions, and artifacts of other cultures tend in Schafer's work to be ransacked for those elements that conform to Western literary, mythical, or psychological archetypes and appropriated in the service of an essentially colonizing artistic vision. Interestingly, Schafer's interest in non-Western modes of expression is primarily an interest in form. "[O]ne does not interpret rituals so much by their contents, Schafer argues, "as by their forms: the special spaces and times they occupy, the ritual objects they employ, the roles of the participants, the decorum and ceremony" ("Theatre of Confluence II" 15). And the forms, he suggests, are both "deliberately structured" ("Princess" 24) and reflect universal archetypes that are "more or less unchanging" (qtd. in Everett-Green, "Polemics").

Schafer's theatrical work, apart from the early opera *Loving* (1965), consists of the *Patria* cycle, a monumental work, begun in the late 1960s and still, after a prologue, six completed parts (with four more in various stages of development), and an epilogue, very much in progress. [11] Throughout the work, archetypal, mythical, and mystical sources are tapped and harnessed to Schafer's essentially mythopoeic/ dialectical vision of the achievement of unity. Structurally, however, the Patria cycle as a whole is determinedly unfinished "and open ended—"a kind of picaresque," as Schafer describes it—and at the same time curiously closed (qtd. in Everett-Green, "Polemics"). He notes, for example, that

> At the end of *The Princess and the Stars*, which is the prologue, the sun descends and says to Wolf, "Go and look for your princess. It will take you through many lifetimes, and many forms." But the archetypes are more or less unchanging. There's an accumulation of experience which makes the characters more complete, but which doesn't necessarily amount to psychological growth. (qtd. in Everett-Green, "Polemics")

As this passage suggests, there are potentially an infinite number of performances, "episodes," works, or events that can be produced within and under the auspices of the

Patria cycle, in which Schafer displays a genius for recycling his earlier work. The cycle's component parts, moreover, are designed to stand on their own, have never been performed together, have only been performed out of sequence, and indeed relate to one another only in terms of deep structure and a fund of generalized, overarching mythical source materials. However, the fact that there is an existing prologue and a planned epilogue together with an insistent assertion of universal and unchanging archetypes, suggests that any openness to the structure is more apparent than real. And, as Schafer indicates in *"Patria" and the Theatre of Confluence*, the epilogue to the series, invoking an all-encompassing closure, brings it "full cycle, concluding at the lake from which it first began" (214).

Where the cycle begins is with its so-called prologue, *The Princess and the Stars* (1981), which is staged at dawn on the shore of a lake in the autumn and which establishes the (invented) "legend" on which the whole cycle is based. It tells the story of the Princess, daughter of the Sun-God, who falls to Earth listening to the cry of the (male) Wolf, the double of the Moon. Once there, she is accidentally wounded by the Wolf and captured beneath the lake by the Three-Horned Enemy. The Wolf then sets out in search of the Princess to seek forgiveness and compassion, through which he will find and redeem both himself and the "patria" and inherit the Moon. In Schafer's account the rest of the cycle follows directly from this scenario:

> The unifying motive of the *Patria* works is Wolf's journeys through the many labyrinths of life in search of the spiritual power which can both release and transfigure him. He will travel under many names and assume many guises: impersonating a human as the displaced immigrant D.P.; as the Greek hero Theseus; as the dead Pharaoh seeking to be raised to heaven by the sun; or as the King in the "chymical marriage" or heiros-gamos of the alchemists. At times he may assume a great pre-eminence; at other times he may be chased away as a fool, a criminal, or a "beast. As the labyrinthine nature of his wanderings intensifies, the Princess becomes personified for him in the figure of Ariadne, who helped Theseus escape the Cretan labyrinth in the well known Greek myth. The thread-gift provided by Ariadne in the *Patria* series is the thread of music. Ariadne's gift is her haunting voice; this is what sustains and transforms Theseus-Wolf during his journeying.
>
> Each of the *Patria* pieces is designed to exist on its own and many explore different theatrical settings and techniques, though all follow the theme of Wolf's search for his spirit in the guise of the Princess as it was introduced in *The Princess of the Stars*. ("Princess" 22)

The structure of the cycle as a whole, and of each of the constituent parts through which this narrative is played out, is a combination of, first, Hegelian dialectic, in which equal opposites contest with one another but in which, ultimately, their conflict brings about a synthesis that represents for Schafer the mystic unity of all creation, and, second, a mythopoeic pattern of renewal that is rooted in theories based on structuralist anthropology as articulated in Frazer's *The Golden Bough* and in the work of literary theorists such as Frye and Barber (see chapter 2 [of Knowles's *The Theatre of Form and the Production of Meaning* —ed.). Thus, the *Patria* cycle is cyclic, beginning with initiation and moving quickly to separation or fall (in the seasonal or biblical sense), as represented in the prologue, *The Princess of the Stars*, it then moves through various kinds of descent into mazes, labyrinths, or necropolises, configured as quest journeys "for unity and the homeland" (*Patria* 11). Eventually, it moves out of these dark, nighttime, or wintertime experiences of deprivation, trial, barrenness, or confrontation to various kinds of rebirth and apotheosis configured as reunion, sunrise, the arrival of spring, or the ascent into heaven. The final, joyous reconciliation is completed in what Schafer calls the epilogue (*And Wolf Shall Inherit the Moon*), which is not yet completed but is outlined in some detail in *"Patria" and the Theatre of Confluence*. Individual parts of the cycle play variations on this overall shape, as the focus shifts from the early parts of the narrative (in *Patria 1: The Characteristics Man, Patria 2: Requiem for the Party Girl*, and *Patria 3: The Greatest Show*); through the "half-way point" (*Patria* 154) in *Patria 4: The Alchemical Theatre of Hermes Trismegistus*, [12] in which separation is recapitulated and union foreshadowed in the alchemical conjunction of Sol and Luna (*Patria* 154); to the final movements toward group (*Patria 5: The Crown of Ariadne* and *Patria 6: Ra* [13]) and individual (*Patria 7: Asteria* [14]) emergence from the labyrinth at dawn; to various kinds of harmony and unity (*Patria 8–10*, projected); culminating in the reunion and apotheosis of the Princess and the Wolf in the epilogue (*And Wolf Shall Inherit the Moon*).

Like the universalist and transcultural appropriation and deployment of the (conflated) languages, legends, and myths of other cultures in the *Patria* cycle, Schafer's use of this familiar mythical narrative structure (which is, of course, fundamentally Western and most clearly embodied in Greek mythology and the Christian Bible) can be seen in its political and social effects to be ultimately conservative and culturally affirmative, not only in its invocation of closure but also in its reinscription of traditional gender roles. According to Schafer, the Princess and the Wolf, or Ariadne and Theseus, are animus and anima symbols, the poles of the cycle's dialectic that are "ultimately destined to blend together in perfect wholeness" and are treated throughout the cycle "as equal partners" (*Patria* 161). They might also be seen, however, as the embodiments of essentialist male and female principles (sometimes also called by Schafer "Dionysian and Appollonian" [15]) that conflate sex and gender, reinscribe restrictive gender roles, and reinforce as universal gendered behaviours that are anything but equal. "The female" in the *Patria* plays—as embodied variously in the Princess, Ariadne, and others—exists primarily as an inactive muse, guide, helper, or embodiment of spirit for the central, active, and clearly more important male— embodied by Wolf, Theseus, D.P., and others. The "universal" mythic quest, then, is represented by "Wolf's search for his spirit in the guise of the Princess" (*Patria* 82), who exerts no agency and occupies no independent subject position. As Schafer says of *Patria 2: Requiem for the Party Girl*, in which Ariadne is imprisoned in a mental institution, "Ariadne, like Uroboros, the self-devouring snake, is caught in an unsettled circularity where she will remain until Wolf, through redemptive love, can restore her to her native element in the heavens" (*Patria* 82). [16]

In narrative terms, then, the *Patria* cycle can be seen to employ and embody a deep structure that is deeply conservative, elitist, antidemocratic, colonialist, culturally appropriative, and antifeminist. What's more, while Schafer can write intoxicatingly about the magnificent and mystical moments and transmogrifications in the cycle, the actual staging of those moments, as he and his creative team move from the conception to the act, can too often be awkward, embarrassing, or even risible. Too often, in Urjo Kareda's phrase, "the drama … is at once both snobbishly obscure and condescendingly obvious" ("R. Murray Schafer").

But it is too easy to dismiss Schafer because of his apparent arrogance and frequent failures. In spite of his political positions and his deployment of culturally affirmative forms of narrative, moreover, the effects of his work in performance can in practice (or reception) be far from closed, monolithic, or repressive. Not surprisingly, this is partly because Schafer, a self-styled maverick who enjoys making unfashionably reactionary public statements, is simultaneously unwilling to align himself openly with "political ideologies" of any kind (which in effect means resisting consistent or identifiable political positions) and deeply critical of current social "realities." The early parts of the *Patria* cycle are, in fact, conceived in part as plays of social protest. In "The Theatre of Confluence," written during the planning stages of the cycle, Schafer evinces an interest in Brecht (45) and indicates his intention to create "pocket opera": "I wanted an aggressive, present-tense opera. Swift, direct, agitational. Not a palliative. Not ceremonial drugging. Not prettifying" (47). He is, moreover, consistently critical of the cultural status quo, often on the ground of its colonialism. The orchestra, for example, he condemns as "a very colonial exhibition. Almost all the instruments are made from materials from plundered territories: ebony, ivory, granadilla. They're all things that have come from cultures and peoples that have been subdued" (qtd. in Everett-Green, "Polemics"). In *"Patria" and the Theatre of Confluence*, moreover, he describes *Patria 1*, which deals with the societal rejection and eventual suicide of a recent immigrant to Canada, as "a work of social protest" and instructs the director to make the work "as political as desired" (66). *Patria 2* he describes as having been based on what he felt were the "deplorable" conditions at Riverview Mental Hospital in Essondale, British Columbia (76).

More significantly, on the structural level, Schafer's interest in mystical, mythical, and alchemical transformations serves fundamentally to shape his artistic vision and inevitably opens the way for transformation of the social formation. Schafer clearly and explicitly believes that "This must be the first purpose of art. To effect a change in our existential condition. This is the first purpose. To change us" ("Theatre of Confluence II" 5).

It is Schafer's interest in change, or transformation (to the degree that his director in a publicity flyer, can refer to *Patria 4* as "a nightly transformation"), that leads to his reliance on ritual forms and on the figuring forth for his audience of change as both a personal and a social possibility. Admittedly, his articulation of this principle is most often couched in individualist, mystical, or "existentialist" rhetoric, as when Schafer insists that, if the rituals *of Patria 6: Ra* are not performed properly and with complete faith in their efficacy, "the sun may not rise" (*Patria* 181), or when he approvingly quotes Mircea Eliade's *Rites and Symbols of Initiation*: "In philosophical terms, initiation is equivalent to a basic change in existential condition; the novice emerges from his ordeal endowed with a totally different being from that which he possessed before his initiation; he has become *another*" (178). "When properly performed and experienced," Schafer argues elsewhere, rituals "can facilitate existential changes or become a palingenesis of spiritual renewal" ("Theatre of Confluence II" 15).

But his rituals can also potentially go beyond individual renewal (of what is, implicitly, already there) to figure forth social change and the emergence of new orders. Existential changes and spiritual renewal, of course, happen within the individual rather than the social realm, but Schafer seems, again, to share with his neo-Romantic but socially radical 1960s forebears, such as Jean-Jacques Lebel, the belief that "if there's still a chance of changing life it resides in the transformation of the human being" (Lebel 268).The ritual structures of the *Patria* series, I would argue, whether or not this is the intent of Schafer and his creative team, can be seen to function structurally to implant change as a social as well as an existential possibility and therefore, potentially at least, to work against the complacency of audiences in the face of a repressive social order. As Schafer argues, the purpose of all rituals is "to prepare one for the change" (*Patria* 177). And the most potent disruptions of what seems clearly to be a culturally affirmative narrative structure of the *Patria* works, and therefore of their socially reproductive potential, derive from their deployment of space, their focus on liminal moments and locations, and the ways in which this deployment and focus affect audiences' experiences.

When Schafer addresses the question of form in his essay "The Theatre of Confluence," he talks first about space and spatial relationships, noting that "the moment an architect encloses space in the form of a building he makes a social comment about the people who are to inhabit that space" (39). Later, in *"Patria" and the Theatre of Confluence,* he goes further: "The moment you organize space you dictate the social actions permitted in that space" (60). Schafer's interest in environmental theatre, then, has directly to do with creating possibilities for social actions that are constrained by traditional theatrical environments: "one has three options with regard to the conventional theatre: to be sentimental about it, to be exploitative, or to leave it behind" (*Patria* 60). While in *Patria* Schafer opts for exploitation, as the cycle proceeds he increasingly moves out of traditional theatrical environments, designing a kind of observation gallery for *Patria* 2 at the Stratford Festival's Third Stage [17] and then moving toward remote nontheatrical spaces ranging from lake- or oceanside settings (at the shifting boundary between water and land) to (carnivalesque) fairgrounds, train stations (as points of departure and arrival), and parks (as meeting places between city and country, art and nature). Eschewing traditional audience-stage configurations, theatrical settings, and standard curtain times, these settings are notable primarily for their liminality: each functions as a site of transition between realms, taking place at dusk, midnight, or dawn on shorelines, fairgrounds, and train stations—ironically, in the case of *Patria 4*, at Toronto's Union

Station. And in deploying these settings, of course, Schafer is seeking what he calls "nodal points" (*Patria* 177), what Sarah Hood calls "the moments of transformation at the heart of life." That many of these settings are outdoor, natural environments is also no accident, since "What distinguishes [a natural environment] from the traditional theatrical setting is that it is a living environment and therefore utterly changeable at any moment" (Schafer, "Princess" 23). And the move to a changeable environment is a move outside the mechanisms of normal social (and theatrical) control:

> When musicians play across a lake at a distance of half a kilometer or more, how are they conducted or supervised? Of what value then are conductors and managers? ... Can we arrange a contract to remove the hazard of rain? And what about the managerial staff? We need boatmen not caretakers, trailblazers not electricians, naturalists not publicists. (28)

From his earliest statements about "The Theatre of Confluence," preceding the creation of any part of the *Patria* series itself, Schafer has expressed an interest in "transformable environments," in part because such environments "would bring about a theatrical *form* which was more fluid" but also because they would provide "a form of possibilities" (42; emphasis added), at least some of which are social.

The reconfiguration of space in the *Patria* series, finally, is more than simply a question of a movement outdoors. Schafer has said that "the metaphor for the whole series has been the labyrinth" (*Patria* 11), and, as he points out in his proposals for *Patria 7: Asteria,* "the intricate structure [of the labyrinth] is not merely the scenery to the drama: it is the drama" (*Patria* 195). The translation of the labyrinth from verbal metaphor to physical realization, where it can become part of the audience's *experience* of the show rather than simply its understanding, is partially realized in *Patria 3: The Greatest Show* and *Patria 6: Ra* and is planned for more thoroughgoing realization on the level of individual audience participation in *Patria 7.*

Patria 3 may serve briefly as an example of the tensions between democratic and resistant multiplicity and the elitist universalist, or culturally affirmative aspects of the work as a whole, particularly as performed in its constituent parts.[18] *The Greatest Show* is set in a fairground where, for the audience members, as reviewer Pamela Young notes, "the fair itself becomes a kind of labyrinth" in which they become "trapped."[19] The setting, consisting of various carnivalesque attractions and monstrosities at tents and booths scattered throughout the fairground, is intriguingly reminiscent of Ben Jonson's *Bartholomew Fair,* as Schafer himself notes (*Patria* 125), in which the same tensions occur between the desire for authorial control of meaning, interpretation, and text and the anarchic, Rabelaisian, populist energies of Bakhtinian carnival, as writers with expressed contempt for "the masses" nevertheless create genial, unsettling, but audience-empowering fairs/shows.[20]

Schafer summarizes the action of *The Greatest Show:*

> Wolf and Ariadne appear as spectators but the Showman, Sam Galupi, compels them to volunteer for two magic acts in which Ariadne is chopped into pieces and Wolf is made to disappear. While the police stalk the grounds hunting for Wolf (who is suspected of some unspecified crime) pieces of Ariadne's anatomy begin to appear in some of the side shows. From a burlesque beginning, the show becomes more macabre until the magicians, attempting to reconstitute the hero and heroine, bungle the job and produce Three-Horned Enemy, who destroys the entire fairgrounds. (*Patria* 210–11)

The mythological underpinnings of the story, the gendering of the hero and heroine, and the linearity of the plot are clear from this account and familiar from the rest of the cycle, though also apparent is the failure of the action to come to a satisfying conclusion, at least as experienced by audiences in the isolated performance of this portion of the cycle.

The show's elitist and universalist tendencies, together with its disturbing orientalism and misogyny, are evident even in the published script,[21] in which a combination of orientalist exoticism and enacted violence against women, both presented more or less as entertainment, is readily apparent. Even in the script, however, some sense of the apparent and potentially empowering anarchy of the event in performance is legible, as when Schafer comments in the introduction, placing the work in the context of the entire cycle, that "the plot of *Patria 3* crumbles, or at least is reduced to small-scale counterplotting and frog-croaking[,] … and the main themes are all splodged [sic] like a bad paint job" (2). Indeed, it is difficult at times to know when or whether a particular side-show event contributes to or deflects attention from the "main action." The script also includes stylistic impurities and heterogeneities, together with irreverently self-parodic sections, as when "Professor Earnest Beauty" lectures on the mythological themes of the *Patria* series, "with special reference to the Beauty and the Beast and Theseus and Ariadne myths" (Category I, 1) at a venue called "the University Theatre," where Schafer himself is later called to give "a short introductory talk to *Patria 3: The Greatest Show*" (Introduction 40), for which he "wears a Tibetan jacket and looks like the aging doyen of some East-West cult of marginal credibility" (Category I, 27). Finally, the script acknowledges its own fragmentary nature as the score for an event that "NO ONE WILL GRASP … AT A SINGLE VISIT" (Category A, 3). But, as Schafer asks in the introduction, "So what if instead of a five-act fauteuil monstrosity we produce a confection of 100 atrocities; amusing, ironical, linked only in the head of the wandering visitor?" (3)

But it is not necessarily linking that goes on in the mind of the wandering visitor, or the linking may not be in the construction of a unified or coherent whole. One of the best accounts of the experience of the play, as opposed to its plot, themes, or setting, is provided by the associate director of the Peterborough productions in 1987 and 1988, who focuses on "the autocritical theatricality" of the show and on the ways in which "The security of your ontological status as 'audience' is … disrupted" (Neill 221, 217): "The questions echo in our minds. Where are the Ideals? The Nobility? The

Divinity? There is no Wizard Oil to cure the world's woes, and Zip the Idiot might well be running the show. The darkness extends beyond the theatre, and the monsters still smile" (221). Reviews of the production tended to focus less on the mythmaking, the role of this work in the larger cycle, or the ultimate containment of the show's anarchic energy than on the discontinuity and randomness of the experience of the show in performance. As Everett-Green described it in *The Globe and Mail,*

> The spectators literally roam around inside the work, happening upon bits of it in random order. Some acts can only be seen after winning at a carnival game, others by being in a certain spot at, the appropriate time.
>
> The pieces of the puzzle do not link together as narrative, but as doodles in different styles on similar themes. Their random progress steadily widens the reference of Schafer's symbols, and makes the contrast of his themes—creation and dismemberment, heroism and betrayal—more violent. ("Peek")

Martha Tancock, reviewing the production for the Peterborough *Examiner,* was more direct and perhaps less positive about the experience. Describing the show as "fuel for the irrational," "a clever conundrum whose impact is both stimulating and unsettling," she thought that, "buffeted between warring forces, the audience is played for a fool.... This show is a Pandora's box of distractions and deceptions that tease and taunt but never really satisfy."

However much it is later contained, then, the physicalization of the labyrinth in *The Greatest Show* (its shift from the realm of allegory to that of audience experience), particularly on the level of individual audience participation, can be a powerful experience of fragmentation, dispersal, chaos, or perhaps even freedom that is unforgettable—and arguably has more lasting impact than the openly orchestrated closure effected in most of the parts and in the cycle as a whole.

* * *

If the deep structures of R. Murray Schafer's *Patria* cycle and the cultural work that they perform are replete with contradictions between the populist and the elitist, the mystical/prophetic voice and the irreverent voice of social satire, the totalizing vision and the fragmenting spatial practice, then the environmental theatre of Hillar Liitoja and his Toronto company, DNA Theatre, is perhaps even more fraught with contradiction. Like Schafer's, Liitoja's roots are in music, including piano studies in Toronto with Anton Kuerti and in Paris with Pierre Sancan; in the American and European avant-garde, including an early fascination with the work of Richard Schechner, Andre Gregory, Tadeuz Kantor, Jan Fabre, and particularly Richard Foreman, with whom Liitoja served an apprenticeship in the early 1980s; and in the poetry and poetics of Ezra Pound, which are the subject of no fewer than his first nine theatrical productions. [22] Like Schafer, too, Liitoja works not from scripts but from "scores," time charts that plot his works' characteristically fragmented individual performances and actions, light and sound cues, in what is ultimately, as Nigel Hunt says, a "musical structure" in which "the director becomes an editor or conductor" keeping the disparate segments in sync (46). [23] Finally, Liitoja shares with Schafer an attitude to audience that is fundamentally dismissive—"I don't concern myself with the audience. I concern myself with the vision" (Gilbert et al. 26)—and an attitude to process that is individualist rather than collaborative: "I'm not interested in actors. I'm interested in performers. An actor portrays a character, plays a role; whereas a performer does what I tell them [sic] to do" (22). Indeed, he sounds much like Schafer as an antidemocratic modernist individualist, [24] rejecting the idea of theatre as a cooperative form and claiming to

> have no fear whatsoever of presenting my vision, undiluted. I want all the power of all the decisions. I do not want to break, even remotely, the boundaries between a set designer, a lighting designer, and a musical arranger. I want to do it all myself.
>
> The best work I've ever seen has always been exclusively the product of one man's [sic] vision. (20)

While actors talk of input into the process—actor Andrew Scorer claims that "there's actually more creative input from the actors than is usual in a play" (qtd. in Hunt 46) and Liitoja himself admits that he solicits and sometimes incorporates their ideas, he also "makes the final decision as to what goes in, what goes out, where whatever goes, and how many times it's repeated" (Gilbert et al. 20). As Sky Gilbert, another regular Liitoja performer, puts it, "paradoxically, one feels very much a part of the process and at the same time at the mercy of a rather sado-masochistic hallucinatory imagination" (27).

What this process results in structurally, however, is a shaping of the theatrical experience for audiences that is anything but contained, closed, or comfortable and that is in its effects, on occasion at least, much more socially interventionist than Liitoja routinely admits. [25] The productions are structured spatially and temporally through analogies with music, poetry, and the visual arts rather than with dramatic, mimetic, or narrative literature, they begin before the audience arrives, and audience members are encouraged to wander through the playing area, changing seats and restructuring perspectives at will. Paul Leonard, analyzing "the scenography of Hillar Liitoja," has drawn attention to the ways in which the "environment—both visual and aural—is "material" in DNA's work, something through which audiences move, structuring the apparently random events as "private experience" (31). He argues that, since "there will remain numerous flourishes that are invisible except to one or two audience members," "the aural and visual environment helps to foster a monadic world in which communication is not a social act but a private experience" (31). Nevertheless, this fragmentation can also be seen as empowerment, a democratization of experience that eschews control of focus and gives choice back to audiences whose experiences are at least to some extent self-constructed. DNA shows involve the simultaneous presentation of various actions that can't be "taken in" totally, "a random presentation of fragments of various levels of speech and images," as Paul Lefebvre puts it, "indisputable, real fragments, that destroy the very idea of realism, replacing it magnificently with that of reality" (qtd. in Hunt 49). Liitoja sees this as a challenge to audiences: "I love to see the audience figuring things out—in vain! I love these people being stimulated, their minds trying to figure out what's going on with their senses. … We're stuck in outmoded ways of perception; it's nice to have things jolted and re-evaluated" (qtd. in Hunt 49; ellipsis in original). And Sky Gilbert concurs, arguing that the "often abrasive aesthetics" of Liitoja's work issue in a "frontal assault on our society's way of thinking in which reason is valued over instinct, and narrative over rhythm" (qtd. in Hunt 49).

Although Hunt sees the effects of this assault as "ultimately … non-intellectual" (49), and Leonard as "purely sensory, … devoid of intellectual content" (31), the cultural work that it performs may operate more to frustrate traditional ways of understanding than simply to shift audiences into an asocial (private) or anti-intellectual realm of "physical or emotional reaction" (Leonard 31)—one that merely reinforces individualism or societally dominant binaries between public and private, intellectual and emotional, realms. It may be closer, that is, to Brecht than it seems, and in fact much of the action of most of Liitoja's productions depends on, or can be actively disrupted or diverted by, audience response. As Liitoja said in an interview with journalist Kate Taylor, "there's an unbelievable rigidity, control, and precision … that can be totally shattered by an audience member doing a simple thing" ("To Make").

For most audience members, then, the effects of the shows are anything but comfortingly cathartic: "Let the audience alone to deal with their own trauma!" Liitoja argues. "Why do you want to counsel and comfort them afterwards? (Gilbert et al. 27). As Robert Wallace suggests,

> DNA's refusal to effect "closure" in its work, like its rejection of linear narrative and its reliance on repetition and interruption, frustrates the audience's expectations of the theatre and challenges their assumptions about the world in which the theatre exists. The audience becomes conscious of the necessity for it to act to make meaning of events. (*Producing Marginality* 165)

Wallace's argument, in one sense, has become conventional as a reading of nonlinear, nonmimetic performance, but what makes it convincing here is the inter-section between the structural features that I have been outlining and the subject matter of at least some of the shows, in which social rather than aesthetic concerns constitute the raw material and in which the cultural work performed by Liitoja's chosen structures is most clear. The necessity for an audience to position itself and to "make meaning," not only of performances, actions, and fragments of light, sound, and language, but also of various positions on urgent social issues, shifts the argument beyond the aesthetic and into the social realm. Two productions may serve briefly as cases in point.

The first DNA production that involved Liitoja's writing his own script, *This Is What Happens in Orangeville*, first produced at Toronto's Poor Alex Theatre in 1987, was inspired by the murder in 1984 of two children by a fourteen-year-old boy and his subsequent confinement for insanity. [26] The production, then, replete with the disjunctions and apparently random actions typical of Liitoja's work, such as screwing in and unscrewing light bulbs, timing scenes, bouncing rubber balls, and performing various other stylized activities, was held together by a core group of scenes between the boy and the psychiatrist assigned to his "case." Unlike most such scenes in contemporary plays such as Peter Schafer's *Equus,* however, these sequences devoted to uncovering a satisfactory reason for the boy's behaviour—explaining it away—came to no comfortable conclusion: the boy tells the psychiatrist without regret that he committed the murders to find out what it felt like to kill. Meanwhile, the interview scenes are interspersed, with fragmentary, decontextualized portraits of "ordinary" people in Orangeville, some related to the boy and some not, engaged in quotidian activities, describing their lives or their reactions to the murders, or confronting the audience with their views, their commands, or, in the case of the young girl mentioned earlier, their nakedness.

Taken out of context, many of these ordinary activities seem as inexplicable as the murders, and they blur the distinctions between normalcy and insanity on which our abilities to "come to terms" psychologically with violence that is in fact socially produced depend. Many of these activities, moreover, require a response or conscious reaction of some kind from audience members who are uncomfortably confronted by apparently gratuitous nudity, buttonholed by an apparently imbalanced fellow spectator, or ordered about by an "Ominous Presence" or by aggressive "ladderboys," stripped to the waist. The confrontation of these random acts of theatre in the context of a play about what we have learned to call a random act of violence is telling, and it requires that we, as individual audience members, confront a plea of insanity that seems to make no conventional sense: the, boy seems, at least, to be the coolest, most rational, most "normal" presence in the room, audience members included, and thereby raises telling social questions about what constitutes the normal in a world that appears to have gone mad. The play ends with the playing of an audiotape of a psychiatrist talking with Liitoja about the effects of child murders on society, and the flicking on and off of stage lights and camera flashes, before, in Hunt's phrase, "the audience is left in the dark, then thrown into the light" (48).

The politics of the subject matter and the involvement of the audience are even more overt in Liitoja's 1990 production of *The Panel: A Devastation Concerning AIDS,* later incorporated into the 1991 production *Sick*[27]. After all, the construction of a discourse on AIDS, particularly one that requires audience participation and debate, was in 1990 and remains a risky and overtly political undertaking. As described by Mark Ruzylo, the form of *The Panel* is "a stylized forum discussion focussed on the representation of AIDS in popular culture" (58), in which seven panelists representing different positions on AIDS, plus a varying number of audience members, who either replace panelists at the central table or speak from the "house," engage in improvised discussions of the implications of selected written and visual media representations of

AIDS that vary from performance to performance and that are not seen in advance by the participants. In an effective parody of the oppressive mechanisms of social control and authority, the discussion is regulated by an outrageously outfitted Moderator who outlines an absurdly rigid and arbitrary set of rules and procedural regimens that structures the performance and by a Judge who makes random and destabilizing interjections and who alone is not bound by the Moderator's regulations. This action is surrounded, interrupted, and further destabilized by various other actions, interludes, vignettes, and conversations with audience members and by a woman who screams poetry and shouts out the ingredients of a holistic healing potion that is later sampled by the cast and willing members of the audience.

Not only does the performance allow for the interrogation of dominant representations of AIDS, and not only does it offer what Ruzylo calls "representational mutability" (57) in its refusal to present a single, dominant, or controlling discourse on a disease that has become a discursive battleground in a political struggle over issues of ownership, representation, and control; *The Panel*, as Alan Filewod argues, also "interrogates the politics of the AIDS narrative by restructuring the fundamental relationship of performer (that is, discourse) and audience" ("Acting AIDS" 13). Audience members not only wander the space freely, as in most DNA productions, but they are also invited to participate directly in the show's discussion, incorporated into the structure of the panel, and forced to confront, take into account, and respond to a range of views different from their own in a forum that is determinedly social. As Ruzylo notes, the performance "challenges the spectators' passivity and indifference, no longer allowing them to distance themselves from the social realities of the epidemic" (86), or, in Filewod's words, from "the historical indifference of society to AIDS" ("Acting AIDS" 13).

* * *

> The audience is treated as visitors to an open house in a mental health institution. The audience is required to answer questionnaires, given badges, divided into groups and led up and down stairs and in and out of various rooms that make up Theatre Passe Muraille. As tourists, the audience's response is a detached one: moderately bemused, a little bored and occasionally diverted.
>
> There is a ... frisson of horror, and an evocation of the gas ovens of Nazi Germany, near the play's end when the audience is herded into a darkened elevator and led to the sleep room of the play's title.
>
> —Liam Lacey

As this description *of Sleeproom,* an environmental play written by Sally Clark, Robin Fulford, Daniel MacIvor, and John Mighton and directed by Ken McDougall at Theatre Passe Muraille in January 1993, suggests, not all environmental theatre in Canada functions according to the principles outlined by Schechner, conforms to the practices of Schechner, Schafer, or Liitoja, or sees environmental staging as an enfranchisement of audiences. Indeed, one of Canada's best-known directors of environmental theatre, Richard Rose, follows very different procedures to very different ends. [28]

Rose established his reputation in the early 1980s as an inventive young director with a flare for the innovative use of three-dimensional space. Early in his career, in productions of plays such as Euripedes's *Electra*, he experimented with unusual audience-stage configurations and with devices such as simultaneous staging in order to break down audience complacency about theatre and the world. In *Mein*, a collective creation, Rose and his designer, Dorian Clark, created a black grid-work box in the cramped back space of Theatre Passe Muraille to explore within a single mind the psychology of corporate ambition. In *The Seagull*, he staged a promenade-style production in a temporarily empty shop with a floor-to-ceiling glass wall overlooking Lake Ontario in Toronto's chic Queen's Quay Terminal, while at the other end of the scale he produced the stage version of Michael Ondaatje's *Coming through Slaughter* in Toronto's distinctly downscale Silver Dollar tavern. In John Krizanc's *Prague* and Jason Sherman's *It's All True*, the proscenium stage of Tarragon Theatre was systematically exposed and exploded in complex metatheatrical deconstructions of theatrical space. Until recently, Rose was best known for his production of Krizanc's *Tamara*, a critique of fascism that attempted to deconstruct the totalitarianism of the theatre itself, as audience remembers were invited to put together their own play by following actors of their choice from room to room in Toronto's historic Strachan House. *Tamara* became an international hit when it was remounted by Rose in Los Angeles, New York, and elsewhere. [29] Finally, *Newhouse*, his exploration of contemporary political morality, was staged in a Toronto hockey arena that stood in allegorically for "the political arena" and borrowed elements of allegorical/environmental stagecraft from medieval pageants and morality plays. In production after production, then, Rose has managed to make the play spring, as one reviewer remarked, "almost spontaneously from the building in which it is performed" (qtd. in Knowles, "Richard Rose"). [30]

Although Rose's environmental theatre shares some features with the environmental work of Schechner, Schafer, and Liitoja, it is nevertheless fundamentally different in a number of important ways. Rose differs from Schechner—or at least from the canonical reputation and influence of Schechner's work on environmental theatre—primarily in his understanding and practice of the politicization of space. Where Schechner is interested in enfranchisement, Rose is interested in power; in fact, it may not be stretching the argument too far to suggest that Schechner is engaged in the constitutionally American search for life, liberty, and the pursuit of happiness, while Rose pursues the personal and political implications of Canada's constitutional guarantee of peace, order, and good government.

Schechner's assumption articulated in "The Decline and Fall of the American Avant-Garde" that "frontalism," or proscenium stagecraft, is politically "retrograde," "a conservative retreat" (96), an assumption that has been usefully critiqued by Timothy Murray, is rejected by Rose, who believes that all performance venues, including proscenium stages such as those that he employed in *Mein* and *Prague*, are environments with, in Marvin Carlson's phrase, their own inherent or historically resonant "environmental semiotics" (36). [31] Rose's productions put into practice the more politically nuanced position that environmental theatre is most usefully defined by its acknowledgement rather than mystification of the space that it inhabits, whatever that may be. Similarly, while for Schechner participation is fundamental to environmental theatre and liberatory politics alike, Rose's work (among that of others) has prompted Steve Nelson's observation that "There is a misconception among critics that environmental theatre is an intrinsically participatory experience. … [N]othing could be further from the truth" (92): "Radically altering the audience/ performance contract," Nelson argues, "is no longer the concern. People walk about and get close physically, but the barrier between actor and spectator remains intact" (93). [32] Indeed, for Rose it is crucial that the barrier remain intact: his interest is in allowing audiences to see performance and behaviour clearly, and from close proximity, and he believes that this is impossible both in life and in theatrical productions in which one is too immediately engaged in the self-conscious processes of interaction to see clearly or judge accurately. In Rose's environmental productions, then, with the exception of certain formalized moments of admission to the space, regulation of behaviour, or direct address, actors do not acknowledge the presence of audience members, particularly in intimate scenes, however much they may share spaces. Rose's productions construct their audiences as voyeurs rather than as participants, visitors who exercise some apparent choice, however severely limited, in the selection of what to look at and the piecing together of the story but who have no influence over the action. They tend to experience, moreover, none of the felt sense of control over the gaze, superior knowledge, or objective viewpoint available through standard proscenium stagecraft, and in productions such as *Tamara* they are constantly aware of scenes going on "offstage," as it were, before other audience members, to which they are not privy.

In spite of Krizanc's claims about the democratization of focus in *Tamara*, then, and Alberto Manguel's hyperbolic claims for it as "the first democratic play" (5), giving audiences more freedom than they have ever had in the theatre, [33] Rose's environmental theatre productions do not take place in open, transformative spaces, nor do they create a sense of audience freedom or enfranchisement. On the contrary, like the production of *Sleeproom* described in the epigraph to this section, in which audiences underwent a test at the outset, were divided into three groups, and were herded through the building that housed the show (but unlike Schafer's *The Greatest Show* or Liitoja's environmental work), Rose's productions, which often explore issues such as censorship, house arrest, fascism, and other mechanisms of social control, tend to employ spaces of entrapment and to point up constraint. Thus, in *Censored*, an adaptation of Mikhail Bulgakov's *A Cabal of Hypocrites*, Rose used a former church interior to house the court of Louis XIV and to explore the relationships between the church, the state, and the arts. The production opened with the audience as extras in Moliere's acting company, cramped backstage (in the theatre lobby/church foyer) awaiting the king's reaction to the first performance of *Tartuffe*. The last act of *Tartuffe* was actually performed offstage, with the actors "exiting" to the lobby to apply makeup and change costumes. Only when *Tartuffe* ended was the audience herded into the playing space proper for the opening of *Censored* itself.

In *Tamara*, which takes place in simultaneous scenes on 10–11 January 1927 throughout Il Vittoriale degli Italiani, the villa of Gabriele d'Annunzio where the Italian nationalist poet is being held in house arrest by Mussolini, the audience is greeted at the door by Capitano Finzi, dressed in a black fascist uniform and standing behind a lectern asking for their "Carta d'identia," issued as part of the program:

> Papers. (*looks at the passport then hands it back to audience member*) Sign there. You will keep this with you at all times. If you are asked to produce your visa, you will do so and you will be required to know its contents. Read it. Anyone found without their papers will be arrested and deported. (Krizanc 20)

(At the beginning of the second act, a missing passport is found, and a female audience member is taken from the room, "interrogated," and asked to scream, "so that your friends suspect nothing," a scream that is heard in other scenes and contributes to the play's action [181].) The passport device is artificial, of course, and audiences tend to find it amusing rather than threatening, but it does point up the real limitations on audience freedom—"the regulations regarding movement in this house" (23)—that are also articulated at the outset, this time by d'Annunzio's valet, Dante Fenzo: audience members may only move between rooms when following one of the characters in the play/ residents of the house ("If you are not following a person you are breaking the law" [24]); if a character closes a door, audience members are not to follow him or her, nor are they to open closed doors; they must move quickly and quietly throughout the "villa"; certain areas are off-limits; they may speak only when spoken to; and so on. At the end, they are more or less ousted from the building, and the doors shut against them.

Newhouse, an adaptation by Rose and D.D. Kugler from Tirso de Molina's *Don Juan (The Trickster of Seville)* and Sophocles's *Oedipus Rex*, includes interrogations of telemedia representation and the political structure of the Canadian government, all focusing on the crisis represented by an unnamed "plague" that is clearly AIDS. The environmental setting in this case orchestrates audience movement as a representation of the manipulable masses as they respond to political speeches, television images, reporters, and theatre itself by following the action from platform to platform and large-scale monitor to monitor. "It was fascinating to watch the crowd surge in a general wave of movement whenever the action moved," Alan Filewod remarks in his interview with Rose and Kugler, who describe the setting as "a kind of cage," inside which the audience was trapped, "a kind of a beast," in Kugler's words, "Totally present but totally excluded" (Rose and Kugler 39).

The hockey rink in which the action was set evoked the political arena, of course, an evocative metaphor when most political conventions in Canada take place in sports facilities and many of Canada's most momentous political events, such as the first election of the separatist Parti Quebecois in 1976, are indelibly associated with hockey arenas (see chapter 5 [of Knowles's *The Theatre of Form and the Production of Meaning*—ed.). More importantly, however, the setting also directly evoked medieval allegorical stagecraft in a number of suggestive ways.

Although it was not immediately apparent to the audience, the set was most clearly derived from medieval staging in its evocation of the body politic as a body. Indeed, the staging evoked the layout of the medieval cathedrals in which the earliest liturgical dramas took place, with their mapping of the head of Christ (the priest in the apse), his outstretched arms (side chapels), and the congregation as corpus. The arena in which *Newhouse* was staged was mapped out with a platform at one end used by the prime minister (the head of government and the source of reasoned argument, as well as the play's Oedipus/Christ figure as sacrificial victim), flanked by banks of television monitors and a small chapel; a "groin" platform at the opposite end, without screens, where Newhouse, the son of the minister of external affairs and the play's Don Juan and Trickster figure, seduced two of his victims; a central platform, also without screens, as the "heart" of the assembly, where action involving emotion took place; and two side platforms, the "lungs," each divided lengthwise by a large screen and used as public areas, the media centre and embassy on one side, the bar and various other locations on the other. In this schema, as Rose and Kugler made clear in their interview with Filewod, the audience, moving through the space as the action shifted from platform to platform in cinematic "edits," functioned as the veins (39). [34]

The allegorical functioning of all this in a play that pitted reason against passion and public against private morality is clear, and the updating of source elements was cleverly done. Sophocles's Chorus, for example, was replaced by a gaggle of reporters and camera operators who followed the public action, broadcasting it "live" to the play's audience and an implied general public. But the revisionings of ancient and medieval staging had political resonances as well. In the case of *Newhouse*'s version of the Greek Chorus, the audience was forced, as Natalie Rewa has pointed out, "to accept the reporter as their collective spokesperson, together with the perspective on events chosen by the camera operator (41). Rewa's analysis of the production's use of space is perceptive and resonates interestingly with Robert Weimann's analysis of the politicized use of *locus* and *platea* in the medieval and early modern theatre (73–85 and *passim*). For Weimann, the platforms, stations, or pageant wagons that served as fixed locations in various types of medieval theatre were also *loci* of power, and the *platea*, the areas between *loci*, which both actors and audience members moved through and which served flexibly to signify variable locations, were public spaces. In Michel de Certeau's formulation, the latter represents a (timeless) "space" of authority rather than a (temporal) "place," where meanings can be negotiated rather than simply communicated from speaker to auditor (17–18). In this schema, the *loci* of the medieval theatre—heaven, hell, and allegorical sites such as "the world," "the flesh," and so on—were fixed centres of universal truth and stable, naturalized power structures, sites from which strategy, in de Certeau's terms, could be deployed in attempts to fix meanings and social structures in the interests of the currently dominant. The shifting significations of the *platea*, on the other hand, institutionally powerless, were what de Certeau would consider the tactical (and potentially resistant) social sites of negotiated meaning operating through time and therefore through constantly shifting positionalities (de Certeau 35–39).

Newhouse, in which the relationship between fixed stages and open floor space resembled the medieval relationship between *locus* and *platea*, then, employed some of the social and political significations of this scheme but adapted them to the world of late capitalism in ways that took into account post-modern information networks and the shifting meanings of place and space themselves. Here the sites of institutionalized power, the *loci*, were not fixed in "place" but virtually omnipresent. Scenes occurring on them were (strategically) broadcast throughout the arena on large-scale screens and monitors that intruded on the experiences of audience members wherever they were, required no movement or activity on their part, and mimicked a post-(economic)-border, free-trade world in which power is located in (cyber)space rather than in specific seats of government, in communication networks and international capital rather than in capital cities. "Private" scenes, in this configuration, took place on various stages, were not broadcast, but required audiences to move throughout the arena and act as "live" witnesses to what amounted to private, tactical acts of negotiation with the dominant or even with sexual and physical resistance, however (self-) destructive or manipulative. The extremes of the production— extremes of intellect and desire—were represented, on the one hand, by the neoconservative televangelist, a figure modelled on the physical image and some of the writings of Stephen Hawking, who never appeared in person but inhabited the space only through televised broadcasts calling for mandatory testing for "the plague." His disembodied intellectual position was treated with some seriousness and was opposed in the play, on the other hand, by the resistant but sheer physical irresponsibility of the libertine Newhouse/Don Juan as embodied desire, who never appeared on camera but whose physicality and physical magnetism—his body—challenged and resisted containment by the play's represented mechanisms of social control. Between these poles, negotiating between the extremes and engaging in both public and private scenes, moved the production's everyman, the public's and the audience's political spokesperson and their eventual scapegoat, the prime minister. This character was ultimately caught not only between reason and desire, between his private life and his public principles, but also between his position as national leader and pressure from Washington (as transnational signifier), in a global political economy that, like the disease on which the play focuses, respects no borders between one country and another, one person and another, and one national government and another. And the audience/ public was his (tainted) life blood.

Liitoja's environmental AIDS play, *The Panel*, then, confronted audiences with the need to position themselves in relation to representations and constructions of the social and medical issues and the public perceptions circulating around AIDS, as it required them to position themselves physically and aesthetically in relation to the performance space. *Newhouse*, by creating an allegorical representation of contemporary public life in a global political economy, making physical the "role" of the public, was, in Filewod's words, "a significant departure from the norm of Canadian political theatre in Canada. Its treatment of AIDS remove[d] the issue from the politics of personal relationships and medical treatment and place[d] it in the arena of public social policy" (Rose and Kugler 33). It did so, perhaps more frighteningly, through a reconfiguration of public and private space, represented and constructed by the theatrical environment as the virtually antidemocratic space of the manipulable circulation of capital, power, information, and disease across national, legal, and personal boundaries.

(1999)

Notes

¹ I am using the terms "post-naturalist" and "post-modernist" here and throughout this chapter in their hyphenated forms in an attempt to limit the meaning, particularly of the latter term, to formal experiments that develop out of, though they may overlap chronologically with, naturalistic or modernist predecessors and that take place primarily since the inception of "late capitalism" (c. 1970), as opposed to the period of industrial capitalism out of and in response to which modernism emerged.

² Schechner published his "Six Axioms for Environmental Theater," coining the term, in *The Drama Review 12* (1968): 41–64, and his book *Environmental Theater* in 1973. They were revised, reintroduced, and reissued together in 1994 as *Environmental Theater: An Expanded New Edition Including "Six Axioms for Environmental Theater."* The other major theorist of the period was Michael Kirby, whose influential "Happenings: An Introduction" and "The New Theatre," together with his and Schechner's "Interview with John Cage," are usefully republished in Sandford. The most thorough taxonomy and history of environmental theatre, (too) broadly defined as "staging that is non-frontal" (1), is Arnold Aronson's *The History and Theory of Environmental Scenography*. Criticisms of these histories might usefully and accurately be levelled in the way that criticisms have been levelled at America- and Eurocentric histories of performance art, with which they overlap.

³ For ritual shamanism and magic, see especially Schechner, *Environmental Theater* 174–92. In "The Decline and Fall of the (American) Avant-Garde," he argues that "to experiment with the space of the whole theater, and to bring the theatrical event into the world outside the theater building, is to investigate most directly the relationship between performers and spectators, and between theatrical events and social life" (29). However, Steve Nelson's 1989 reassessment, "Redecorating the Fourth Wall: Environmental Theatre Today" (which treats John Krizanc's *Tamara* as an American play of the late 1980s, without mentioning the author or the show's 1981 origins in Toronto), questions the political efficacy or even intent of most

American environmental theatre in the 1980s. Timothy Murray's "The Theatricality of the Van-Guard: Ideology and Contemporary American Theatre" offers a very different critique, based on Althusser, of what Murray sees as Schechner's somewhat simplistic equation of proscenium stagecraft, or "frontalism," with political conservatism, while simultaneously throwing into question the automatic assumption that the "avant-garde" (or the "van-guard") and nonfrontal staging are by definition politically interventionist.

⁴ This is my own account of *Stage* (or *Groove*; its name changed between the conception, including the publicity, and the act, but it never became clear whether confusion about the change was part of the show), written and directed by Wendy Agnew and Darren O'Donnell with Dr. Josef Raza and produced by Pow Pow Unbound at Buddies in Bad Times Theatre in March 1993.

⁵ Everett-Green quotes Schafer as saying, "I love the natural environment of Canada. I'm not so pleased about the society, which is becoming increasingly vulgar, and hostile to quality…. That's why I like to go to Europe, where they still understand what quality means." He also objects to "a slippage towards funding multicultural entertainments rather than Canadian entertainments [sic]…. I'm not in favour of multiculturalism. I think you should forget wherever you came from, and live where you are, and build a culture based in Canadian social and climatological experiences" ("Polemics").

⁶ The most thorough account of Schafer's theatrical work is his own, in *"Patria" and the Theatre of Confluence*, which includes copious illustrations ranging from scores that incorporate the composer's doodles, through environmental plans, to production photographs. David Burgess notes the similarity of the "theatre of confluence" to Richard Wagner's *Gesamptkunstwerk* (35), and Everett-Green cites Wagner, together with Richard Strauss and Benjamin Britten ("Schafer") and Alban Berg ("Undisciplined"), as analogues and influences. Schafer himself acknowledges Wagner (*Patria* 22–23 and *passim*; "Princess" 25). He also cites Reinhardt (*Patria* 67), D.H. Lawrence ("Princess" 27; "Theatre of Confluence II" 19), Joyce (*Patria* 23, 141), Eliot (*Patria* 141), and Eliot's mythological source, Frazer's *The Golden Bough* ("Theatre of Confluence II" 10). He links himself with Kandinsky, Klee, and the Bauhaus (*Patria* 23; "Theatre of Confluence" 33), as well as with Dada (by way of Tzara, Breton, and Schwitter) (*Patria* 79; "Theatre of Confluence" 36), the Russian constructivists (*Patria* 126), and the Italian Futurists (by way of T.F. Marinetti, whom he quotes at length on "variety theatre" as an analogue to his own "theatre of confluence") (*Patria* 132–34). His director, Thom Sokoloski, indicates in an interview with Burgess that Schafer has talked about Reinhardt, Meyerhold, Vahktangov, Artaud, and the Russian constructivists (39), and Ulla Colgrass cites among Schafer's influences and interests Cocteau, Klee, Fuller, Schoenberg, Webern, and Eliot, as well as Pound (35).

⁷ *My Cassell's Latin English/English Latin Dictionary* defines *patria* as "fatherland, see patrius." *Patrius*, in turn, is defined as "of or relating to a father, fatherly, paternal."

[8] "Immigrants" are the subject of *Patria 1 : The Characteristics Man* (renamed *Wolfman* in 1991 in *"Patria" and the Theatre of Confluence*), in which the central character, "D.P.," is reduced to despair and suicide. In his discussion of this work in *Patria*, Schafer feels obliged to make clear his opposition to immigration, on the ground that "the country [is] already overpopulated" (58). For other critiques of democracy, see "Theatre of Confluence" 37–38.

[9] See also Schafer, "Princess" 23–26, on his borrowing, as he calls it, from Native legends and languages; "Princess" 26, together with "Theatre of Confluence II" 15–17, on Japanese ritual, including the tea ceremony; and *Patria* 65–66 and "Theatre of Confluence" 33–34 on Japanese forms, including Kabuki, read through Eisenstein. Schafer indicates, moreover, his hope to complete *Patria* 10, in which his hero Wolf/Theseus will "go to the East to seek enlightenment, just as I have frequently sought it myself in oriental art and religion" (*Patria* 213). On the Catholic Mass as an "integrated ritual" see "Theatre of Confluence" 34. Schafer also cites "Eskimo," Balinese, and other "primitive" forms in "Theatre of Confluence II" 18. The *Patria* cycle itself draws directly on *The Tibetan Book of the Dead* (*Patria* 84) and on Greek, Egyptian, and other sources for mythological grounding/valorization. Schafer's general, Rousseauesque principles of primitivism are articulated in "Theatre of Confluence II" 5–7. His explanation of his use of "foreign or invented languages" is also revealing (particularly in light of his views on multiculturalism and the fact that, in *Patria* 2, Ariadne alone speaks English, while the evil doctors and nurses who attend her are linguistically constructed as Other): "The reason is that today more than ever before in history we live in a linguistic polyglot which has resulted in the polluting of all consistent linguistic paradigms. At times nothing seems to remain to us but a mass of jargon and gibberish" (*Patria* 76).

[10] See also, of course, Derrida's more general theoretical critique in *Of Grammatology* 97–268 of "the privileged place ... Rousseau occup[ies] in the history of logocentrism" (97).

[11] Schafer provides a useful synopsis of all parts, completed and in progress, in "*Patria: The Work in Progress*" (*Patria* 209–14).

[12] *Patria 4* was called *The Black Theatre of Hermes Trismegistus* when it was first produced at the Festival de Liege, Belgium, in 1989. The name was changed for the 1992 production at Union Station in Toronto as part of the DuMaurier World Stage.

[13] The structure of *Patria* 6 most clearly embodies in microcosm that of the cycle as a whole. As Schafer describes it, "the form of *Ra* is tripartite, with an introduction leading to the Halls of Preparation, the descent into the Duat (Underworld), culminating in death followed by rebirth and concluding with the ascent towards the rising sun of the new dawn" (*Patria* 178).

[14] Schafer calls *Patria* 7, not yet completed, a "dance drama" in which "the apotheosis has begun" (*Patria* 157).

[15] "The clash of Dionysian and Apollonian themes is everywhere evident in the story" (*Patria* 159).

[16] This reinscription of traditional and repressive gender roles is apparent from the beginning of Schafer's theatrical career. His first work for the stage, the 1965 opera *Loving*, represents archetypically "female" or "feminine" attitudes (used interchangeably) as "vanity" (which Schafer defines as "the desire to be and remain attractive to the male"), "modesty," and "passion." The male archetypes that he employs, meanwhile, are Don Juan, the Warrior, and the Poet (*Patria* 16).

[17] Schafer intended this gallery to be two-sided, but his director, Michael Bawtree, presented him with a central pit surrounded on four sides by tiered rows of seating.

[18] I am not taking into account here a number of the ramifications of *The Greatest Show*'s relationship with its immediate community as audience, as participant, and as sponsor, ramifications that align it at once with populist disruption, local empowerment, and reification of local power structures, since these issues are similar to those covered in chapter 4 [of Knowles's *The Theatre of Form and the Production of Meaning* —ed.]. It is nevertheless worth noting these tensions, the ways in which local support for the project were marshalled through provincially and federally elected representatives and local corporations, who supported the production financially and in letters (see Adams; Domm; and Grant), circulated in the press kit for the production, about the economic benefits to the community to be gained through tourism, employment, and other opportunities for "the community's businesses and service establishments" (Grant). Schafer argued somewhat differently about what he called the social agenda of the production:

> my attempt to break down this horrible division between the professional and the amateur, the entertainer and the entertained, to find some way in which not only the actors, the musicians and the others involved in the performances, somehow in the middle between professionals and the amateurs, but also the entire audience (so called) is involved and participates. ("Text" 37)

[19] Schafer describes "the invigorating environment of this spatial variety which is never geometrical or finished off but is broken unpredictability by wing flats, soffits and coulisses, suggestive of the labyrinth which is the subtext of the entire work" (*Patria* 125).

[20] See, especially, Jonson's induction scene (*Bartholomew Fair* 9–13), in which a playwright's representative negotiates the terms of artistic judgement with the audience. It is interesting to note a similar tension in Schafer's love for football, a populist sport that is often experienced by audiences as carnival but that nevertheless depends on militaristic and masculinist strategies of planning and control. Colgrass, describing Schafer's childhood, makes the comparison:

> He was an avid football player and read every book he could find on football strategy. A young team he coached in the High Park Y.M.C.A.

League for five years became unbeatable, and this leadership in sports is probably relevant to his ability to direct "a cast of thousands" in his later elaborate dramas. Perhaps his love of ritual and the need to physically act out his musical ideas are also connected with his early years in sports. (33)

Schafer himself claims that "in *Patria 1* I have tried to create a work as exciting as a football game" (*Patria* 66).

[21] The script is not continuously paginated. The introduction and the scenes set at each venue begin at page 1 and proceed to the end of their own sections. My parenthetical quotations from the script will therefore indicate both section and page number.

[22] I am drawing biographical information on Liitoja from Hunt 45–46. Only one script by Liitoja has been published, *The Last Supper,* but it is not one of his environmental works and is atypical in almost every respect. My account of Liitoja and DNA is based on personal experience, secondary sources, and a videotape of a 1993 production, *The Panel.*

[23] One reviewer called Liitoja's nine-and-a-half-hour *Hamlet* "a symphonic score" (qtd. in Leonard 30), and Hunt describes the structure of *The Last Pound* as being "based on the classical sonata form (presentation of two themes, transmutation, and final recapitulation)" (46). A sample score for *Private Performances,* including Liitoja's notes, was published as "Liitoja Scores" in *Theatrum.*

[24] Liitoja also shares with his modernist predecessors a tendency to treat life— including a disturbing number of naked girls in his productions—as "raw material" for his art (Hunt 46). Hunt rightly points to "the nudity of the young girl" in *This Is What Happens in Orangeville* as "more exploitative of women than suggestive of innocence" (49).

[25] The press kit circulated by DNA includes a page entitled "Features," which outlines elements central to its productions and gives a flavour of its sensibilities:

> Spectators are seated spectators throughout the performers spectators space. The spectators performance occurs spectators amongst the performers spectators spectators who are spectators performers clearly seen spectators and become spectators part of spectators the performance spectators.
> 1. There is much happening simultaneously at the same time.
> 2. Caress, blind, shout, faint, scream, Pound [sic], stop, blast, cry, flash, turn, hold, bang, flicker, jump, touch, fade, wait, stun, freeze.
> 3. Performers may be planted in the audience. Who is the performer?
> 4. Different cycles are pitted against each other.
> 5. Multiple repetitions.
> 6. Totality of the work and each performance begins before the spectator is admitted.

[26] I am indebted to Nigel Hunt's essay "Hillar Liitoja: Chaos and Control" throughout my discussion of *This Is What Happens in Orangeville.*

[27] I am indebted to Mark Ruzylo's thesis "The Representation of AIDS in Four Canadian Plays" throughout my discussion of *The Panel.*

[28] In discussing Rose's environmental work, I am including his collaborators at Toronto's Necessary Angel Theatre, particularly playwright John Krizanc, dramaturg D.D. Kugler, and designers Dorian L. Clark and Graeme S. Thomson. Rose has worked extensively in various kinds of theatre in Canada and the United States and is by no means defined by his environmental theatre work, which was concentrated in the 1980s.

[29] For an analysis of *Tamara* and *Prague* as political plays, see Knowles, "Truth." On the different cultural work performed by *Tamara* as produced in Toronto, Los Angeles, and New York, see Knowles, "Reading Material."

[30] This paragraph is adapted from the opening of my article "Richard Rose in Rehearsal" (134).

[31] An illustration of particularly resonant environmental semiotics, and one that illustrates how site-specific the cultural work performed by theatrical productions can be, occurred in the Los Angeles production of *Tamara*, performed at the Hollywood America Legion building. As Krizanc describes it,

> Early in act two, the Fascist captain, Finzi, interrogates the suspicious-looking new chauffeur, Mario:
> FINZI: "Are you now, or have you ever been, a member of the communist party?"
> MARIO: "No."
> FINZI: "I ask again: are you a Communist?"
> MARIO: "No."
> FINZI: "Have you ever known a Communist?"
> MARIO: "No."
> FINZI: "Three times you answer no."
> When the scene was first rehearsed, the temperature in the room seemed to drop twenty degrees. Everyone got goose bumps. The actor playing Mario broke character and asked, "Can you feel it?"
> We could. Thirty years ago, the building had housed the hearings concerning the Hollywood Ten. Those words have become synonymous with McCarthyism and I had put them in the play to draw the parallel between McCarthyism and fascism. Every house has its ghosts. ("Innocents" 37–38).

[32] In fact, Marvin Carlson argues that, whatever the audience-stage relationship, "the actor remains an uncanny, disturbing 'other,' inhabiting a world with its own rules, like a space traveler within a personal capsule, which the audience, however physically close, can never truly penetrate" (130).

[33] In an interview with Jon Kaplan, Krizanc said, "I wanted to give people more freedom than they've ever had in the theatre. I wanted to give choices back to the audience" ("Tamara" 137). Richard Plant, 197–98, argues that the play somewhat dangerously gives the illusion of freedom of choice to audiences whose decision-making and field of vision are in fact tightly constrained, and this may account for its having been successfully appropriated by Toronto millionaire Moses Znaimer and produced as a *divertissement* for audiences of the rich and famous in New York and Los Angeles. I argue elsewhere, however, that even there "the stars, would-be stars, and star-gazers that constituted so large a percentage of *Tamara's* American audience may have looked, at the end of the evening, at the pathetic figure of their fellow artist Gabriele d'Annunzio on his hands and knees, snorting cocaine from the feet of a corpse, and seen themselves" ("Reading Material" 275).

[34] Natalie Rewa provides a useful explication of the functioning of the setting to which I am indebted here, together with a map of the floor plan for the production by Graeme Thomson and John-Kelly Cuthbertson.

Works Cited

Adams, Peter. Letter. n.d. Press Kit. Schafer, *Patria 3: The Greatest Show*.

Aronson, Arnold. *The History and Theory of Environmental Scenography*. Ann Arbor: UMI, 1981.

Burgess, David. "Schafer's *Patria Three*: The Cycle Continues." *Canadian Theatre Review* 55 (1988): 34–42.

Carlson, Marvin. *Places of Performance: The Semiotics of Theatre Architecture*. Ithaca: Cornell UP, 1989.

Colgrass, Ulla. "Artistic Farming: The Many Talents of Murray Schafer." *Canadian Forum* March 1989: 33–36.

de Certeau, Michel. *The Practice of Everyday Life*. Trans. Steven Rendall. Berkeley: U of California P, 1984.

Derrida, Jacques. *Of Grammatology*. Trans. Gayatri Chakravorty Spivack. Baltimore: Johns Hopkins UP, 1976.

Domm, Bill. Letter. 29 February 1988. Press Kit. Schafer, *Patria 3: The Greatest Show*.

Eliade, Mercia. *Rites and Symbols of Initiation*. Trans. Willard R. Trask. New York: Harper, 1965.

Everett-Green, Robert. "A Peel at Schafer's Greatest." Rev. of *Patria 3: The Greatest Show*, preview version, by R. Murray Schafer, Theatre Autumn Leaf at Crary Park, Peterborough. *The Globe and Mail* 10 August 1987: C11.

———. "Polemics and Poetry." *The Globe and Mail* 16 February 1991: C8.

———. "Schafer, Peterborough Festival Embark on Long-Term Alliance." *The Globe and Mail* 28 June 1989: C19.

———. "Undisciplined Script Detracts from *Patria*'s Superb Music." Rev. of *Patria 1: The Characteristics Man*, by R. Murray Schafer, Canadian Opera Company/Shaw Festival at the Texaco Opera Theatre. *The Globe and Mail* 23 November 1987: C8.

Filewod, Alan. "Acting AIDS: Gender and Audience in Canadian Plays about HIV." Paper presented at the Association of Canadian Theatre History meetings, May 1991.

Frazer, James G. *The Golden Bough: A Study in Magic and Religion*. 1890. London: Oxford UP, 1994.

Gilbert, Sky, et al. "New Directions on Directing: A Panel." *Theatrum* 10 (1988): 19–27.

Grant, J.K. (Quaker Oats Company). Letter. 8 March 1988. Press Kit. Schafer, *Patria 3: The Greatest Show*.

Hood, Sarah B. Rev. of *"Patria" and the Theatre of Confluence*, by R. Murray Schafer. *Theatrum* 26 (1991–92): 10.

Hunt, Nigel. "Hillar Liitoja: Chaos and Control." *Canadian Theatre Review* 52 (1987): 45–49.

Hutcheon, Linda. *The Politics of Postmodernism*. London: Routledge, 1989.

Jonson, Ben. *Bartholomew Fair*. 1614. Ed. E.A. Horsman. Manchester: Manchester UP, 1979.

Kareda, Urjo. "R. Murray Schafer without the Panoramic Explosions." Rev. of *Patria 2: Requiem for the Party Girl*, concert version, by R. Murray Schafer, Theatre Autumn Leaf with Arraymusic at the DuMaurier Theatre Centre. *The Globe and Mail* 20 October 1993: C5.

Kirby, Michael. "Happenings: An Introduction." Sandford 1–28.

———. "The New Theatre." Sandford 29–47

Kirby, Michael and Richard Schechner. "An Interview with John Cage." Sandford 51–71.

Kirchhoff, H.J. "Encounters with the Nude and the Rude." Rev. of *Groove*, by Wendy Agnew and Darren O'Donnell, Pow Pow Unbound at Buddies in Bad Times Theatre. *The Globe and Mail* 5 March 1993: C5.

Knowles, Ric[hard Paul]. "Reading Material: Transfers, Remounts, and the Production of Meaning in Contemporary Toronto Drama and Theatre." *Essays on Canadian Writing* 51–52 (1993–94): 258–95.

———. "Richard Rose in Rehearsal." *Canadian Theatre Review* 42 (1985): 134–40.

———. *The Theatre of Form and the Production of Meaning: Contemporary Canadian Dramaturgies.* Toronto: ECW, 1999.

———. "'The Truth Must Out': The Political Plays of John Krizanc." *Canadian Drama/L'Art dramatique canadien* 13.1 (1987): 27–33.

Krizanc, John. "Innocents Abroad." *Saturday Night* November 1984: 34–38.

———. *Tamara.* Toronto: Stoddart, 1989.

———. "Tamara Takes Off." Interview with Jon Kaplan. *Canadian Theatre Review* 44 (1985): 135–38.

Lacey, Liam. "An Exercise in Virtual Tourism." Rev. of *Sleeproom*, by Sally Clark et al., Theatre Passe Muraille. *The Globe and Mail* 8 January 1993: C6.

Lebel, Jean-Jacques. "On the Necessity of Violation." Sandford 268–84.

Leonard, Paul. "The Scenography of Hillar Liitoja: Privacy and Senses." *Canadian Theatre Review* 70 (1992): 29–31.

Liitoja, Hillar. *The Last Supper.* Toronto: ArtBiz, 1995.

———. "Liitoja Scores." *Theatrum* 8 (1987): 19–21.

———. "To Make Your Spirits Soar." Interview with Kate Taylor. *The Globe and Mail* 1 May 1993: C3.

Manguel, Alberto. Foreword. Krizanc, *Tamara* 3–7.

Murray, Timothy. "The Theatricality of the Van-Guard: Ideology and Contemporary American Theatre." *Performing Arts Journal* 24 (1984): 93–99.

Neill, Mary. "The Play-within-the-Play in R. Murray Schafer's *The Greatest Show.*" Schafer, *Patria* 216–21.

Nelson, Steve. "Redecorating the Fourth Wall: Environmental Theatre Today." *TDR* 33.3 (1989): 72–94.

Plant, Richard. "The Deconstruction of Pleasure: John Krizanc's *Tamara*, Richard Rose, and the Necessary Angel Theatre Company." *On-Stage and Off-Stage: English-Canadian Drama in Discourse.* Ed. Albert-Reiner Glaap. St. John's: Breakwater, 1996. 189–200.

Rewa, Natalie. "All News Newhouse." *Canadian Theatre Review* 61 (1989): 40–42.

Rose, Richard, and D.D. Kugler. "The Words Are Too Important." Interview with Alan Filewod. *Canadian Theatre Review* 61 (1989): 33–39.

Ruzylo, Mark. "The Representation of AIDS in Four Canadian Plays." MA thesis, U of Guelph, 1993.

Sandford, Mariellen R. *Happenings and Other Acts*. London: Routledge, 1995

Schafer, R. Murray. *Patria 3: The Greatest Show*. Indian River, ON: Arcana, 1987.

———. *"Patria" and the Theatre of Confluence*. Indian River, ON: Arcana, 1991.

———. "The Princess of the Stars." *Canadian Theatre Review* 47 (1986): 20–28.

———. "The Text: Schafer on *The Greatest Show*." Interview with David Burgess. Burgess 37–38.

———. "The Theatre of Confluence (Note in Advance of Action)." *Open Letter* 4th ser. 4–5 (1979): 30–48.

———. "The Theatre of Confluence II." *Canadian Theatre Review* 47 (1986): 5–19.

Schechner, Richard. "The Decline and Fall of the (American) Avant-Garde." *The End of Humanism*. New York: Performing Arts Journal, 1982. 11–76,

———. *Environmental Theater: An Expanded New Edition Including "Six Axioms for Environmental Theater."* New York: Applause, 1994.

Sokoloski, Thom. "The Staging: A Three-Dimensional Illusion." Interview with David Burgess. Burgess 39–40.

Suvin, Darko. "Reflections on Happenings." Sandford 285–309.

Tancock, Martha. "Greatest Show Is Clever Conundrum." *Peterborough Examiner* 7 August 1987.

Wallace, Robert. *Producing Marginality: Theatre and Criticism in Canada*. Saskatoon: Fifth House, 1990.

Weimann, Robert. *Shakespeare and the Popular Tradition in the Theatre*. Baltimore: Johns Hopkins UP, 1978.

Young, Pamela. "Midway of Black Magic." *Maclean's* 5 September 1988: 70.

Shawna Dempsey and Lorri Millan:
Lesbian National Parks & Services

by Kathryn Walter

Shawna Dempsey and Lorri Millan arrived in Banff in their turquoise 1963 Pontiac Laurentian, dressed from head to toe in khaki gear. From their boots to their caps, they inhabited the uniforms of Park Rangers, complete with accessories. With the jingle of their key chains, you could hear them coming, but only a close look at their badges gave away their participation in the Lesbian National Parks & Services. As "out" as this name may seem, in actuality it was subtly inserted into public view. The name of this organization appeared on Shawna's and Lorri's bodies with such formality and apparent legitimacy that for all intents and purposes it normalized the word *lesbian*. But it was the charm exhibited by Shawna and Lorri that gave their cause the most credibility and ultimately enabled their lesbian identities to enter a potentially threatening mainstream. The Rangers uniforms and badges lent authority that allowed the two artists to move freely in the vast heterosexual midst, giving directions, taking photos and otherwise lending helping hands. Policies were drafted and circulated, and a recruitment day was organized in Central Park. Apart from an occasional break to do laundry, Shawna and Lorri wore their uniforms for the duration of their stay in Banff, becoming a part of the Western vernacular.

Word got around town that the Lesbian Rangers were out and about, as their brochure ended up in the hands of tourists and town residents alike, including the family of the woman portrayed on the brochure's cover. Shawna and Lorri had appropriated this photograph from a book about the Rocky Mountains published in the 1960s, and as it turned out, the woman depicted was alive and well and living on the outskirts of Banff. There was a buzz around town about this, and news got back to the Centre by word of mouth. But before any authorities were alerted or mistrust grew, the Rangers politely printed a new cover and carried on with their duties. The new brochure featured an illustrious portrait of the Rangers posing against a vista of the town. Even the administration at Banff National Park were relatively respectful, regarding the friendly impostors with more awe than suspicion. Perhaps this acceptance resulted from the Lesbian Rangers' propensity to take their own advice, watching their step, ensuring that the wilderness belongs to everyone.

This private investigation was conducted by means of public interaction. Taking full responsibility for their actions, the Rangers met their audience face-to-face. Their encounters with people took place in real space, a we-are-in-this-boat-together kind of space, and in the process, a private and marginalized lifestyle was publicized; the invisible was made visible; homosexuality "came out," and a situation that was potentially contentious became matter-of-fact. Shawna and Lorri's performance was a parody, an amusing inquiry into the authority of the park ranger but, at the same time, it was a gesture of pride based on lived experience. Theirs was a play about everyday issues, and with humour in their ardent actions they engaged their audience and communicated their commitment to a way of life. There was the odd occasion of homophobic outburst, but the Rangers subdued any preconceived fears of a population dominated by Reform Party mentality. Shawna and Lorri were truly the most endearing activists this site had ever seen.

(1999)

Field Reports from the Lesbian National Parks & Services

by Shawna Dempsey and Lorri Millan

LESBIAN NATIONAL PARKS & SERVICES
National Headquarters: 485 Wardlaw Avenue, Winnipeg, Manitoba Canada R3L 0L9
Ph. 204-453-8845 Fax 204-453-8845 email finger@escape.ca

Ranger Lorri Millan

FIELD REPORT NO. 13
DATE: July 10, 1997
LOCATION: Banff Avenue (southbound near Caribou Street)
TIME: 11:37

Patrolling Banff Avenue this morning, we encountered a young male *Homo sapiens.* Displaying a certain strain of XY behaviour, the male shouted, "Fucking homos," before bounding away into the throng. (We were fascinated to observe that his survival instincts were clearly intact, despite the other developmental problems he exhibited.)

• • •

LESBIAN NATIONAL PARKS & SERVICES
National Headquarters: 485 Wardlaw Avenue, Winnipeg, Manitoba Canada R3L 0L9
Ph. 204-453-8845 Fax 204-453-8845 email finger@escape.ca

Ranger Shawna Dempsey

FIELD REPORT NO. 27
DATE: July 14, 1997
LOCATION: Banff townsite
TIME: 13:00

Leading a group of potential homosexual naturalists on a brief tour of the town this afternoon, we paused to examine various sites (the invisible Lesbian Heritage House and Gardens, etc.). We were delighted that so many of the participants were seniors, proving once again that interest in the gay outdoors is not limited by age. We met at the Whyte Museum, and proceeded on a set course (highlighting various flora and fauna groups) to the Walter Phillips Gallery. The only difficulty encountered was that some of the participants insisted on referring to the trek as an "Art Walk," which we felt created doubt regarding the rigour of our scientific method. However, we, the field rangers, are confident that standards are being upheld.

• • •

LESBIAN NATIONAL PARKS & SERVICES
National Headquarters: 485 Wardlaw Avenue, Winnipeg, Manitoba Canada R3L 0L9
Ph. 204-453-8845 Fax 204-453-8845 email finger@escape.ca

Ranger Shawna Dempsey

FIELD REPORT NO. 33
DATE: July 19, 1997
LOCATION: The Banff Centre for the Arts
TIME: Various

Many residents at The Banff Centre for the Arts consistently exhibit "Ranger Envy." This is evident in their behaviour, including (but not limited to) attempting to buy the world-famous green-and-tan uniform, and when thwarted, asking to "try on" various parts of the regulation gear and then cleverly "forgetting" to return them.

• • •

LESBIAN NATIONAL PARKS & SERVICES
National Headquarters: 485 Wardlaw Avenue, Winnipeg, Manitoba Canada R3L 0L9
Ph. 204-453-8845 Fax 204-453-8845 email finger@escape.ca

Ranger Lorri Millan

FIELD REPORT NO. 47
DATE: July 21, 1997
LOCATION: Campsite, Two Jack Lake
TIME: 21:47

Patrolling the campsite, Ranger Dempsey and I sighted a pair of bewildered short-haired females. Clothed in colourful cotton, they carried the clear markings of the not-uncommon "Helper" lesbian. Because they displayed signs of confusion and fatigue, we approached cautiously. After contact was established, we ascertained that they were suffering from disorientation as a result of being separated from their urban pack, or "community." Casual contact with the Lesbian Rangers seemed to allay their fears, acting as a stop-gap until they could migrate home.

• • •

LESBIAN NATIONAL PARKS & SERVICES
National Headquarters: 485 Wardlaw Avenue, Winnipeg, Manitoba Canada R3L 0L9
Ph. 204-453-8845 Fax 204-453-8845 email finger@escape.ca

Ranger Shawna Dempsey

FIELD REPORT NO. 56
DATE: July 24, 1997
LOCATION: Central Park
TIME: 15:00

Today's recruitment drive was very successful. The colourful "Lesbian National Parks and Services WANT YOU!" banner and the pink lemonade attracted countless passersby, who were most interested in the service and how they might become involved. Among our more animated guests was a day camp of thirsty children who were very excited by our Junior Ranger programs. (On a personal note, I must say it is extremely satisfying to have eager young faces look up at our crisply uniformed selves with naked awe and respect.)

• • •

LESBIAN NATIONAL PARKS & SERVICES
National Headquarters: 485 Wardlaw Avenue, Winnipeg, Manitoba Canada R3L 0L9
Ph. 204-453-8845 Fax 204-453-8845 email finger@escape.ca

FINAL REPORT
DATE: August 1, 1997

BACKGROUND:

The first field study of the recently formed Lesbian National Parks & Services was conducted in Banff for a period of nineteen days, July 7–25 inclusive. Banff was chosen because of its wealth of natural habitat, dearth of lesbian plant and wildlife and a largely tourist human population who display some interest in the environment, and were therefore seen as potentially impressionable/educatable/vulnerable to LNPS.

GOALS:

Rangers Dempsey and Millan sought to:
• promote the introduction of gay and lesbian flora and fauna into the Banff area
• identify and nurture the small existing feral homosexual population
• educate regarding the importance of lesbian wildlife in any healthy environment

METHODOLOGY:

Week 1 – needs assessment and general survey of the area
Week 2 – implementation of homosexual agenda
Week 3 – recruitment

FINDINGS:

The lack of openly lesbian populations of any species was even more marked than initially feared. However, the Banff area itself is distinguished by an ethic of "unlimited growth," as evidenced by the exponential increase in tourism (five million visitors annually in 1997, which is expected to double in the next decade). After much careful study, we concluded that it seems possible that within this framework the introduction of homosexual species indigenous to the area might also lead to exponential multiplication, transforming the gay-wasteland-that-is-Banff into a virtual Galapagos of homosexual wildlife.

CONCLUSION:

Despite the challenges encountered by our first field team, the Rangers succeeded in establishing a beachhead in the heterosexual wilderness. We feel that the team's approach (exploiting rampant consumerism as a model by which to achieve explosive homo growth) will be studied for years to come and can be used to help form new and even more effective strategies for the furthering of Lesbian National Parks & Services' ambitions. We see a strong possibility for a more out and positive future, but it is crucial that our work (introduction, protection, preservation, advocacy) in the Banff area continue. Furthermore, we are confident that the Lesbian Rangers, armed with their experiences at Banff National Park, are now ready to proceed to other ecosystems throughout the country.

Report submitted by Lesbian Rangers Shawna Dempsey and Lorri Millan.

(1999)

**Lesbian National Parks
& Services and You!**

by Shawna Dempsey and Lorri Millan

Lesbian National Parks & Services
and You!

Founded in 1997, the Lesbian Ranger Corps is a fast-growing and dynamic force of professionals dedicated to the preservation, management and proliferation of lesbian wildlife in all its forms. But we can't do it alone. There are many ways you can become involved with Lesbian National Parks & Services. We'd like to take this opportunity to answer a few frequently asked questions.

Who is allowed to wear the world-famous khaki-and-green Lesbian Ranger uniform?

Only those who have passed our extensive and rigorous screening and training tests are inducted into the much-respected Lesbian Ranger force. Our education program (including biology and survival techniques) is not for the faint of heart, but can be oh so rewarding. If you are considering a career in lesbianism, we welcome you. Contact Lesbian National Parks & Services without delay.

Is there a place for men in the Lesbian Rangers?

Male members find the induction process particularly challenging. However, with true commitment, becoming a Lesbian Ranger is within everyone's grasp.

I believe in the Ranger ethic and want to be involved but can't make a full-time commitment. Is there a place for me in the Corps?

Serve in the Lesbian Ranger Reserve! Designed to meet the needs of your busy, fast-paced lifestyle, the Reserve offers you the flexibility you need and still allows you to make a commitment to serve in times of crisis. Enjoy the camaraderie of monthly meetings, educational retreats and seasonal cookouts.

Is there a way for my kids to become involved?

Yes! The Junior Rangers is designed to introduce your child to the wondrous experience of lesbian wildlife and wilderness fun. Watch your child's eyes light up as she earns merit badges, makes friends and learns leadership skills. And she'll love her pint-sized uniform! Start a Pack in your neighbourhood today.

How can I take the Lesbian Ranger spirit back to my neighbourhood?

Wherever you go, whatever you do, ask not what lesbianism can do for you, but what you can do for lesbianism.

Remember, whether you live in a large urban centre or a small rural community, on a mountainside or on the vast, open prairie, Lesbian National Parks & Services depends on all citizens to create an ecosystem better suited to the diversity of lesbian wildlife just waiting to flourish. Lesbian National Parks & Services wants you! We need you. Together, we can make a difference.

Write to: Lesbian National Parks & Services Headquarters
485 Wardlaw Avenue
Winnipeg, MB
Canada
R3L 0L9

Or e-mail: finger@escape.ca

(1999)

Eyewitness Account

by Kyo Maclear

Visitors have started carrying around Lesbian Park Rangers pamphlets as conversation pieces. (I've noticed more than a few Banff Centre residents with conspicuously stuffed jacket pockets.) The pamphlet, an official-looking guide, replete with references to mythical lesbian landmarks, appropriates the bizarre idioms of Tourist Board copy to insinuate other routes into Banff's social and historical wilderness. The ecological views of Lorri and Shawna garner such warm and wide reception that it would seem that lesbians can finally come out of the woods of obscurity.

The Lesbian Park Rangers, unlike the Mounties co-opted by Disney, can be touted as 100 per cent Canadian. Lorri with her Erik Estrada glasses and Shawna with her Ranger hat periodically tipped to passersby both appear well-scrubbed and approachable. In fact, they are strikingly less officious than their "real-life" counterparts. Their witty banter and deadpan delivery have made them favourites on the Banff Centre campus and in town.

It is amazing, but I have yet to see them out of uniform or off-duty. The tone of their performance has been sustained, their personae have been played "straight," so to speak, for three whole weeks. Gradually the surrogate rangers are becoming ever more real, ever more familiar. Of course, there are repeated references to "the funny lesbians in costume," but the conceptual satire seems to have titillated visitors (myself included) to the point that we have become willing participants in the masquerade. Are we falling prey to parody? Or is the fiction unravelling the real, its centre and margins?

This would be side-show entertainment were it not for the highly suggestive and involving nature of the performance. The Rangers' starched uniforms and earnest demeanour have encouraged a Pavlovian response—visitors all seeming to cry, "Lead me!" At a certain level I can understand the reaction, having been semiologically trained during a fourth-grade trip to Algonquin Park to see rangers as "my friends." Less immediately obvious, however, are the broader implications of the masquerade.

Lorri and Shawna, you see, have fused stereotypes to create a new social breed. The first thing they want us to know is that nothing is what it seems: not the mythical "lesbian" (demonized as a social threat, target and outsider), or the equally fictionalized "ranger" (celebrated as a front-line guardian of the Canadian wilderness). The Lesbian Park Rangers make it clear that social scripts, determining who will be loved, hated and revered, can be easily scrambled. Identities can be cross-wired and reprogrammed because they are based on unstable attributes.

Thus, Lorri and Shawna test social definitions and values. They know it is difficult to vilify someone who is there to protect and guide you (hence homophobes, who are so insanely resistant to seeing gays and lesbians in care-giving professions), and even harder when that "someone" bears a striking resemblance to an erstwhile Canadian folk hero.

(1999)

The Local and Global "Language"
of Environmental Sound [1]

by Hildegard Westerkamp

When I rode on a camel in the desert of Rajasthan, India, in November of 1992, I documented the journey with a sound recording. I expected to hear mostly the silence of the desert and camel sounds, which were intriguingly foreign to me. What I had not anticipated, but should have known after several months in India, were the many people that we encountered: vendors selling drinks, musicians playing the indigenous music of the desert, and curious children running alongside the camel trek of tourists and their guides.

Later, when I listened back to the recording I was struck by my reaction to it: on the one hand I felt a deep affection for the camel that had carried me into the desert and into a highly local soundscape of desert silence, the voices of people who lived in the nearby village of Sam and of the intensely beautiful and energetic music of that region; on the other hand I felt the cold reality that we were just another group of no-name tourists with money.

This reaction caused me to explore the inherent tensions of that situation and my experience of it in a performance piece for tape and spoken voice called *Camelvoice*. It became the beginning of a larger work, entitled "India Sound Journal." (My original presentation at Sound Escape began with a live performance of *Camelvoice*, the full transcription of which can be found in the Appendix at the end of this paper.) I want to highlight three points here, all of which connect in some way to *Camelvoice* and are imbedded in my topic about the global and local "language" of environmental sound.

The first one addresses the widespread attraction these days towards recording and composing with environmental sound and how the relatively affordable and portable audio technology has encouraged this trend. Connected to this growing interest is an often indiscriminate and uninformed use of the words soundscape and acoustic ecology. In other words, there seems to be a belief that if one works with environmental sounds one is automatically a soundscape artist and an acoustic ecologist.

The second point addresses the question of place. An incredible number of human beings are on the move across the globe nowadays, whether they are travellers and emigrants who go to new places by choice or refugees who are forced to leave their countries and settle in foreign territory. The resulting figures of displaced people are high. Questions of place and where we belong tend to accompany many of us who are on the move, as a way to orient ourselves in a world where "change itself has become the most pervasive and dependable part of life" (Suzuki 172).

The third point has to do with ecology. Whenever we address issues about place, about the local in relation to the globe as a whole, questions inevitably emerge about how we can possibly find a relationship that is ecologically balanced. Two Canadian books that promised to give some insight into these questions and could perhaps help to connect to the topic of environmental sound, listening and acoustic ecology became my conversation partners while preparing this paper. They were David Suzuki's and Amanda McConnell's *The Sacred Balance: Rediscovering Our Place in Nature* (1997) and Grant Copeland's *Acts of Balance: Profits, People and Place* (1999).

Finding a balance between the local and the global is becoming exceedingly urgent when we consider that "the rapid globalization of the world economy benefits transnational corporations at the expense of community-based economies, especially in developing countries" (Copeland 6). In order for specific characteristics of a place, and thereby a sense of place to survive in the face of sweeping corporate homogenization, it has become a matter of survival to preserve, highlight or recreate local, regional identities. But this is a complex task when this same corporate world has also established a transportation and communication net that works to seduce us into escaping the constraints of home and of the familiar, promises paradise in distant parts of the world, or connects us instantaneously with people all over the globe. Many ecologists have recognized that any environmental issue is nowadays primarily an economic issue (Copeland); in order to withstand global corporations and their destructive approach to the environment, workable local economies have to be created and supported. Ironically, community groups, environmental groups and NGO's have discovered that email and the internet are important and subversive tools of communication among communities across the world for information exchange of how best to work locally in the face of corporate globalization.

Given this current scenario, how can listening, recording and composing with environmental sound play a role in finding a balance between the local and the global? Can we claim that we are engaged in an ecological act when exploring the soundscape in such a fashion? *Camelvoice*, is probably pointing mostly at the inherent contradictions that we face when we work with environmental sound. Suzuki states that:

> Today we can see the beginnings of a new way of thinking about the world—as sets of relationships rather than separated objects—which we call ecology....We belong to, are made of, that world that surrounds us, and we respond to it in ways beyond knowing. (198–99)

But as soon as we record any sound it inevitably becomes an *object* out of context and, when played back, it does not belong to the place that surrounds the listener. Doesn't that imply that the act of recording any environmental sound and the act of listening to such recordings is in direct contradiction to the central meanings of ecology?

Strictly speaking the answer must be yes, as the *original* relationships between ear, sound and environment no longer exist.

Canadian composer Michael Coghlan was recently quoted as saying,

> I see myself as an acoustical ecologist. For instance, certain sounds are disappearing—horses' hooves clopping and the clink of glass milk bottles. It occurred to me that, as nature becomes more eroded by urban expansion, many streams will dry up. Once you record the sounds of the streams, you've got a sample of something ecological." (4)

Assuming that he was quoted correctly, I must disagree with this composer wholeheartedly. A sound sample in itself—even if it is preserving a disappearing sound—cannot be something ecological. In fact, to say it this way is a contradiction in terms. A sample, by definition, is taken out of its context and thereby loses all relationship to its former place and time and its original environmental, social, cultural and political meanings.

To give this composer the benefit of the doubt, his quote may have fallen victim to the same process of sampling that he seems to use in composing with environmental sound. In that case one could perhaps rephrase his last sentence—"*Once you record the sounds of the streams, you've got a sample of something ecological*"—by saying that the recorded sounds can potentially become the compositional language with which to "speak" about endangered waterways and thus address issues of ecology. The sounds then become a tool with which to raise awareness in his listeners about the state of the streams, with the ultimate goal of preserving them. To record and archive the sounds or even to compose with them is not in itself ecological. But the conscious application of recorded sounds as a "language" powerful enough to change our perception and to instigate environmental change could perhaps be understood as a type of ecological act.

It is at this juncture that it becomes interesting and hopefully ecologically effective to work with the sounds of the environment. It does not really matter whether we use our ears in listening walks, or present recorded soundscapes or environmental compositions to better understand the significance and the meanings of sound in our lives. All these actions are based on listening and making our relationship to place a conscious one. In fact, it may be our *responsibility* to get to know the tools of sound communication technology if we want to work effectively as acoustic ecologists. They can be utilized to counteract the dominating corporate/commercial "tone" in the media by creating alternative expressions.

In *Camelvoice*, the camel's sounds have not only been taken out of its desert context, I also have extracted very specific sounds from a much longer recording. Plus, I am replaying them in my home environment which is diametrically opposed to that of the desert. We cannot smell the camel, we do not see it, we cannot touch it. There cannot be a true living exchange between us and the recorded animal. I don't actually need to tell the listener this, as the piece itself points out exactly that and was created precisely for that reason: to speak of the many contradictions and to ask what in fact we are carrying home with us when we have made such a recording. My strongest memory of that experience is that I heard everything, including the desert silence, amplified through my headphones and that I have no idea what the place sounded like without that mediation. The fact that this camel's task was to carry foreign visitors on a desert ride, placed it squarely at the crossroads between global and local economies; that is, by carrying its load, the tourist, it participates in the economic exchanges of the global tourist industry and in that act becomes the vehicle for the people in this desert village, Sam, Rajasthan, to earn a living and strengthen the local economy. And it is the *recording*—not the live experience—that caused me to create *Camelvoice* and question the camel's place and situation.

Grant Copeland states that "No more than five corporations now control more than 50 per cent of the global markets for consumer durables, automotive products, airlines, aerospace, electronic components, electricity and electronics, and steel" (6). By flying with the airlines, using the electricity in hotels, renting taxis, bringing our electronics such as cameras, videos and sound recording equipment, we are participating in and are totally dependent on the workings of the global economy, in order to have this unique desert experience. And the camel's body is the pivotal point in this specific meeting of global and local economies—a formidable burden to carry for any living being. At the moment of the recording in 1992, this camel with all its quirky personality traits still belonged to a family group in this village. A growing tourist industry could eventually ruin this relationship by making the monetary exchange more important than the actual experience between people, camel and environment. We have already seen this happen to horses all over the world who are trained into docile lifeless creatures for the comfort and safety of the paying tourist.

At the beginning of this text most readers would not have heard of this camel. Now you have at least heard the story of our meeting, our limited relationship. Although we know that the story cannot replace the live situation, perhaps it can be the beginning of a conversation that we need to have with and about living beings in our world. Suzuki quotes ecologist Joseph Meeker as saying that:

> Learning to converse well with the world can begin by listening carefully to the messages sent ceaselessly by our bodies and by the other forms of life that share this planet. The best conversations are still those that play on the variations on that great and ancient theme, "I'm here; Where are you?" (197).

In some way *Camelvoice* is such a conversation, although when I made the piece, I never thought of it in that way. Suzuki claims that:

> The evolutionary context of human history makes it plausible that the human genome—the DNA blueprint that makes us what we are— has over time acquired a genetically programmed need to be in the company of other species. Edward O. Wilson has coined the term "biophilia" (based on the Greek words for "life" and "love") for this need. He defines biophilia as "the innate tendency to focus on life and

life-like processes." It leads to an "emotional affiliation of human beings to other living beings...Multiple strands of emotional response are woven into symbols composing a large part of culture." In urban environments, our genetically programmed need to be with other species is usually thwarted, leaving us yearning. (177)

Camelvoice is part of a larger compositional project that has allowed me to find access, and to create an "emotional affiliation," to a culture that would have continued to feel very foreign to me without this. And I can only hope that the combination of my writing about it and transcribing the piece is a meaningful continuation for you, the reader, as well, of that same conversation with the world.

Computers, sound software, and recording equipment are made by some of the largest, most powerful corporations. So if we choose to use audio technology for our soundscape work, we are automatically partaking in the global market economy. But rather than making commercials for a large corporation about camel rides in the desert, we can choose to put ourselves in the same spot as the camel; into that pivotal point between the global and the local. We can use these tools to reveal the details and specific characteristics of a place and to celebrate its uniqueness. For, the more deeply a place or a culture understands and honors its own unique character, the harder it is for a corporation to eliminate a local sense of place. We can choose to do with the language of sound what the corporate world does or what the subversive poet does with the language of words. Suzuki states that

> Language weaves worlds of being and meaning; but this is a double-edged sword. ...The propaganda of destructive forest practices informs us that "the clearcut is a temporary meadow." Definition identifies, specifies and limits a thing, describes what it is and what it is not: it is the tool of our great classifying brain. Poetry, in contrast, is the tool of synthesis, of narrative. It struggles with boundaries in an effort to mean more, include more, to find the universal in the particular. It is the dance of words, creating more-than-meaning, reattaching the name, the thing, to everything around it. (201–02)

Using recorded environmental sound as a type of language in one's compositions can also be a double-edged sword. Rather than using the soundscape as a large resource of sound samples for abstract musical ideas, a sound piece can be a *vehicle* for deeper understanding of acoustic environmental issues and issues of perception, a *vehicle* for creating "more-than-meaning." Such work is not an end product but, ideally, a beginning from which to create new relationships to place and time for both composer and listener.

Because the natural environment itself is threatened by corporate invasion, and because urbanization has alienated many of us from nature, there are substantial reasons why we would want to highlight and amplify nature's sonic language, its plight, its endangered position. As Suzuki claims, "A human-engineered habitat of asphalt, concrete and glass reinforces our belief that we live outside of and above nature, immune to uncertainty and the unexpected of the wild" (180).

Certainly, the sound of traffic, air-conditioning, background and foreground music, construction, gardening equipment, electrical hums, among many others, are the acoustic expressions of this disconnection from the natural world. They are soundwalls that prevent us from hearing distance, space and the more subtle sounds of acoustic exchange among humans and other living beings. Everything that ties us to the global market makes itself heard in broadband hums. This includes, ironically, the hum of computer hard drives in studios where environmental sound works are created. I am also convinced that many of the papers for this international conference on acoustic ecology [where this paper was first delivered] were written to the accompaniment of this all pervasive hum. But because we can block out what we do not want to hear while thinking and writing, even people like us, who supposedly are aware of their surrounding soundscapes, often choose not to notice. Were we to record these humming soundscapes and play them back as you read this, I think we would all be appalled by what we hear.

This leads me to conclude that, despite the fact that acoustic ecologists share an honest concern for the quality of the soundscape, we have not resolved the contradictions between our actual soundscapes and what we talk, write and compose about. The fact is that any continuous broadband sound separates us from the world around us. And this, in the long-run, can only impoverish our relationship to the natural world, and to the people around us. Suzuki writes that:

> When we forget that we are embedded in the natural world, we also forget that what we do to our surroundings we are doing to ourselves. …Ecopsychologists argue that the damage we do to ourselves and our surroundings is caused by our separation from nature. Instead of trying to adjust to the existing social order and accept the status quo, they argue that for true mental health we must challenge the norm and take into account the interrelatedness of people and all other life forms. (179)

Challenging today's status quo literally means silencing, turning off, reducing the hums that are symbolic of corporate global thinking and that, like a cancerous growth, destroy the local, subtle elements of place and culture, destroy precisely that which gives a place its specific character and thus its vitality and energy. It also requires that we continuously strengthen our own listening attention, whether we are listening with our bare ears or through audio technology. And this, in turn, strengthens our relationship to and understanding of the soundscape as a whole. Creating soundscape pieces from that position of understanding enables us to speak the language of environmental sound with real care for the ecological balance of the soundscape. As Suzuki notes: "If we can see (as we once saw very well) that our conversation with the planet is reciprocal and mutually creative, then we cannot help walk carefully in that field of meaning" (206).

But of course, with soundscape recordings and compositions we can only create repeatable excerpts from our sound environment for such a conversation, no matter how sensitively they have been put together. Perhaps the ultimate ecological step is to let go of our incessant drive to reproduce sound, to shape it, to broadcast it into the world. Similarly to what Pablo Neruda suggests in this excerpt of his poem *Keeping Quiet* (original title *A Callarse*):

> If we were not so single-minded
> about keeping our lives moving,
> and for once could do nothing,
> perhaps a huge silence
> might interrupt this sadness
> of never understanding ourselves
> and of threatening ourselves with death.
> Perhaps the earth can teach us
> as when everything seems dead
> and later proves to be alive.

We may simply want to stop and listen. After some time we may begin to hear the truly local, the here-and-now, and after some more time we may hear the *inner world tone* that, according to Sikh wisdom, underlies everything and connects us through our consciousness both to the here and now and to the globe as a whole. Because this may be the only thing left, should the global economy collapse and the electricity shut off.

(2002)

Appendix: Transcription of *Camelvoice*

TAPE	TEXT
(camel sounds, some men's voices)	(live spoken voice)
1) snort	At this moment it's November 28, 1992— I'm riding on a camel—
2) snort	—a camel in the desert near Jaisalmer, in Rajasthan, India.
3) /	Actually at this moment it is July 1st, 2000.
4) quiet grunt	I'm riding through the electroacoustic ether,
5) bah!	together with my camel,
6) bah! oh!	at "SoundEscape" in Peterborough, Ontario.

7) "back"   This is a talk about the *Local and*

8) oooh   *Global "Language" of Environmental Sound.*

9) long gurgle   My name is Hildegard Westerkamp and this is an excerpt
   "oh dear"   from the India Sound Journal".

10) "picture"   Everyone knows where I am.

11) long gurgle   Everyone can see me, I mean the real me, body and all.
    "that's nice"

12) ah   But no one can see the camel. It's all voice.

13) oh oh   Camelvoice in Rajasthan.

14) gurgle   Audience and I in Peterborough. All body and voice.
                             We do not see the camel. The camel doesn't see us.
                             Camelvoice disembodied.

15) chewing   Sometimes I *do* show a slide of me recording the camel.
                             Me laughing, the camel smirking. In Rajasthan.
                             —But not today.

16) long gurgle   Camelvoice November 1992.

17) burp   Here in Peterborough, July 1st, 2000
                             at Sound Escape.
                             Riding through the electroacoustic ether
                             disembodied
                             from the sand, the heat, it's voice.

18) chewing   Where is the camel at this moment?
    "he'll eat it"   Where is it eating?
                             Who is riding it?
                             Recording its voice?
                             Photographing its body?

19) one chew   Where is it now? Reproduced many times all over this
                             uhm... Global Village?

20) lips flapping   Is it still the same camel, chewing and digesting loudly in
                             the village of Sam, Rajasthan?

21) "posing"

Note

[1] This paper was originally presented at "Sound Escape, An International Conference on Acoustic Ecology," Peterborough, Ontario, Canada, June 28–July 2, 2000.

Works Cited

Cochlan, Michael. "Interview." *Focus on Research*. Toronto: York University (Winter 2000): 4.

Copeland, Grant. *Acts of Balance: Profits, People and Place*. Gabriola Island: New Society, 1999.

Suzuki, David, with Amanda McConnell. *The Sacred Balance: Rediscovering Our Place in Nature*. Vancouver and Toronto: Douglas and McIntyre, 1997.

Things I've Learned from Theatre SKAM

by Sean Dixon

Do your best to conduct the first week of rehearsal away from the city.
If there's an off-site location where you want to do a show, ask.
Take lots of photographs.
You can evoke a hole in the ground with a bare floor and descend into it.
  It is possible.

Don't use the term "kinesthetic pleasures" in an interview.
Eat lots of fibre.

You can get more levels of playing areas out of a restaurant patio than most A-house
  stages.
If you're in front of the audience, you're on the stage. If you're upstage of the
  performers and the audience can see you, duck.

If you can play a fiddle and also a trumpet, then it's likely you can play both at the
  same time.
Talk faster.
You can be sexy without taking your clothes off.
Also, you can play a horse without a lot of fuss.
A turn of the head can be as good as a lighting change.
A turn around the audience can be as good as a lighting change, too.
Live music first – before lighting, before set, before canned music. In our culture
  of the Xerox, culture of the Copy, the strength of theatre is in being, as much as
  possible, the Real McCoy.

The audience knows that you're the ones who are telling the story. You're sharing the
  performance area with them. You don't have to hide from them. (Unless you're
  upstage of the stage and not performing, in which case, duck.)
Theatre is not TV with coughing and line flubs.

If you need that railroad tie badly enough, you can lift it. And you can remove the
  slugs from it, too.

The event is of paramount importance.

Chances are that the man in the security vehicle who drives up beside the audience,
  upstaging the proceedings, is only acting out of curiosity.

When the stage direction says she doesn't ever move of her own volition, it looks like she won't ever move of her own volition, even when there's a mosquito sucking the blood out of her cheek.

When you need a playing area, don't rule out car roofs, BFI bins, loading docks, skids. Stones walls. Stairs. Scaffolding. Tree branches. Hillsides.

The audience will define the playing area, even if the elements have taken everything else away.

A hammock is a great thing to have onstage.

A hole in the ground is an excellent thing to have onstage.

A hillside is an excellent, excellent thing to have onstage. But if there are train tracks running along the top of it, be careful.

As many songs as possible.

Close your eyes and roll into the light.

When the train goes by, wave.

Pray it isn't a freight.

It is better to enter while playing the banjo than it is to enter and then start playing the banjo.

When the stage direction says she carries her on her back, it looks like she's going to make darn sure to carry her on her back, and keep an eye on her as well, to brush away any mosquitoes that might land on her cheek.

When the stage direction says he throws her up in the air, it looks like he's going to try and throw her up in the air.

But when the stage direction says there has to be a working manual railroad car on stage, along with tracks for it to ride along – why, that's just a lot of hooey.

And, while we're on the subject, when the stage direction says there is a warehouse door, locked and bolted, it's likely you can get away with a small old-fashioned shutter tied at shoulder height to a pole and swinging in the wind, a shutter you have to hold with one hand while you knock with the other, and it will do the work of the door as long as you have endowed it with a sense of doorness, and lockedness, and boltedness. Belief is everything. Well, belief is everything as long as it is accompanied by wit. You can even carve a little mail slot into it.

The audience, you see, has an imagination and will employ it.

A man holding a toy airplane and walking solemnly across the space will convey the sense of a large airplane flying across a country with that man inside it. Particularly if he's singing.

If you're tired of using realistic-looking firearms in your shows (particularly when your lead actor has had real guns trained on him, and dogs, as he lay flat on the concrete, face down, arms out, palms up, in a serious, unexpected, show-stopping encounter with the police), you can use cell phones instead; you can use farm implements instead. Anything but real guns. Anything but real guns…

You can install a secret door and pull off a magic trick in the middle of effing nowhere.

When performing outdoors there will sometimes be rain, there will sometimes even be rain on opening night. But Robertson Davies got it wrong in *Tempest Tost*: find somewhere to do the show, tell the story with what elements you can, and the audience will be thrilled and grateful.

With faith and hard work you can bring all kinds of shit to life.

You can step from a cookshack doorway onto a mountaintop just by saying the words and then seeming to see it.
A human face is far more expressive than a lighting state.

The occasional train is okay. Constant traffic noise is a bit of a grind, though.
The back loading dock of Wonderbucks on Commercial Drive in Vancouver is a great place to do theatre. Especially when they let you open the loading dock door and pile the boxes in the exposed storage room in theatrical ways.

A shared sensibility, a shared aesthetic, a shared vocabulary, means a company.
A company means strong theatre. There's really no question about that.

Are you in, is not a question. It's a statement.

(2002)

Out and About: The Performance Art
of Shawna Dempsey and Lorri Millan

by Jennifer Fisher

> The live in all facets of life is decreasing. People have their cell phones, their palm pilots, their MP3 players, their laptops. They go to movies, play video games, watch TV, read magazines. We have less reason to interact in real time and real space, and we are social creatures! People's sense of community is so fractured these days that coming together to experience a live performance—that age-old, one-on-one human connection—is still vitally important to our species.
> —Shawna Dempsey (Dempsey & Millan, Personal Interview)

> While other forms of media communicate, there is something about being live in front of another person, or group of people, that contains empathy and a true possibility of change. This is unique to the performance of live work. Maybe it's because we are all breathing together, maybe it's because one of us could drop dead. Maybe it's because there's a risk. This is important to acknowledge and take advantage of.
> —Lorri Millan (Dempsey & Millan, Personal Interview)

Since beginning their collaboration in 1989, Shawna Dempsey and Lorri Millan's performances have developed rhizomatically, presenting brilliantly scripted cabaret style monologues of iconic females, rap songs by feminine anatomical parts, discursive meditations on lesbian life, and more recently, site-specific, conceptually-centred interventions that they term *real world performances*. The duo's embodiment of familiar gender stereotypes fluently navigates the tightrope between fine art and popular culture with spectacles that involve the body as a medium to colour artistic expression. Moreover, speaking from the contradictory standpoint of a living body— as simultaneously cultural object and embodied subject—ups the stakes of a distinctly feminist politics. [1] Their performances characteristically instill a sense of comfort in the micropolitical practices of daily life: audiences settle in and relax their suspicions, only to find themselves carried into, and participating in, a liberal lacing of humour that drives a spectacular detournement.

Dempsey and Millan met in Toronto during a performance zeitgeist that included The Clichettes, Tanya Mars, Nightwood Theatre, and Sheila Gostick. Shawna was completing a degree in theatre production at York University (and worked as the technician for The Clichettes), and Lorri was working in a variety of media including photography, drawing, and writing songs (Dempsey & Millan, Personal Interview).

Performance provided an effective nexus to embody their feminist concerns within an art practice, becoming their primary medium and pivotal to their interdisciplinary work that included video, film, and print media.

The conceptual thrust of Dempsey & Millan was consistent with the theory boom underway in gender studies including the influences of deconstruction and identity politics during the 1980s. While seriously critiquing dominant power structures, their performances deploy a tone of playfulness and humour to posit alternative subjectivities for women. Their work mobilizes razor-sharp parody as an edge of critical resistance. Their extensive *oeuvre* of performances presents the struggles of gay and feminist subjects within the shared pleasures of subcultural identification. Each spectacle characteristically frames a familiar female icon, and then articulates a divergent fable, often one that impels audiences to recognize their own queerness self-reflexively, whatever its modulations of difference or unconventionality. Fixed perspectives give way while swept up charmingly in a participatory situational enjoyment. An affective politics of "peopleness" drives the work which is clearly evident in the artists' likability and heart-centred interactions, even when involving communication between positions of difference. Ultimately, Dempsey & Millan's boldly courageous assertions can be appreciated on many levels at once by diverse audiences, whether feminist, gay and lesbian, or the local, national, and international art and academic communities.

Dempsey & Millan's finely realized *mise-en-scènes*, costumes, and scriptwriting are heirs to, and consistent with, the formalism of Robert Wilson and Meredith Monk. Shawna apprenticed with Monk in New York from 1983–84, which also instilled important cues concerning collaboration, as Monk was then working with Ping Chong. Other important performance inspirations include postmodern dance which staged everyday movements in highly conceptual contexts, and Laurie Anderson's synthesis of new media within the performance art genre. In addition to 1980s feminist Toronto performance, the duo acknowledge the importance of Lydia Lunch and Karen Finley.

The process of creating each work begins with collectively envisioning an image. The performance is generated by expanding upon this image or iconic figure, giving her a character, gestures, scripting her language, and framing the work in a theatrical or paratheatrical setting. [2] The representational strategies deployed by Dempsey & Millan at once recognize the disciplinary forces of patriarchal culture and redress the relegation of the lesbian to "other." As their staging both appropriates and subverts conventional women's roles, so, too, their cabaret performances present a distinctly phallic, powerful performer while simultaneously deconstructing a phallocentric visual economy (Wray 195). Annie Martin insightfully elucidates the split subjectivity of Shawna's onstage persona, noting that her performance of an apparently "unique interiority" is at once authentic and inauthentic, as what she voices "as her own," is simultaneously Lorri's co-written script. As Martin points out, the "me/not me" aspect of the performed speech, the space between authentic and inauthentic, is precisely that zone where new "possible" selves are forged (Martin 43–44).

Virtually every performance involves an elaborately constructed costume—itself an art object—that is enlivened by the performance. Femme characters carry nostalgic resonances of Betty Crocker or Barbie, yet refuse to be contained by patriarchy. In turn, butch characters usurp patriarchal authority for distinctly lesbian presences and enjoyments. Likewise, the minutely inflected textual scripts effectively hijack the authority of their originating discursive formations, whether women's magazines, television advertisements, science fiction films, grocery stores, national parks wildlife services, or Eaton's catalogues.

A suite of performances explores the dress as a ceremonial costume and icon of feminine identity. In these pieces, cloth is replaced by sculptural materials that extend the metaphoric impact of sartorial iconography to embrace a multiple, heteroge- neous, and contradictory feminist standpoint (Harding 243). In *Object/Subject of Desire* (1989),[3] Shawna appears in a paper ballgown, elegant as a debutante at a "coming out" ball. Wearing the rustling paper as brittle as the gender codes that contain her, she asserts herself as a desiring subject: "I want you…" While one might initially assume this desire to be heterosexual, the twist is the performer's explicit assertion of lesbian desire. The material comprising the costume for *The Thin Skin of Normal* (1993), an off-shoulder evening gown, is Saran Wrap bristling with four-inch roofing nails. This icon references 1970s advice columns that suggest, to keep their marriages alive, housewives greet their husbands dressed in cling wrap. Rendered porcupine, a curvy theory-savvy feminist becomes prophylactic to reductive habits of polarized femininity. In turn, *Arborite Housedress* (1994) is performed in a wearable sculpture "dress" made of wood, laminate, chrome kitchen hardware, and cloth. Weighted within her wearable architecture, a patriarchally colonized "housewife" reveals her anxieties in assuming power:

> Eve took a wrong turn [out of paradise] but her first mistake was getting behind the wheel in the first place … It had serious repercussions for her, her family and human history but it also hurt Adam's feelings… and that's not very nice is it? (Dempsey & Millan, *Live*)

In *Plastic Bride* (1996), Shawna appears nude under a clear plastic wedding gown, merging the architecture of the bride's dress with the visible conventions of forensic evidence. She asks the audience if they've ever had one of those dreams where they were wearing the wrong outfit. At issue is self-ammonizing fashion, the risks of being killed by a fashion mistake. *Growing Up Suite* (1994), backed up by Montreal's Choeur Maha, reflects on lesbian coming of age in Scarborough. The lady's underwear pages of the Eaton's catalogue becomes a source of budding sexual fantasy where "industrial strength underwear concealing unimaginable body parts… so powerful they needed hardware to keep then in place" (Dempsey and Milan, *Live*). This thematic continues in *The Eaton's Catalogue [1976]* (1998) as a classic tableau vivant of The Three Graces within a functioning fountain. Faucets protrude from the bodices of 1970s evening gowns, from which water flows. In these retro-cyborgs, actual hardware displaces heavily constructed lady's brassieres (Fisher and Drobnick).

In each of these performances, costumes present the "constructedness" of sartorial femininity. Fashion, whether butch or femme, becomes a resonant signifier of social change employed to deconstruct patriarchy and project utopian-feminist impulses (Gaines 1).[4] Yet, while the forms of nostalgic fashion may mimic forms of patriarchy, Dempsey & Millan pry open the duo's ideological content to rescripting. Forms of language, gesture, and cultural referents—such as Eaton's department store catalogues—polysemously acknowledge a different viewing subject. The collaborator's "people palette" (Dempsey & Millan, Personal Interview) expanded with *A Day in the Life of a Bull Dyke* which presents Lorri as an alluring butch icon starring in a B noir video. The confessional voice-over narrates the poignant struggles of the lesbian—defined as she is by homosexual desires and physical acts—and empathetically enters into the subjectivity of desiring lesbianism.[5]

The perpetually controversial *We're Talking Vulva* (1990) is a cheeky anatomy lesson given by Shawna embodied in a five-foot tall vulva costume. Her rap intro interpolates a distinctly female audience: "… that's why I'm here, to say hello, to show you around down below. Hi Girls!" (*We're Talking Vulva*). Presented as a perky "subject," the vulva gets her hair coloured, goes shopping for vegetables, and works out. This educational video is an entertaining consciousness raising of the functions, cultures, and enjoyments of female genitalia.[6]

Dempsey & Millan skillfully mobilize the power of stories to reshape ideologies of gender through a set of narrative works which retell popular myths from a lesbian feminist perspective (Dempsey & Millan, Personal Interview). Conventional narratives of media culture shift as wittily wrought narratives make central—if only for the duration of the performance—a queer standpoint. The strategic resituation of cultural codes have important epistemological consequences and affirm art's capacity to effectively place a wedge in hegemonic structures. *Mary Medusa* (1992) invests a mythological icon with a kaleidoscope of identities: mythical personage, homemaker, and corporate superwoman, to articulate a subjectivity located in the gaps between how the feminine is conventionalized, and how women actually want to live. This piece explores women's challenges of living out idealized roles, ultimately moving into an exploration of (monstrous) female excesses of desire: "A woman out of control is a frightening thing!" In *Looking Backward 3000* (2000), a professor speculates about contemporary life in the year 3000. Speaking an archaic TV English gleaned from videos of "Dynasty" and the "Regis and Kathy Lee Show," she itemizes in sci-fi-ese her speculations on the demise of global communication. *The Short Tale of Little Lezzie Borden* (2001) retells the story of the Victorian murderess Lizzie Borden as a contemporary tale of kleptomania, appropriating the rhetorical tone of women's fashion magazines: "This is not a weapon… this is a hatchet… not a tool, an accessory… and accessories create interest (Dempsey & Millan, website)." And *Lesbian Love Story of the Lone Ranger and Tonto* (1997) casts an alternative to the male dominant racist Ranger and Tonto legend.

Outside the gallery, cabaret, or proscenium, Dempsey & Millan's performances are paratheatrical, blurring the edge between performer and audience, and have been staged as interventions in shopping malls, the Manitoba provincial legislature, and National Parks. In *Smile Girl* (1993), Shawna appears in a suite of public settings and events assuming a classic cigarette-girl mode of self-display as she hands out breath mints and safe sex information. In *Golden Boy Awards* (1992–94), Shawna assumes the mythical subjectivity of the "golden boy" sculpture atop the Manitoba provincial legislature building in an agit-prop award ceremony that singles out unwitting politicians known for unscrupulous activity.

For *Grocery Store* (2002), Dempsey & Millan collaborated with media diva Jake Moore and graphic designer Zab to create an actual grocery store in Ace Art Gallery to sell food and essentials that are otherwise unavailable in Winnipeg's Exchange District. The project involved radio ads, a circular of advertising specials, and a mail-in coupon campaign to the mayor petitioning for an increase in downtown services. The intent was to raise public concern and provoke a response from civic politicians who had been making planning decisions that had adversely affected this largely artists' community. And in *Scentbar* (2003) Shawna and Lorri appropriate the uniform of scientific authority. Dressed in white lab coats, Shawna undertakes a "scientific" questionnaire into the feelings and general attitudes of her subjects. Findings are codified, and then Lorri creates a personal perfume combining such unconventional, yet highly affective, scents as "light industry," "grannie's purse," "rental car," and "regret" (Dempsey & Millan, *Scentbar*).

Lesbian National Parks and Services (1997–present) comprises a complex discursive masquerade involving uniforms, social interactions, brochures, field reports, and a book-length *Field Guide to North America*. For lesbians living in a heterosexist culture, creating a reality is an act of both resistance and self-preservation (Dempsey & Millan, Personal Interview), and Dempsey & Millan developed the characters of the Lesbian Rangers to insert an explicitly lesbian presence into the landscape. Initially conceived for a Banff Centre residency, Shawna and Lorri arrived in the rocky mountain tourist town in their turquoise 1963 Pontiac Laurentian, wearing their "official" park ranger uniforms, and, remarkably, remained "in character" for the duration of their stay.[7] The performance consisted of patrolling Banff, politely interacting in deadpan "ranger speak," earnestly giving confused shoppers directions, or edifying tourists about the lesbian geography of the flora and fauna of Banff. They also handed out wryly written brochures which indicate Banff's historical and biological homosexual presence. Appearing as innocuous as Girl Guides or Boy Scouts serving pink lemonade, a soft-sell recruitment drive "to expand the core of lesbian rangers" had no incendiary effect. This piece both normalizes (often invisible) lesbianism and points out the constructedness of nature.[8]

Repositioning recreation from a homosexual standpoint, the rangers suddenly found themselves part of an ever-unfolding, parallel universe. Performance became something that happened not only between walls or within a video monitor, or between pages, or in a particular time frame (Dempsey & Millan, Personal Interview).

Like reality TV shows, the conceptual premise drove events that were unpredictably compelling in themselves. The piece became a situational testing of the authority given to those in uniform. People did tend to give them a lot of respect, and felt entitled to interact, and thus enter into the performance.

Both Shawna and Lorri emphatically credit each other as their most important influence. While the two were involved romantically for years, their post-relationship communication comprises a mature working partnership of openness, a dynamic mutual respect, friendship, and what Janice Williamson has termed an "informed intuition" that comes from a working experience and knowledge of each other (Bell and Williamson 65). They challenge assumptions that collaboration is inherently limiting or some shared compromise, instead asserting that they find it expanding: "doing their own work" *is* doing collaborative work (Dempsey & Millan, Personal Interview).

Having now collaborated for over fourteen years, their creative process exhibits performative rigour, incisive scripting, and conceptual resolution. Yet at the same time, they have avoided the rigidity of mimicking previous successes. They have developed tolerance for the trials and errors attendant to emergent creativity and have not pressured themselves to be "brilliant" all the time. With what was to become Lesbian Rangers, for example, they began by attempting a complex theoretical work, but then came the realization that what they really wanted to do was dress up in the uniform (Dempsey & Millan, Personal Interview). The paratheatrical intersubjectivity that this piece impelled could not have been predicted as the experiential laboratory for the interrogation of uniformed authority it became.

As Lisa Gabrielle Mark perceptively notes about Dempsey & Millan's practice, the question of authority itself is destabilized when it is shared by more than one person (Mark 36). Given the challenges of surviving as full-time artists, can the personal be other than political? What has emerged is a politics of collaboration that challenges the notion of the autonomous artist itself.

(2004)

Notes

[1] In Dempsey and Millan's words, "we really have to believe in what we're doing to put [our] bodies out there" (Personal Interview).

[2] Richard Schechner (105) defines "paratheatre" as the blurring of boundaries between the performer and the audience, or artist and beholder in significant ways.

[3] Please note that within this text, the dates given for the performances indicate the year they were first staged.

⁴ Jane Gaines has argued: "In popular discourse there is no difference between a woman and her attire. She is what she wears" (1).

⁵ The simultaneous magazine drag of *A Day in The Life*, is a brilliant masquerade of *Life* magazine. The embodiment of Lorri for the first time had a powerful effect on how the collaboration was perceived because it made Lorri a visible participant. After that point there were no more arguments with performing venues about two airfares.

⁶ *We're Talking Vulva* brought the revelation that performance needn't be obscure, but an art form where a simple idea can satisfy (and provoke) on different levels simultaneously. The controversy pertaining to this piece has been surprisingly long-standing. Hallwalls Gallery in Buffalo lost their National Endowment for the Arts funding for an entire year because this video appeared in their support material. A similarly reactionary controversy ballooned at the University of Winnipeg over Dempsey & Millan's artists' talk for fourteen-year-old students, generating six months of press coverage as "Vege-gate." Most of the vitriol was generated by those who hadn't actually seen the work.

⁷ *Lesbian National Parks and Services* was initiated by Dempsey & Millan at the curatorial proposition of Kathryn Walter for the exhibition *Private Investigations* at the Banff Centre.

⁸ Margot Francis argues that while Dempsey & Millan's Lesbian Rangers subvert heteronormativity, their subversion of nature still depends on their whiteness, and the racial history of colonizing the outdoors.

Works Cited

Bell, Lynn and Williamson, Janice. "Public Warning! Sexing Public Spheres: A Conversation with Shawna Dempsey and Lorri Millan." *Tessera* 25 (1998–1999): 57–78.

Dempsey, Shawna & Millan, Lorri. *Scentbar*, Five Holes: reminiSCENT, curated by Jim Drobnick and Paul Coulliard, Toronto, September 20, 2003.

———. Website: www.fingerinthedyke.ca

———. *A Live Decade: 1989–1999*, video of selected performances. Winnipeg: Finger in the Dyke Productions, 1999.

———. Personal interview. August 6, 2003.

Dempsey, Ranger Shawna and Millan, Ranger Lorri. *Lesbian National Parks and Services Field Guide to North America*. Toronto: Pedlar Press, 2002.

Fisher, Jennifer and Drobnick, Jim. *CounterPoses*. Montreal: Oboro & Display Cult, 2002.

Francis, Margot. "'Unsettling Sites…': The Lesbian National Parks and Services." *Fuse* 22.4 (2000): 41–45.

Gaines, Jane M. "Fabricating the Female Body." *Fabrications: Costume and the Female Body*. Ed. Charlotte Herzog and Jane M Gaines. London: Routledge, 1990. 1–27.

Harding, Sandra. "Rethinking Standpoint Epistemology: What is 'Strong Objectivity'?" *Feminism and Science*. Ed. Evelyn Fox Keller and Helen E. Longino Oxford: Oxford UP, 1996. 235–48.

Mark, Lisa Gabrielle. "Hijacking Cabaret," *Border Crossings* 14.1 (Winter 1995): 35–38.

Martin, Annie. "Shawna Dempsey and Lorri Millan," *Parachute* 75 (1994): 43–44.

Schechner, Richard. *Between Theatre and Anthropology* Philadelphia: U of Pennsylvania P, 1985.

We're Talking Vulva. Dir. Tracey Traeger and Shawna Dempsey. String of Girls Productions, 1990.

Wray, B.J. "Structure, Size and Play: The Case of the Talking Vulva," *Decomposition: Post-Disciplinary Performance*. Ed. Sue-Ellen Case, Philip Brett and Susan Leigh Foster. Bloomington: Indiana UP, 2000. 188–91.

Deep-Mapping a Morning on 3A: The found and the Fabricated of *The Weyburn Project*

by Andrew Houston

> Absence is either the trace of a previous presence, it contains memory;
> or the trace of a possible presence, it contains immanence.
> —Peter Eisenman (4–5)

What Remains

By the spring of 2001, I had been living in Saskatchewan for almost four years. During this time, I discovered that a province famous for its slow decline of population—particularly of youth leaving for lucrative employment and bright futures elsewhere—and for its photographs of barren-looking homesteads and soon-to-be torn-down grain elevators was actually a place blessed with absence. Saskatchewan's abandoned buildings are potentially some of the greatest archival treasures that exist in all of Canada. Several decades of relatively slow economic growth has created an environment where what remains from the past has been left, in some cases virtually undisturbed, in the very spot where it was placed years ago. While many see old, empty buildings as a measure of decline and even the death of a culture, I see them for their immanence as a performative archive and as a resource for rebirth through reconsideration of what remains of both the building and its embedded culture.

Regina is rich with vacant and semi-vacant buildings of historical interest. While I taught at the University of Regina, I was able to indulge my interest in such buildings by launching a site-specific dramaturgy class wherein the students and I began to realize the great potential for site-specific performance that existed throughout the city. Out of this class came performances in the dome of the provincial legislature, a gentleman's social club, and a cowboy bar; all were created with the aim of animating the various layers of history inscribed in these environments, especially the stories and feelings shared by the public around a problem in the past, that something was not quite right about the history of these places. From this series of animations, collectively called *The Host/The Ghost/The Witness*, there emerged two multimedia performances exploring the problematic past embedded in place; each of these buildings was experienced as a host to all manner of narratives (ghosts) that could be brought to life through various media (animation) for witnesses or an audience curious about these sites.

In the second of these two performances, *The Museum of Miss Fortune*, it became obvious to me that two prevailing motifs exist in this kind of work—the first is that of an archive, the second is that of a map. As each intersects with performance, the focus becomes less a matter of the rare archival object, or the best route through a space, and more about exploring the ideas and sensations found in creating a relationship to the past. I will return to the archive later. As for the map, Mike Pearson, formerly of the Welsh site-specific theatre company Brith Gof, has gradually taken his practice in the direction of a hybrid between theatre and archaeology and sees mapping as a central narrative device when we begin to think about using environments as a resource for creation. He calls this process "deep-mapping" and defines it the following way:

> Reflecting eighteenth-century antiquarian approaches to place which included history, folklore, natural history and hearsay, the deep-map attempts to record and represent the grain and patina of place through juxtapositions and interpenetrations of the historical and the contemporary, the political and the poetic, the factual and the fictional, the discursive and the sensual; the conflation of oral testimony, anthology, memoir, biography, natural history, and everything you might ever want to say about a place (Pearson and Shanks 64–5).

The term was coined in relation to William Least Heat-Moon's *PrairyErth* (1991), an account of Chase County in the American Midwest that conflates all of the above ways of getting the measure of a place and that offers essentially everything you needed to know about a particular place—in this case, Kansas. Here the scope and function of the map is broad and multifaceted, representing not just the logic and structure of the social fabric through its impact on the environment and local inhabitants, but also how the social and the cultural are lived and felt in such a place. A key concept is that of sensorium—"culturally and historically located arrays of the senses and sensibility" (Pearson and Shanks 54). Pearson introduces sensorium as a way of working against the dualism of mind and body. As a site-specific performance goes about animating a building, one of the first concerns is how best to map this sensorium, to navigate through a space wherein this sensual subtext is a factor of navigation.

In Saskatchewan, I was thinking a lot about the influence of maps on my approach to site-specific performance, when scenographer Kathleen Irwin, videographer Richard Diener and I were first invited down to Weyburn to visit the Souris Valley Extended Care Centre, formerly known as the Saskatchewan Mental Hospital. Trenna Keating, an artist I had worked with in previous site projects, grew up in Weyburn, in "the shadow of the asylum," wanted us to consider creating a performance in the building. During this first reconnaissance mission, the four of us spent about five hours walking the halls of this massive facility, spellbound by the feel of the place. It felt like walking forever, as we came across hallway after hallway that appeared to vanish far into the beam of sunlight from a distant window. Walking from hallway to staircase, from room to room, we encountered a continuous bombardment of the senses: the smells, the temperature changes, the exhaustion from trying to see it all, the feeling of floors and walls polished and pristine in one place, stained and peeling in another. These hallways, staircases and rooms offered us a sensorium of the past; as each surface revealed itself to be a palimpsest of the traces left from the many who had journeyed through these passageways before us, we began to think about how best to map an encounter with the ineffable past of this place.

Walking is surely the preferred form of navigating the sensorium of a given site, for both artist and audience alike; both parties do a good deal of walking in this process of discovery; the former establish the parameters of this map, while the latter embark on a journey through the site governed by the map, conveyed through the signs, symbols and actions of performance. Michel de Certeau is probably best known as a philosopher to comment on the practice of walking: he links the act of walking through a given environment with linguistic formations; the act of walking is akin to the act of enunciating one's relationship to surroundings, to place: "[t]o walk is to lack a place. It is the indefinite process of being absent and in search of a proper" (de Certeau 103). Nick Kaye posits de Certeau's walker in the context of site-specific performance when he states:

> The walker is thus always in the process of *acting out*, of performing the contingencies of a particular spatial practice, which, although subject to the place, can never wholly realize or be resolved into this underlying order [...] de Certeau's walker realizes the site in its transitive sense, always in the act or effort of locating, and never in the settled order, the "proper place," of the location itself (Kaye 5–6).

Kaye reminds us *pace* de Certeau that any attempt to fix the location through the "symbolic (named)" participates in this movement. Here, where space, like the spoken word, is realized in a practice that can never rest in the order it implies, so the representation offered by "'the word' *moves one on* from 'site'" (Kaye 6). Just as these spatial practices function in the *absence* of place, in their inability to realize the order and stability of the proper, so the "'symbolic (named)' is tied to the experience of lacking a place precisely because representation, by definition, presents itself in the *absence* of its object, the referent" (Kaye 6). Thus, in the act of navigation, of mapping and walking a route through what is left of the Weyburn hospital, our attempts to come to terms with the past are always acts that construct a kind of removal from the idea that an authentic sense of the past can be found purely in what remains, or in any putative attempt to "locate" or reconstruct what has been. Rather in the way our mapping— our words and acts—create a fabricated gesture toward the found, we may find that the immanence of the absence in what remains of the Saskatchewan Mental Hospital at Weyburn and between the found and the fabricated is the journey towards the life of the past we seek.

The Found: The Saskatchewan Mental Hospital at Weyburn

The Saskatchewan Mental Hospital at Weyburn took about sixteen months to build. When it was finished in December of 1920, it was one of the largest buildings in the

British Empire. When the hospital opened, it was on the cutting edge of mental health care and espoused a treatment known as "work and water" (Robillard 6). A good day of healthy labour, preferably out of doors, was regarded as healthy for the mind and body, and if hard work was not enough to calm and control some patients, they were treated with ice baths. This treatment may seem inhumane; yet it was nothing compared to the insulin, electro-shock and lobotomy treatments that followed. These practices were, in fact, a compassionate attempt to handle a disease that was little understood, frightening and completely debilitating. The hospital primarily served the needs of the mentally ill but was also a kind of "holding tank" for those in the community who "did not fit in" (Blakley 21). In the 1950s, the hospital was in the avant-garde of drug experimentation (especially lysergic acid diethylamide-25 or LSD—the term "psychedelic" was coined there). Pharmaceuticals were eventually successful in emptying the hospital in the mid-1960s. By the time of my first visit in 2001, the building was called the Souris Valley Extended Care Centre; it had officially ceased being a mental hospital in 1971, but it was still home to about fifty patients who were never able to return to the community for various reasons, as well as about 145 extended-care residents. Parts of the building have been home to a number of community organizations and activities, including the Soo-Line boxing club, a daycare and a dry cleaner. Since 1971, the Centre has also housed a dance school and the Southeast Regional College, although by 2001 neither was still residing in the building. The hospital's massive footprint is comprised of three wings that span off of a central structure; the whole building measures about one-and-a-half kilometres all the way around. For the most part, all activity now occurs in the building's core and its southeast wing; the rest of the structure is either empty or used for storing old equipment.

Architect Arthur Allen claims that the design of the Weyburn Hospital came from English and American precedents in a nineteenth-century medical movement for the moral management of insanity and that this moral architecture matched current ideas of public order based on obedience and regularity:

> In the Weyburn design, massive scale, long approaches on an infinite prairie, rigid symmetry in gardens, walks and facades, an ornate lobby with a golden staircase and a prominent central dome gave an overpowering sense of authority to the institution. Like the palaces of absolutist monarchs, the aesthetics of tyrannical design were used to subdue the willfulness of deviant individuals. If awe is defined as a mixture of reverence and fear, the architect of Weyburn imposed that feeling on anyone in or near his building. Imagine the impact on people struggling with badly damaged self-esteem and accustomed to life in small houses in very wide open places (Allen 20).

During the six months following our first visit, I went on several more reconnaissance missions with Kathleen and Richard, as we attempted to get the measure of this massive building as the resource for the creation of a performance. Site-specific performances are generally conceived for, mounted within and conditioned by the particulars of a found space upon which strategies of animation may go to work. Animation may happen through a variety of media—theatre, dance, music, visual art, video and film. All forms of animation rely for their conception and their interpretation on the complex coexistence, superimposition and interpenetration of a number of contexts, either cultural, political, economic or historical, and on two basic orders: the found—or that which is of the site, its material existence—and the fabricated—or that which is brought to the site in the form of animation. Strategies of animation are inseparable from the site, and often the site is the only context in which they are intelligible. As Pearson reminds us, "Performance recontextualises such sites: it is the latest occupation of a location at which other occupations—their material traces and histories—are still apparent: site is not just an interesting, and disinterested, backdrop" (Pearson and Shanks 26). Indeed, the challenge and the reward to the artist in a site-specific work is the historical, political, cultural and economic reality of the materials found with which to make the work. As Allen suggests, the Weyburn hospital is a building with a profile that resonates; indeed, all who have had contact with this place, either as workers, patients, members of the community or anyone who has had an association with any of these people, seem to have a story about the place.

Over the next few months, it became obvious that many people in southern Saskatchewan had stories to tell about the hospital. By early 2002, we had received approval and significant support, both in-kind and financial, from the Souris Valley Extended Care Centre board of directors, the South Central Health District, the University of Regina, the Saskatchewan Arts Board and the Saskatchewan History and Folklore Society. We launched a website aimed at gathering the many stories that people seemed ready to tell about "the Mental." The website was an attempt to gather all manner of narrative about the Saskatchewan Hospital at Weyburn, from history to folklore, legend, myth and anecdote; we wanted people to share stories about working there, visiting a friend or family, or living in a town notoriously connected to a provincially infamous asylum. The website was a great success; by mid-May, we had nearly 100 stories. The website also gave us access to many retired psychiatric nurses, with whom we could conduct interviews and ask questions about the history of working in the hospital.

Our agreement with the South Central Health District included a clause stating that we were not to interview patients as part of our research. [1] What might have at first seemed like a restriction, in fact turned out to be a valuable filter in the process. As an artist approaching the Saskatchewan Mental Hospital at Weyburn, I could best relate to the many who had gone there to work. In particular, I could relate to the psychiatric nurses; most came to Weyburn from other parts of the province in search of employment. Like me, they wanted to understand the plight of those subjected to this institution; despite lack of experience and previous training, the new nurses did their best to understand and accommodate the environment in which they found themselves. Those who arrived at Weyburn before the 1950s—before the advent of tranquilizers and other drugs that made patient care easier—had to cope with problems in as creative a fashion as possible and usually with a good sense of humour.

From the perspective of an educator like myself, there is a familiar quality in these stories about the tenacious battle for modest gains. Nurse Sherrie E. Tutt describes some of the struggles and discoveries she made while working with a GPI patient named Grace:[2]

> We started with toilet training. Darting back and forth, blocking her escape one way and then another, I gradually worked Grace toward the toilets. Getting her to sit was another matter. Mostly she didn't. Next came the shower. Bathing was not something she did on her own, so if I was going to be able to tolerate the smell, we had to hit the showers. Now the showers were three-sided affairs barely big enough for someone my size, let alone someone hers. I was getting pretty good at herding by this time. We got to the shower door. She stopped. And wouldn't budge. First I tried pushing, then pulling. She just stood there. Finally, worn out, frustrated and almost in tears, I turned around and butted her with my backside. By this time a crowd of my fellow student nurses had gathered and were doubled up howling with laughter. I collapsed against the wall, laughing myself. Grace looked at us like we were from another planet, and then she stepped into the shower. Clean, but wet, we headed for the locker room in hopes of finding some of her own clothes. Nothing. She'd long since grown out of her own clothes. But I did find lipstick, a comb, and her pair of glasses. She stood docile as ever as I put lipstick on her thin lips, fluffed her hair, put on her glasses and held up a mirror. She looked in it, really looked. And for the first time I saw a glimmer of expression in her dull gray eyes. And her lips twitched, ever so slightly ("Excavations").

Fortunately, many retired psychiatric nurses were excited about our project; by early spring, we had recorded about two dozen interviews, and it was discovered that a good number of our interviewees were keen to play an active role in the performance. We had gathered many hours of videotape in these interviews that we couldn't possibly incorporate in detail into the performance; so, as a way to remedy this situation and somehow sustain the oral history of this community, I decided that the audience should be led through the site by these retired nurses. At this point, we had started to map a journey for the audience to follow through the site; now we needed to find ways to animate the "depth" of the sensorium along this route. Some of the video interviews had been rigged to occur while I went for a walk with the interview subject through the site; without fail as we went from hall to hall, through door after door, different stories would be triggered by these surroundings. Gradually more and more stories were told, reflections were shared, opinions ventured, desires revealed. I knew I had come a long way with this group when stories of misbehaviour and subversion surfaced. I had discovered how these people truly navigated and survived in this work place, and I wanted the audience to hear this as well.

We arranged the use of the southwest wing of the building. This part of the old hospital was especially attractive to us because it was entirely empty; most of it had not been used in almost twenty years, and it was the only wing of the hospital with the original roof still in place. There are various layers to the history of the south-west wing. When it was still functioning as part of the hospital, it was the male wing, for both patients and staff, and in the true hierarchical sense that has historically governed all hospitals in Europe and North America, this meant that the top floor (D) was the domain of medical staff and was in this case a residence for male nurses. With the significant decomposition of the old roof, this floor was in the greatest state of decay; its combination of utilitarian architecture—the windows high on the wall, the spare layout of the rooms and washrooms—paradoxically combined with the seemingly extravagant designs of peeling paint, eroded floorboards, and puddles fecund with mossy growth. Floor C was a domain for patients who received various treatments: It was here that every ministration from the corporal manipulations of cold water baths to insulin and electro-shock therapy occurred. Floor C also told the story of decades of drug treatments; here were the scars of every drug used to control agitated patients, from Paraldehyde through LSD, and on to the more modern drugs like Moditen and Largactil. Historian Quint Patrick has said "You could smell Paraldehyde from thirty feet away so one can only imagine what it tasted like (Patrick 6). As rooms closed off to the world for the last thirty years were wrenched open for us, the metallic smell of many of these treatments lingered with the mould on windowpanes and in the carpets, gradually giving way to the forces of nature. Floor B was full of rooms with hundreds of beds and wheelchairs stored end-to-end, as if in silent mimicry of the late 1940s, when the hospital, built to house about 1,000 patients, held nearly 3,000. This was an administration floor, as it could be accessed from each end of the wing: the one side connected to the hospital's main building, and the other provided entry to a parking lot via an elaborate stairway. Finally, Floor A, the basement, was the location of the refractory ward, the place where even the advent of tranquilizers had not diminished the often brutal physical contact between staff and patient. In addition to being the floor that provided solitary confinement for violent patients, Floor A was the home of the Soo-Line boxing club, a community centre for a more sporting form of violence, right down the hall from what had once been padded rooms.

While *The Weyburn Project* became a multidisciplinary performance that used all four floors of the southwest wing, I want to focus on a segment of the project that took place on the second floor (Floor B) and was based on a day in the life of Helen Flaaten (née Helen Gawiuk) on 3A, a refractory ward with ten side rooms and ninety patients. Before I address this particular story and the dramaturgical fabrication that became its performance, I want to briefly describe Floor B and how what was found there prompted our animation approach. In the mid-1940s, before it had become a storage floor for hospital beds and wheelchairs, Floor B had been the administration centre for the Weyburn campus of the Southeast Regional College. As we entered the south-west wing from the parking lot, immediately on the left was what had been the college's administration offices. The college had vacated the premises nearly five years earlier, so these rooms were covered in a layer of dust and dead flies, but beneath this lay thousands of discarded papers, file folders and other office material. Although this floor had been deserted for some time, the debris that remained made it look as though the former inhabitants had left in a hurry. Perhaps the greatest draw for me to this work is that the process of speculating about the found never ends, and an important link between artist and audience is made as both parties follow a line of questioning through the site, wondering about every object and its placement. We found thousands of documents relating to the college, its operation, its students and staff. As an employee of an institution not unlike this one, I was shocked: How could they—the movers? the clerical staff? perhaps the soon-to-be-laid-off staff of the college—just leave everything this way? Among the piles of administrative debris, I pondered the possible revenge of fed-up workers with what they had been asked to do. There was also a good deal of havoc apparent in the way old typewriters, old computer paraphernalia and other office equipment had been left, tipped over, piled up—again, looking as though they had been discarded in a hurry. Or perhaps someone had ransacked all of this equipment and material since the college moved out. One could only speculate.

What was left of the Southeast Regional College contrasted with the hospital materials stored down the hall. The beds in several rooms, the wheelchairs in others— all neatly piled or parked in an orderly fashion. The world of the college and the old hospital intersected wonderfully in that the rows of beds and chairs were often lined up before the chalkboards that had been installed in the old ward rooms. In some cases, this equipment bore the stains, the scratches, the cracks and wear marks of con- stant use. Occasionally we would even find a nameplate or patient number. Indeed, as the material in the backs of these chairs sagged or the castor of one of the beds looked dysfunctional, it seemed that these objects had taken on the attributes and qualities of their former inhabitants. As we pondered the links between the apparently panic-stricken leftovers of an administration with the apparent purgatorial order of the hospital leftovers, ideas for a dramaturgical weave of these two worlds began to take hold.

The Fabricated: A Morning on 3A

Our interviews with the retired psychiatric nurses revealed an important theme of pride taken in the ability to do a job well that required a great deal of physical and mental strength and stamina. The nurses spoke in glowing terms about how their dis- cipline and strength helped them survive the frequently punishing work conditions they faced. Prior to changes in provincial labour laws in 1946, nurses worked twelve hours per day, six days per week. This arduous weekly routine was augmented by a military-style, stern and arbitrary discipline that was exemplified by the hospital's chief attendants. Percy Cole, a veteran of World War I served as chief attendant in the hospital's first decade, and was perhaps the greatest example of this approach. Under Cole, a nurse learned that

> one was never quite sure where he would be required to work, as all postings were put up on a big bulletin board to be read before going to

work. Frequently a person who was on the 7 a.m. to 7 p.m. shift would come to work in the morning only to find he had been posted for the evening or 7 p.m. to 7 a.m. shift. He would have to go back home to bed at 1 p.m. and return at 7 p.m. the same day (Patrick 43).

Before the early 1950s and the invention of tranquilizers to subdue patients, our research found that nurses had little to rely upon in the task of caring for the mentally ill, other than ward supervision and a written code of ethics. In order to contain the more dangerous, erratic behaviour of the patients in their charge, the nurses who worked at the Weyburn hospital in these first three decades were able to survive their work essentially because they were more disciplined, more organized and either faster or stronger than the patients. It was an environment ruled by survival of the fittest, governed by a slim volume of rules.

We began an animation of Floor B with an abridged version of the nurse's code of ethics and Helen Flaaten's narrative, "Working on 3A." With four actors in their early twenties and a twenty-minute physical score that incorporated these texts, the performance took our audience from a day room artist's installation near the southwest wing entrance, [3] through the network of hallways, wards and side rooms that made up the majority of Floor B, and down the main hallway to a staircase to Floor C. The physical movement of this work was enhanced by a musical military-style march composed by Lindsay Stetner and performed by an ensemble of musicians placed down the main hallway, toward the exit to Floor C. The effect of this placement was that the physical journey of the actors and audience through this routine brought them closer to the throbbing tempo of the music—perhaps echoing the throbbing a nurse feels in the ears after a stressful bout of activity on an over-crowded ward. The main hallway is about 150 metres long, and its tile, plaster and concrete surfaces give it a harsh and reverberating acoustic quality. As the performers and audience walk briskly down the hall toward the playing musicians, the impact of this march can be felt in the body, like an assault. Mike Pearson suggests that we might consider this kind of animation in site-specific performance as constituting a kind of stratigraphy of layers: of text, of physical action, music and/or soundtrack, scenography and/or architecture (and their subordinate moments). Dramatic material can be conceived and manipulated in each of these strata, which may carry different themes or structures in parallel. From moment to moment, such layers may alter the dynamics or dramatic significance (Pearson and Shanks 24–5). Here, the march of music and action provides a layer of understanding to the cold, hard surfaces of the hospital hallway that are *felt* in the way the spectators must follow the route established for them; this embodied "sensoria" opens up a realm of speculation for those on this journey about the working lives of the nurses at the Weyburn hospital that is in part ineffable—beyond language.

Helen Flaaten's text is a cross between the kind of report every nurse had to write at the end of each shift, chronicling the activities on the ward over the previous twelve hours, and a primer on how to survive working with mentally ill patients who could become unexpectedly violent. It includes instructions on how best to provide food to a presumably hostile patient in solitary confinement, by "set[ting] the plate on the cement floor close to the door, hav[ing a] broom handy to push the plate in quickly" ("Excavations"), and it describes how things can get out of hand:

> One could never count on a totally quiet time when cleaning up the side rooms, taking the residents to the bathroom and preparing them for bed. One incident: the resident decided she was going to smash windows, before we could subdue her she had smashed about 3 windows, cutting her wrists in several places, bleeding severely. Call the doctor: suture the severe cuts, give the resident a sedative ("Excavations").

We staged this text in part as lessons to our audience, taking full advantage of the chalkboards and other such scholastic modifications made to the architecture of the ward rooms on Floor B. The other significant resonance between the college and hospital, developed in our animation of this floor, was in the way we used sheets of paper. Another common theme among the retired nurses we interviewed was the problem of too much paperwork on the job. Apparently, the preponderance of paperwork is a problem among both those who work in health care and in post-secondary education; I was reminded of stories from each institution as our interviewees described how every instance of contact with a "client" had to be recorded at the end of the shift in a "lengthy report" to be "read by the night nurse in charge, signed and returned in the morning" ("Excavations"). Considering that one of the first things we found on Floor B were piles and piles of paper from the college, it occurred to me that for administration, sheets of paper often represent or stand in for patients or pupils, and this is something these institutions have in common. Furthermore, just as attendance is an important part of a student's evaluation in class, a significant part of each nurse's report was a "head count." In the physical score created to animate Floor B, sheets of paper became metaphorical patients as well as students; our four nurses counted them, moved piles of them, stamped them with ink, collected them for organization and finally found themselves chaotically entangled with them.

An aspect of Pearson's stratigraphy has to do with the spatial dimension of metaphor. As a layering of text, action, music and scenography overlays a site's cultural, historical and architectural features, the associative quality of metaphorical elements between the found and the fabricated gains a certain depth. In this respect, the sheets of paper operate as both a parataxis and a hypotaxis connecting the various historical uses of Floor B. A parataxis is the placing of clauses, or other fabricated elements, one after another, without any explicit means of coordination, subordination or predictable cohesion. Here, pieces of paper were ordered on the floor to represent patients' beds or students' desks, alongside piles of tangled paper that were reminiscent of the many patches of peeling paint and other indicators of decay or disarray found in the site. As they witness the performers manipulate and manoeuver this paper, the spectators are free to make connections and associations between the various ways in which sheets of paper may be associated with bed sheets or are emblematic of health care, education and the bureaucracy embedded in this site. The hypotaxis is the subordination of one clause or layer of meaning to another in cohesion of density. The hypotaxis is a palimpsest. In one respect, the spectators experience a nurse lecturing before a chalkboard to be an animation of the Southeast Regional College; as she begins to instruct us about various disciplinary measures, the reference point of the lesson becomes multiple, and when she produces a bottle of sedative pills, we are transported to the time of the hospital. The classroom is seen to be fabricated out of a hospital ward; the papers on the floor are no longer students' desks, but patients' beds.

Mapping the Performative Archive in *The Weyburn Project*

Site-specific performances demand a great deal from the spectator. Spectators become witnesses to these events in the sense that they are present, not merely as observers, but also as participants who play an active role in the mapping of the site, the unfolding of the event. It is the work of the witness in the *The Weyburn Project* to piece together the found and the fabricated. As each person navigates a route through the site, he or she will embody different meanings of the event based upon how they have "read" the map. This reading is not only seen but felt, as the sensorium includes *proxemic* dimensions, an audience's physical proximity to the sweat, the dust and the stains of the performance's elements; it includes a *haptic* experience in so far as witnesses are welcome to get a feel for where they are in the site through physical contact with the work's elements; finally, it includes the *kinesthetic* dimension of walking, the act of physically working out the most appropriate route between the found and the fabricated of history. In the way site-specific performance allows a felt knowledge of the past, it may be seen as a significant reconsideration of the idea of an archive.

Rebecca Schneider reminds us that the Greek root of the word "archive" refers to the "house" of Archon; by extension, "the architecture of a social memory which demands visible or materially traceable remains is the architecture of a particular social power over memory" (Schneider 102). She questions the role of performance in relation to the archive as a "site" of the past and wonders if the logic of the archive demands that performance disappear in favour of discrete remains. Schneider proposes a performative relationship to the archival "house" and the objects found there in the same way that I am proposing a performative relationship to the Saskatchewan Hospital at Weyburn and what was found there. Schneider emphasizes the value of re-enactment as a way of keeping memory alive and making sure that this embodied, performative sense of history does not disappear. Although the ontological status of a performance such as *The Weyburn Project* is ephemeral—it happened in 2002, and now it is over—Schneider reminds us that the practices of a performative archive do remain in the residue left through body-to-body transmission during the fabricated enactment. To approach history as an act of securing "any incident backward—the repeated act of securing memory" (Schneider 103) is to rethink the site of history in ritual repetition. This is not to say that we have reached the "end of history," nor is it to say that history didn't happen or that to access it is impossible;

rather, it is a call to reawaken the sensorium in our approach to history. Schneider explains this in terms of how we may experience history through the body:

> It is rather to resituate the site of *any knowing* as body-to-body trans-
> mission. Whether that ritual repetition is the attendance to documents
> in the library (the acts of acquisitions, the acts of reading, writing, edu-
> cation) or the family of oral tales of lineage, or the myriad traumatic
> re-enactments engaged in both consciously and unconsciously, we
> refigure history onto body-to-body transmission. In line with this
> configuration performance does not disappear, but remains as a ritual
> act—ritual acts which, by occlusion and inclusion, *script* disappearance.
> We are reading, then, our performative relations to documents and to
> documents' ritual status as performatives within a culture that privileges
> object remains. We are reading, then, the document as performative act,
> and as a site of performance (Schneider 103).

Schneider brings the sensorium of embodied experience to historical archive in the same way that I would like to suggest that site-specific performance may reawaken the sensorium in our approach to theatre. As theatre becomes less an event ruled by what is seen in the archival "houses" where it is traditionally practiced and departs these houses to become an embodied engagement with actual environments, the potential for new understanding of theatre practice and the world it navigates exists. For those who walked, witnessed and brought to life the deep-map experience of *The Weyburn Project*, I am confident that what remains is now a matter of what resides immanently within each person whose being still resonates with the routine of a morning on 3A.

(2005)

Notes

[1] In fact, the website attracted stories and information from former patients. We decided these stories should be represented on the website, but only referred to in more abstract ways in the performance. The story of Gordon Smith, however, who was wrongfully admitted to the hospital as a nine-year-old boy, features promi-nently in the documentary film created about *The Weyburn Project*, entitled "Weyburn: An Archaeology of Madness" (for details see: http://uregina.ca/wey-burn_project/pages/video.html).

[2] GPI stands for General Paresis of the Insane. It is the final stage of syphilis and is incurable. In the early 1950s, the time of this story, it was considered untreatable.

[3] After our audience had been "processed" in a manner similar to what would have happened to patients entering the hospital for the first time, they were escorted by

a guide (a retired nurse) to a day room that had become Gerry Anne Segwick's installation exploring the "Hallmark card" experience of being hospitalized; here they waited to be taken through Floor B. The inspiration and resource for this installation had been a box of discarded cards sent to patients that had been left in one of the many storage rooms to which we had access during our research.

Works Cited

Allen, Arthur. "The Last Asylum." *On/Site Review* (Summer 2000): 20–21.

Blakley, Al. "Treatment*s*." Robillard 20–2.

De Certeau, Michel. *The Practices of Everyday Life* Berkeley, CA.: U of California P, 1984.

Eisenman, Peter. *Moving Arrows, Eros and Other Errors: An Architecture of Absence* London: Architectural Association, 1986.

"Excavations: Stories about Weyburn." *The Weyburn Project.* 11 September 2004. http://uregina.ca/weyburn_project/pages/weyburnhist.html.

Kaye, Nick. *Site-Specific Art – performance, place and documentation* London: Routledge, 2000.

Pearson, Mike and Michael Shanks. *Theatre/Archaeology*. London: Routledge, 2001.

Quint, Patrick. "History." Robillard 1–13.

Robillard, Ane, ed. *Under the Dome: The Life and Times of the Saskatchewan Hospital, Weyburn*. Weyburn: Souris Valley History Book Committee, 1986.

Schneider, Rebecca. "Performance Remains." *Performance Research* 6.2 (2001): 100–08.

Sex, Cars and Shopping:
Meditations on Social Disabilities

by Andrew Templeton

Can a community suffer from disability? Is it possible to define the behaviour of a society as dysfunctional? As I write this, George W. Bush has been re-elected president of the United States. If the polls are to be trusted, this outcome should baffle the majority of Canadians (and, I'd venture to guess, an even bigger majority of *CTR* readers). In the wake of the election result, much of the analysis in the media has focused on how the Bush campaign was able to exploit key "hot button" issues, including a sense of fear in the United States about the rest of the world. It would seem that for many Americans concepts such as conciliation and consensus building (not to mention an ability to speak French) are seen as signs of weakness, perhaps even effeminacy. It is clear that many Americans define themselves through a military framework—their heroes are soldiers—a very alien concept to a demilitarized nation such as Canada. Can a culture that can be so easily moved to fear, isolationism and wilful ignorance be considered mentally balanced?

By the same token, can a culture that seeks emotional security from objects, or one that allows corporations to define and exploit inadequacies the public might feel about themselves, be considered healthy? What about one that objectifies and commodifies the human body while at the same time creating a plethora of sexual anxieties? How healthy is a society that constantly tells itself that individuals don't measure up—in the type of furniture they own, the size of their cocks, the shape of their tits or the type of car they drive? What does it say about us collectively? What does it say about us as individuals that few—if any—of us can escape these pressures unscathed?

While we might recognize these processes at work generally in our society, how capable are we of identifying them in our immediate surroundings or measuring the impact they have on us as individuals? The exploration of such issues—what might be termed cultural dysfunctions—is at the heart of recent work by Vancouver's Radix Theatre. As a site-specific company, they have attempted to examine familiar environments through different conceptual lenses and, in the process, force audience members to re-evaluate their personal responses to these environments. A uniting theme that runs through the three productions I will be considering is the tension between the illusion of promise (whether the furniture showroom, sex or the car) and the largely unrecognized reality of disappointment when these objects fail to deliver. That illusion should be a central theme for a theatre company is, of course, highly appropriate.

Radix likes to term its productions "meditations," and this is a useful description of both the creators' process and the audiences' experience. All three of the shows under consideration are non-narrative and were developed through a collaborative process. They have a collage feel about them, of elements being built around a central theme or concept that is then refined and further developed. Refreshingly, for a company interested in exploring social issues, there is no polemic, no didacticism, no set answers. Radix—bravely in my view—leaves the audience to draw its own conclusions, not just as to how to respond to the issues being raised but as to how the production actually tackles them. In a sense, the productions are like mysteries that each audience member must solve for herself. Audiences are engaged directly, and it is this sense of experience, and the individual response to that experience, that is at the very core of Radix's work. Radix's notion of site-specific, therefore, has two key components: the inherent theatricality of any and all human spaces and the impact that those spaces have on us as individuals (and, by extension, how those spaces demand that we perform).

In terms of theatrical space, a branch of IKEA would seem to be a natural. After all, what are IKEA showrooms if not stage sets? Set in the Richmond, BC, branch of IKEA, *The Swedish Play* (2002), was originally conceived by Andreas Kahre and developed by him in collaboration with Radix co-Artistic Directors Andrew Laurenson and Paul Ternes. Described by Radix as "invisible theatre," the piece involved performers' and audience members' moving through the "performance space" during store hours, with shoppers generally unaware that an event was taking place. Audience members put on headphones and were instructed to choose either the comedy or tragedy tour, which they followed through a soundtrack. These soundtracks contained a collage of sounds and samples, including discourses on theatrical forms and post-modern theory and sound clips from old movies. The soundtracks were designed to obstruct any sense of narrative development. They were meant to create unease and to stop the audience from assuming its traditional role as passive spectator. This, perhaps not surprisingly, met with resistance from some critics and audience members. According to Paul Ternes, co-artistic director of Radix and one of the co-creators, those who simply followed the program were likely to be disappointed, perhaps because there was no show to get in a traditional sense. Those audience members who were willing and able to "break the rules" of theatrical experience, to engage directly in the process, clearly got more out of the experience.

A more traditional approach would have seen narrative scenes inspired by and using the showrooms to comment on consumer culture. While this would have created a more familiar experience for the audience, it is highly unlikely that it would have encouraged them to re-examine the environment in any meaningful way. Probably, it would simply have extended the illusions that consumer culture indulges in and have left the audience unchallenged in their assumptions about how that culture affects them. In short, the audience might have "got" the message, but it is unlikely that they would have "felt" it in any meaningful way. By undermining narrative and audience expectations, by making the experience "difficult," Radix was, in effect making a more fundamental point about the nature of consumerism and the reality of the showrooms (and perhaps theatre more generally). Whether they succeeded is for others to judge, but there is a certain purity of thought in their approach. By disrupting narrative, by reinforcing the artificial nature of the theatrical experience, they forced the audience to consider, in a real sense, the artificiality of the showroom and, hopefully, the processes at work below the surface of consumer culture.

Like many contemporary businesses, IKEA is really selling brand and lifestyle. Its method of operation is to create a sense of unease in the consumer—there is something lacking in his life, something that can be cured through IKEA's products. This has proven to be far more effective than focusing on the practical or the necessary aspects of goods. After all, the exploitation of dissatisfaction and unease is a well that can be returned to again and again. Those shelving units didn't make you happy? Well, maybe you should try these ones instead. This exploitation could not occur if a sense of dissatisfaction about self-worth weren't already at work in our culture. When combined with a sense that value is measured in objects, dissatisfaction creates an exploitative environment, an environment that looks like furniture showrooms (where money can buy you happiness). Yet, self-evidently, objects cannot cure such fundamental failings. There is no salvation available through consuming, no measurable happiness except for the brief excitement of ownership. These lifestyles are all style and no life.

The Swedish Play mirrored the consumer experience of seeking comfort from illusions and the ultimate frustration that results. The show was more than an exploration of the possibility of showrooms as potential theatre sets. By never seducing the audience into illusion, by isolating them with headphones, the show provided an opportunity to respond to the environment in a new way—to see that the furniture was really wood held together with threaded screws; to see that the displays were manifestations and manipulation of their desires.

Headphones isolate the audience from their environment and even from the performance itself (especially when the soundtracks are equally dis-associative, like those used during *The Swedish Play*). Just as the world seems different when you wear a Walkman, so does a performance heard through headphones. It turns attention back to the individual, forcing her to negotiate reality in a new way. This demonstrates an interest that Radix has in the human body as one of the "sites" that they explore with their work. Indeed, the human body was the subject of *SexMachine* (2003), a production based on the writings of Wilhelm Reich, a pioneer in body-centred psychotherapy. It was conceived and directed by Ternes, who co-created the piece with Laurenson, Alison Dowsett, Noah Drew, Emma Howes, Billy Marchenski, Tanya Marquardt, John Popkin and Sarah Wendt. Set in Vancouver's historic Shelly Building, audience members were treated as if they were arriving at a sex clinic for a tour and possible treatment. Actors dressed in lab coats greeted audience members and asked them to remove their shoes and put on hygienic surgical socks and then gave them a "treatment" on a hip-shaking machine. After a (non-pornographic) video installation, the audience was led past a series of performance installations set in different offices and glimpsed through open doors. These included an orgasm-inducing exercise bike, writhing naked bodies and a psychiatrist with electrodes strapped to his head reading out his fantasies. The production ended with the audience exiting through a maze of red-lit bubble-wrap and emerging, through a taut opening, into a small room, bright with white light—a form of plastic rebirth.

As with *The Swedish Play, SexMachine* toyed with audience expectations. Not surprisingly, they arrived in a state of heightened expectation about what they were about to witness. Those expecting a licentious bacchanalia would have been disappointed. Instead, they were treated to a tableau of sexual dysfunction and an exploration of the sexual repression and guilt that pervades our culture (despite all our claims to sexual openness). This wasn't a Sixties transgressive celebration of sexuality. It was, rather, a performance of sex in need of therapy, sex in need of correction—again, an exploration of what lies beneath.

It must say something about our culture that a show like *SexMachine* can be produced without raising an eyebrow, and yet we have such a strained relationship with the sex act itself. In a very real sense, we have isolated ourselves from it, and even those who revel in their sexuality, such as swingers and blog-keepers, seem, in some fundamental way, to be responding to the repression at work in our society. For most of us, our personal sexuality remains hidden, while at the same time we are saturated with sexual imagery (that often isn't very sexy). There seems to be a disconnect between our innate, sensual natures and the way we communicate sexually in our culture; therefore, a "sex show" set in an office environment is a perfect metaphor. Setting sexual expectations, fantasies and, perhaps above all, naked bodies in sterile, functional offices confronted the audience with their own (and society's) relationship to their sexuality, their own desires and their relations to other bodies. This says something about the sexual isolation that we now experience. Here we are, sexual creatures, existing in sterile boxes. It also evokes how we have isolated sexuality from our own lives, and how, as a community, we apprehend sex as a commodity (almost exclusively visual)—on Internet porn sites, in advertising or on television programs. Sex is used as a tool to sell products. And, as with the lifestyle anxieties that *The Swedish Play* attempted to uncover, so the use of sexual imagery taps into anxieties about our own personal sexuality. Instead of enjoying sensual pleasure, we are bombarded with images of what sexuality should be. Just as, say a car company, might use sexual imagery to sell its product, so Radix used sex to sell *SexMachine*. We have removed sexuality from our lives in a damaging way and placed it in sterile environments.

I think it's important to recognize that the show started and ended with a form of physical contact: the hip-shaking machine and the bubble-wrapped maze. This last element is particularly striking. After being confronted with images of strange, disconnected sexuality, audience members were left to navigate their own way back out into the world. There was no human connection, only the touch of plastic. These sexually alive individuals were alone, with no sensual connection. They were not touching another human being.

This lack of direct human contact was also a subtle theme at work in *Half a Tank* (2004). Conceived and directed by Laurenson and co-created by Laurenson, Ternes, Kahre, Ron Samworth and Sean Lang, *Half a Tank* was described as part auto-circus, part drive-in theatre. Set in a parking lot, the production was built around a central conceit—the breaking of the five hundred-thousand-mile barrier on the odometer of an old car, a 1970s Diplomat. This (literal) milestone was achieved by the car's being driven the last few miles in circles while the audience watched from the comfort (and safety) of their own cars. The production effortlessly evoked the sense of a small-town, community event. In part, this was created by the on-air chatter of Bob Piston (Laurenson), the host of CKAR, who introduced the elements that made up the spectacle, which included an audience singalong, a car symphony and a Darwinian Derby, where audience members were given remote control cars, which they had to keep out of the way of the Diplomat's massive wheels. The driver (Lang) also performed some impressive driving tricks—at one point hanging out the car window while driving with his feet. These down-home spectacles were punctuated by phases with an almost Zen-like quality—the car simply driving in circles, racking up those miles.

The deliberately low-rent feel created a sense of authenticity, that this really was a community celebrating the life of a car (the history of which—including the fate of the original owner—was referred to throughout the show). In addition, the different elements seemed like "found" objects, growing out of the central idea of the show. The production played with the tension between the isolation of being in cars and the community aspect of the show. As the production progressed, the elements became progressively darker, matching the growing darkness of the night sky overhead. The community space—the space outside the cars—became less safe while the show itself became more recognizably theatrical. This second phase was dramatically ushered in by a "drive-by painting," when a Fifties hot rod entered the space and paintballers shot up the Diplomat, covering it in paint. By this point, the sun had set, and the audience was firmly placed within their cars. As the Diplomat finally neared its milestone, a character was run over and unceremoniously thrown in the trunk. Unable to restart the engine, the driver was forced to push the vehicle the last few yards to achieve the milestone. The show, now fully theatrical, concluded with a dance piece: Creatures in black cloaks made their way through the performance area and took over the car, while Death rode around on a Segway (a two-wheeled person-mover that itself now looked sadly dated). In the end, the Diplomat was towed away and the space cleared, leaving a final image: a burning barrel of oil in the darkness of the parking lot, the only lights coming from those audience members brave enough to risk a flat battery to light up the show.

Half a Tank dealt in the tension between opposites—the joy of the car and the dramatic and negative impact it has had on our culture. Again, the arc of the experience matched the theme of the show, from the undeniable fun and physical joy of the automobile through to the nightmarish conclusion that the oil is rapidly running out. *Half a Tank* explored not just the interior space of the car but also the bleak parking lot, the faded Eighties high-tech of nearby Science World and the glittering sterility of the new downtown towers (largely empty, investment buys) in the near distance. In the first week, the weather was spectacular, the setting sun casting every-thing in a golden hue. The show—certainly the first half—felt like a tailgate party; there was more interaction between audience members, more of a sense of the cars opening out into the environment. On the second weekend, the weather reverted to seasonal norm and it poured with rain. The impact was dramatic, forcing the audience to retreat into the interior space of their cars. Where the first weekend emphasized the joy of the car—its shiny physicality—and car culture, the second was more focused on the interior experience—entrapment and looking at the world through a windscreen.

The interior space of the car—not just any car, but the car that audience mem-bers arrived in and used every day—was an important element in the production. We were witnessing something from within a familiar, interior space. There was a tension between feeling that we were participating in a community event and the strange disengagement that happens when we watch events through our windscreen. This form of disengagement from our surroundings is something that happens whenever we drive. We are removed from the environment; it is something we drive through and, if we notice it at all, we do so from an emotional distance. We can comment freely on the dress sense, weight or behaviour of those shut out on the streets. There is also a sort of performance that takes place when we're driving. Our behaviour—certainly mine—becomes generally more aggressive, less tolerant. The car is loaded with unconscious images of speed and freedom, and anything that impedes that freedom frustrates us. There is a serious disconnect at work in our society. We transport our soft bodies at high speeds inside metal containers, rarely reflecting on the lives, including our own, that we endanger.

For Radix, locations are not simple settings or thematic tools but are integral to decoding experience. Productions evolve directly out of the environment and they provide a vehicle for the audience (the experiencers) to understand that environment in a new way. This, then, leads the experiencers to consider how they—as indi-viduals—interact with that environment and, ultimately, with the innate theatricality of their lives and perhaps, even, of human nature. To Radix, the world is literally a stage. Every environment contains narratives that we—in a largely unconscious manner—interact with. It is also, perhaps, fair to say that, with these three shows, Radix has been evolving a "theatre of disappointment," meditations on how contemporary society has let us down (or perhaps, more precisely, on how we've let each other down by engaging in an unreflective manner inn the empty promises at work in our society).

There is another theatre of disappointment to consider. *Half a Tank* ran just before *Joni Mitchell: River* opened the Vancouver Playhouse's current season. While staging this musical may simply have been response to market demand, it certainly is a sad comment that a musical revue took up one of the (Canadian) slots of one of our mainstage companies. Anyone who knows the Vancouver scene will not be surprised. This is a city where the general public is simply not as engaged in traditional theatre as in other urban centres. This is a city where the outdoors and the shiny and new are valued, a city where, as I write, the Fantastic Four are fighting Doctor Doom downtown. We can only hope that companies like Radix—where the notions of what a theatre experience should be are constantly being redefined—represent a way forward, that a city that prides itself on being active will continue to be attracted to theatre that actively engages them. There is an image of hope that I can share. On the last night of *Half of Tank*, as they left the parking lot, individual audience members took the opportunity to drive in circles around the burning oil barrel. It was a moving testimony to the power of performance to engage the individuals to the point where they take over and become performers. This, I imagine, was a pure Radix moment.

(2005)

Arrivals and Departures:
How Technology Redefines
Site-related Performance

by Kathleen Irwin

> *The end of the twentieth century marks a most significant moment in time for performing arts and technology. ...[O]ur challenge is to imagine a future for the arts that extends well beyond the human imagination that has shaped them in our lifetime. No matter what the time or place of our birth during the first half of this century, we all arrived as analogue babies, enriched and yet encumbered by traditions in the arts that were formed by a myriad of cultures. These traditions gave way to new trends, and in time were embraced by the immigration patterns that formed our nations. The last half of the century is another story; the new arrivals are digital babies...*
>
> —Richard Loveless (283)

In Canada's foremost national English language newspaper is written the following description of Cirque de Soleil's latest production, *KA*, at the MGM Grand Hotel in Las Vegas: "Imagine a Broadway stage that can rise, fall, float, become completely vertical, or tilt, often at alarming, gravity-defying angles, and you'll have some idea of what [director, Robert] Lepage has conceived" (Posner). Commenting on this marriage of super technology and the performing body, Lepage states: "the 19th-century conception of the proscenium stage was based on a vertical world—with God above, man in the middle and the devils below the trap doors ... But the new world is horizontal, as much as vertical. So it should be possible to have a theatre where everything is possible, where there is no floor, no ceiling, no gravity" (qtd in Posner).

Certainly in Cirque de Soleil's mega-million dollar production technology is foregrounded—"[a]ll the theatre's innards lie exposed—winches, cables, conduits" (Posner). However, with all the technological trappings that purport to redefine audience perception in entirely new ways, the conventions remain unaltered. Spectators purchase tickets, sit passively in a darkened theatre and watch the spectacle unfold. It seems that this explosion in entertainment technology has missed the mark in addressing more pertinent issues surrounding the use of interactive strategies, including telematics and telepresence, all of which rely on the subtle role of technology to support cybernetic interface in the world of art and performance.

In relative magnitude, *The Bus Project* falls at the opposite end of the scale from *KA* in terms of technologically enhanced entertainment. Nonetheless, it addresses some of the issues surrounding interactive technology and its use in integrating public art/performance in public places, reaching new audiences and shaking up long cemented perceptions. It exemplifies, as well, the blurring of disciplines and the fading lines that differentiate theatre from site-specific installation and interactive installation practice and questions the merit of aligning such events with a specific discipline.

The appropriation of public space by vested interest groups problematizes issues-based performance and amplifies the threat of such interventions being censured. Furthermore, ambiguity surrounding private space (malls, cinemas, theatres, campuses) and public space disguised as private space (such as the bus depots here cited) situates the consideration of legitimate activity in appropriate place at the centre of performance strategy. While guerrilla performance tactics may, with the necessary planning and derring-do, realize a one-off event, technology can support such intervention and facilitate a subversive performance over a longer duration.

Organized under the rubric of interdisciplinary research, *The Bus Project* was a collaborative, media-based, public art performance/installation undertaken by theatre and inter-media artists, computer scientists and graduate students in June 2004 through the University of Regina. The project was conceived to bring together researchers not normally engaged in conjoined projects (Kathleen Irwin, site-based Scenographer; Rachelle Viader Knowles, inter-media artist; and Daryl Hepting, computer scientist), and to encourage work across conventional disciplines. The project was designed, as well, to employ students in activity that bridged academic and professional environments by mixing up emerging artists and young computer scientists with well-established practitioners. Collaboration was central to the project, both as a means to connect academic research with local issues and to encourage new approaches in the fine arts and sciences, where single authorship is frequently the norm. In the odd way that research develops, blurred authorship and interdisciplinarity became as central to the investigation as were its original concerns that focused on site-specificity, non-conventional spectatorship and technological support for public interaction.

To provide some background, *The Bus Project* was part of SPASM II: The Couture of Contemporaneity, a public art festival organized by PAVED New Media Gallery in Saskatoon, Canada. The event was a significant one that brought together local, national and international artists through collaborative media projects, interdisciplinary works, visual art installations and performance art. Invited by the festival, *The Bus Project* submitted a proposal for an installation that spanned two sites (Regina and Saskatoon) considered adjacent by prairie standards (275 kilometers). The venues proposed were the Saskatchewan Transit Company's bus terminals in the two cities and in an intercity bus. Reflecting the various disciplines of the participants, the project was simultaneously conceived of as a performance, as site-related exhibition and as scientific fieldwork.

Investigating the themes of displacement, mobility, transience and home, *The Bus Project* proposed integrating low-tech bus travel with high tech computer interface using the provincial public transportation network to address more universal concerns of migrancy and dispersal. Here, we were playing with the idea of the bus as a means of containing and disseminating people along with their actual and metaphoric "baggage." As well as installing customized upholstery on an intercity vehicle, we planned to place computer terminals in the bus terminals.

As the project was realized, computer terminals were imbedded in individually designed and fabricated "game stations" or kiosks and were optimally placed to invite public interactivity. When the video game was played, point and click options presented anecdotes of arrivals and departures. These poignant narratives were collected from eight women affiliated with the organization Immigrant Women of Saskatchewan and reflected stories of immigration from Afghanistan, the Ukraine, South Africa, South Korea and Wales. The results, edited into an interactive video game format, explored notions of choice and chance, resilience and transformation. Upon entering the game, the player encountered several on-ramps, each offering the opportunity to click on road signs that indicated destinations within the province—Moose Jaw, Swift Current. These places morphed into the distant places from which each woman had travelled. A player chose, for example, one or several arrival stories by interacting with the video game in the Regina terminal. One had to become a traveller in one's own right, completing the bus trip to Saskatoon, in order to play the parallel departure story. Interacting with the game was encouraged by displaying the kiosk, constructed in brushed steel and shaped like an abstract human form, in the centre of each waiting room next to a row of fast food dispensers. With its customized chassis exhibiting the familiar screen of a video game or automatic teller, it attracted a steady flow of interest (Bus Project).

Carrying the notion of displacement onto the bus itself, several seats were "upholstered" (dyed fabric, resist and appliqué) with culturally marked surfaces that reflected what is carried, worn or left behind in the act of displacement. The upholstered seats were placed in the coveted front row positions. Hence, watching the view and viewing the art (at least sitting on it) were concomitant.

The choice of locating the project at the bus depots exploited the ambiguity of public and private space where watching people at defining moments of arrival and departure is done surreptitiously—like eavesdropping. The strategy of using the game station to disguise stories of displacement, under sometimes difficult circumstances, was a masking device that provided a credible ruse for the curious who stepped up to play a game and found themselves on the receiving end of a very personal anecdote.

While the clients of the bus station accepted the presence of the kiosks without question, not surprisingly, from the start, the administrators were suspicious of the project and our reasons for wanting to situate the game station in the waiting room. Their primary consideration was ostensibly for their customers' well-being and they insisted that the game be unobtrusive and that interactivity be clearly voluntary. Behind their concern was the fear that the content of the game might threaten, disturb or subvert the proper activity of the bus depot. Central to this distrust were issues of race and education. In Saskatchewan, a province where demographics clearly indicate a large and growing undereducated, underemployed aboriginal community, the public transit system represents an affordable means of transport for a frequently itinerant population. That a video game, addressing local issues of migrancy, might, at best confuse or rankle, or at worst inflame, was the central unspoken concern.

When we first approached the authorities to negotiate the placement of the kiosks, their initial strategy was to ignore us or to continuously defer our requests to other or higher authorities. Only after repeated insistence that the Saskatchewan Transportation Company was, in fact, a crown corporation (thus publicly owned and publicly available), we were finally allowed to undertake the installation. Their outright suspicion surrounding the project challenged us at every turn and suggests why the placing of art in public spaces is frequently viewed as a minefield.

The aesthetic of the bus depot is purely utilitarian. Seats are hard and do not invite relaxation. A video camera continually surveys the area; fluorescent lights are harsh, illuminating every corner and eliminating the possibility of illicit activity or even a moment of privacy. The television is tuned to all-news or all-sports channels. It is predominantly a male space. However, the insistence of a female perspective through the anecdotal interviews with immigrant women dealing with personal loss and self-discovery and the reworking of the utilitarian bus seats with hand crafted (women's work) seat covers was incongruous, amusing, ambiguous and compelling. It demanded a redefinition of this gendered space compatible with feminism's blurring of the boundaries between private and public, the personal and the political. The personal revelations in the women's stories brought to mind feminist arts activism of the 70s (e.g. Judy Chicago and Lucy Lippard) that insisted on the radical imposition of an alternative and redefining perspective to unhinge normative notions of female identity. Reflecting on work of that period, Suzanne Lacy writes, "the suppression of an empowered female identity through popular culture's misrepresentations could be counteracted by articulate identity constructions in art" (27). Fortunately, spaces have a way of shifting functions and, at the end of the project, the bus depot was functioning more like a gallery or kind of theatre as the public phoned in to enquire, not the departure time for the intercity bus, but when the arrival of the reupholstered vehicle was expected. In re-imaging the space of the bus station as something other than the usual, the project made it somehow more complex and interesting; a place where class, race and gender clashed and intersected and where a women's perspective might be considered the norm. Perhaps what is most threatening in the transformation or inversion of quotidian space into "art space", however temporary, is that it might happen again, happen anywhere, happen spontaneously and without warning.

What role did technology play in this project? In the rampant drive towards a totally tech-supported lifestyle where BlackBerries and cell phones proliferate, the bus depot was chosen to underscore the mundanity and low-tech quality of intercity bus travel. The role of technology here was to intersect the routine with a *jouissance* or playfulness and to create an interface with the travelling public that offered a virtual, rather more arbitrary, journey around the province than the one on which they were about to embark. Each destination on the virtual tour became a portal to the world through the narratives of the women embedded there.

The virtual journey was inspired by current experiments in algorithmic psychogeography: the notion of the random stroll or drift elaborated into a systematic practice that is sometimes codified into set patterns such as "two to the right, then one to the left." The arbitrariness of the experience, the desire to satisfy one's curiosity about what is around the next corner is key to the psychogeograpic experience and we wanted the same pleasure of discovery and surprise to be part of the video game.

Psychogeography can be broadly defined as the study of how physical surroundings affect mood and behaviour. Psychogeographers practice the art of the *flâneur* or urban wanderer, rehearsed in the literature of, among others, Charles Beaudelaire, Thomas de Quincy, Walter Benjamin, Michel de Certeau and elaborated on by the surrealists in the 30s, the Lettrists in the 50s and the Situationists in the 60s. It is now well-documented on a large number of websites and blog diaries as a contemporary, site-specific practice that combines art and political activism with an agreeable pastime for those who like to "stroll, drift and wander simply for the pleasure of turning the next corner...." (Glowlab). One of the better websites on the subject gives the following insight.

> One of psychogeography's principle means was the dérive. Long a favorite practice of the dadaists, who organized a variety of expeditions, and the surrealists, for whom the geographical form of automatism was an instructive pleasure, the dérive, or drift, was defined by the Situationists as the "technique of locomotion without a goal," in which "one or more persons, during a certain period drop, their usual motives for movement and action, their relations, their work and leisure activities, and let themselves be drawn by the attractions of the terrain and the encounters they find there." The dérive acted as something of a model for the "playful creation" of all human relationships. (Psychogeography)

Of course, unlike the limitless opportunities afforded by random drifting through city streets, the video game offered finite choices and distinct parameters that were quite narrowly defined. The interface used a simple "point and click" method and, at first approach, resembled most an automatic ticket vendor. When the title image on the video screen dissolved into a cartoon-like map of Saskatchewan, the player faced a choice among a number of available destinations although these options were all within the province's borders.

Here, technology was used to mask or disguise the presence of the women in the video games and, simultaneously, to reveal them, somewhat playfully, to those who chose to engage. In general, the expectation when playing video games is to encounter only virtual presences, 2D or 3D animation, never real people. An incongruity is achieved in placing real people in virtual space that raises such questions as: is virtual space a place? If so, is it private or public—will I be caught eavesdropping? If these are real women, am I listening to scripted text or actual, documented memories? Are the memories factual or am I participating in a staged or theatricalized event? While the project employed immigrant women to tell their stories, at least one of the women was an actress, two were inter-media artists and one a scenographer, all cognizant of the mediating camera and their own ability to manipulate it for optimum effect. Each was asked to tell a story, not necessarily adhering to the facts; embroidering was allowed, even encouraged. The women were videoed against carefully chosen backgrounds, the lighting was controlled, several takes were done and the stories severely edited. In the editing, certain words and phrases ("coming home," "I was lonely," "lost") were extracted and superimposed graphically across the screen. In other words, a sort of performance was created.

While the bus depot is defined by leave-taking and homecoming, it is an inhospitable environment of schedules, non-stop television, in-your-face advertising, bad coffee and twenty-four-hour surveillance. The experience of viewing a computer screen and listening intently to an intimate narrative implied the consideration of the human dilemma that inverted normal expectations associated with a cybernetic interface in impersonal settings. Interacting in this way produced an ambivalent response in the random passerby who engaged with the game, making one feel both an interloper and a fellow traveller.

In terms of the interface strategy, the challenge was in providing universal accessibility. We strove to present the game in a way that was recognizable, provocative, intriguing but non-threatening—essentially invisible. It could not draw undue attention to itself. We hoped that by exhibiting similarities to adjacent vending machines, the game would exhibit an organic connection to its locale. At the same time, it would be offer a critique, its presence permitting a more complex reading of that place.

In the relative scale of technology-supported entertainment, *The Bus Project* was not a grand event. Part theatre, part inter-media performance, part installation, it seemed to address current local concerns in a provocative and compelling way that attracted an under-accessed spectatorship, urged the reconsideration of local circumstances in an increasingly homogenized world and reassigned meaning in a place of proscribed activity. It encouraged spectators to view their immediate surroundings in a global context of interlocking networks and immigration patterns where migrancy is the result, not of choice, but of economic and political pressures and contingencies.

Too frequently, the spaces where we live and work are fragmented, commercialized, scrutinized, patrolled and controlled. Within these spaces debate and dissent are screened or outrightly prohibited. Perhaps the overarching achievement of *The Bus Project* was in recognizing that public art can engage people in surprising and vibrant ways, challenging, in the process, conventional notions of appropriate time and place. The project recognized that we live in a highly mobile society engaging in both low-tech and high-tech systems of communication that override conventional notions of linear time and space and that these metaphors can be harnessed to stimulate contemplation, conversation, and possibly debate about the local and global communities where we live and work. As well, the Project underlined the essential role that such performative events play in building and sustaining an urban community by celebrating diversity, inclusivity and how single stories undermine powerful narratives.

If the technology in Cirque de Soleil's *KA* does not, as I contest, redefine audience perception, does *The Bus Project* come any closer to making this lofty claim? As Lucy Lippard claims "[t]o affect perception itself, we need to apply ideas as well as forms to the ways in which people see and act within and on their surroundings" (286). Lippard argues that the challenge of redefining perception is best addressed by reaching out to participant communities and marginalized audiences by whatever means possible and "allowing the art idea to become, finally, part of the social multi-centre rather than an elite enclave, sheltered and hidden from public view or illegibly representing privileged tastes in public view" (286). This reaching out will inevitably result in crossing perceived boundaries and exploring new territories; here the notion of actual place is fundamental. She goes on to suggest that basic shifts in perception are achieved when a work is specific in its ability to engage a spectatorship on the level of their own lived experience; when a work is collaborative to the extent that information, advice and feedback is sought, on some level, from the community in which the work is realized; when the work is generous and open-ended enough to be accessible to a wide variety of people from different classes and cultures; appealing enough to engage the imagination and be memorable; simple and familiar enough, on the surface not to confuse or repel potential viewer/participants; complex enough to hold people's attention and to offer layers of experience to those who participate on different levels; evocative enough to jog memory and emotions; provocative and critical enough to make people consider issues beyond the scope of the work. Fundamental to Lippard's criteria is that the most successful intervention, the event that successfully redefines audience perception, is unobtrusive. It differs least from the space in which it is situated.

In the example of *The Bus Project*, it was, effectively, the seamless support of technology that permitted the situating of the piece in an inhospitable environment and allowed it to claim that space for an extended period of time. Tellingly in the end, the Saskatchewan Transportation Company wholeheartedly endorsed the project, in the process redefining the bus depot, themselves, not merely as a place of beginnings and endings but as "art space" and thereby opening the door to future collaborations.

Initially the project aimed to investigate performative representational strategies in non-traditional spaces, engaging diverse spectatorships and how technology might seamlessly support the universal aims of conjoined research. Inevitably, in assessing the project, there arose other issues that merited consideration. Some secondary issues included blurred authorship, intentionality versus outcomes and assessment strategies in measuring the relative merits of interdisciplinary research.

Among the artists and researchers on this project, only the scenographer had worked extensively on collaborative projects. Theatre is fundamentally a collaborative art and the interdisciplinary mix of contributing artists and technicians brings a depth to the work and, through this creative network, connects it to diverse communities and audiences. Collaborating with multiple artists and communities, both in the process of development and in its reception, broadens a work's intertextual scope. The nature of this work is chaotic—like a train speeding out of control. The job is to hit the brakes at the appropriate moment and bring the train up short in front of the station and on time. The train analogy is apt as it represents the adrenaline rush of the ride as well as the satisfaction of reaching the station. The process is as important as the end result. Equally important is the intersection of participating communities who are not distinct, in many ways, from the category of spectator. Here the lines are tantalizingly blurred.

Buy-in from participant communities is central to this method and where these communities intersect and chafe is usually the focal point of the event and provides the value added moment—the moment of excess meaning that is never intentional—can never be planned for nor repeated. The chaotic process is not easy to negotiate—the big picture is never available to every one at the same time. This is true for the artists and researcher /participants as well as for the spectators. For this reason, results are difficult to measure by traditional yardsticks.

When conventional methods of evaluating artistic merit are difficult or impractical to apply, then criticism must refer to the artists' expressed intentions (although this method does not always take into account the possibility that the artists' stated purposes do not comprehend the multiple, sometimes unconscious, levels on which art operates). While intentions are not necessarily an accurate or definitive indicator of merit, they suggest contexts and criteria through which to evaluate merit. They are important indicators of the values and meanings the artists attach to their work.

Representing a hybrid way of working across multiple disciplines, *The Bus Project* provokes questions about transdisciplinarity. A project of this nature ideally exhibits the richness and depth that results from diverse input. At the same time, its very hybridity makes it difficult to assess by usual discipline-oriented standards and criteria. In mixing things up like this, *The Bus Project* hoped to interrogate conventional ideas regarding creative authorship and explore how blurring problematizes the assessment of eventual outcomes and conventional ways of critiquing the value of art. In scientific or academic terms, the question begging to be asked is: Are the goals of interdisciplinarity best served when individuals retreat to their own disciplines to assess and measure results or should a new model be considered? In artistic terms, the question begging to be asked is: Is it art and, if so, in what category should it be classified and critiqued?

An assessment must ultimately ask the question, is the work a substantial and meaningful addition to cultural or intellectual life? If so, is it equally so for artists and public alike? In the case of multifaceted events, a way of considering these questions may eventually be found in assessing, to the degree possible, the range of possible experiences and outcomes offered. If intentionality is used as one yardstick for attributing merit, then it must also be understood that, in such events, there is an excess of meaning well beyond that intended or imagined by the artists.

My concern, in this paper, has been to interweave issues of blurred disciplinarity and the assessment of its effectiveness, cyber technology and virtual presentation with issues of interactivity in place-specific public art and performance. I contest that it is not the foregrounding of extreme technology that the production of *KA* represents, nor the new connections and crossovers that interdisciplinarity proposes that makes these times challenging and redefining to artists and researchers who deal with visual representational strategies, audience perception and who look to technology for future directions. Rather, the challenge is to understand and use technologies to support innovation that breaks down boundaries between disciplines and communities and makes art increasingly available to under-accessed populations. Technology is pervasive, ubiquitous (hence largely invisible) and can facilitate presenting art in places normally considered purely functional, single use and too "local" for broader cultural consideration. The aim of technology, represented here, is to support the use of pervasive media and investigate how it can evolve in order to support a range of cultural and creative activities.

An example of how this technology is being explored is seen in international networks like PLAN (Pervasive and Locative Arts Network) that considers the broader question that technology opens up—"what kinds of creative, social, economic and political expression become possible when every device we carry, the fabric of the urban environment and even the contours of the Earth become a digital canvas?" (Plan). A new generation of pervasive technologies is enabling artists in every discipline (artists, activists, hardware hackers, bloggers, game programmers, free network builders, semantic web philosophers, economists, and university and industry researchers) to break away from traditional desktop PCs and games consoles and experience interactive media that are directly embedded into the world around them.

Looking to the future, new fields of transdisciplinary research foregrounding the use of pervasive technology and locative media (the combination of mobile devices with locative technologies) will support experiences and social interaction that respond to a participant's physical location and context. Together these convergent fields raise possibilities for new cultural experiences in areas as diverse as performance, installations, games, tourism, heritage, marketing and education.

A key characteristic of this research is its interdisciplinary nature, with many of these projects combining practicing artists and technology developers whose early research has frequently been delivered as public artworks that have yielded new insights into the ways in which participants experience pervasive media and locative technologies—strategies that interrogate the very terms and conditions of the "conventional audience" and may truly reshape their perception.

(2005)

Works Cited

Bus Project, The: http://uregina.ca/Bus_Project/busproject.html.

Glowlab: *Shuffle: Psychogeography with a Deck of Cards and Your Own Two Feet*, www.glowlab.com./shuffle_about.html, April 2005.

Lacy, Suzanne, ed. *Mapping the Terrain: New Genre Public Art.* Seattle, Washington: Bay Press, 1995.

Lippard, R. Lucy. *The Lure of the Local: Senses of Place in a Multicentered Society.* New York: New Press, 1997.

Loveless, Richard L. "Time Past … Time Present … Time Future: Re-envisioning the Aesthetic in Research for Human Performance." *The Routledge Reader in Politics and Performance.* Ed. Lizbeth Goodman and Jane de Gay. London: Routledge, 2000. 283–87.

Plan: Pervasive and Locative Arts Network, http://www.open-plan.org/, April, 2005.

Posner, Michael. "Reinventing the Cirque du Spectacular." *The Globe and Mail* (5 February 2005).

Psychogeography and the Dérive: http://www.geog.leeds.ac.uk/people/a.evans/psy-hcogeog.html, April 2005.

Please Dress Warmly
and Wear Sensible Shoes

by bluemouth inc.

Please Dress Warmly and Wear Sensible Shoes

BLUEMOUTH INC. PRESENTS

An individual brings in a piece of raw material to the group and it gets ground through the collective mill. Two hours, two minutes, two months too late it emerges more or less transformed.

In the spirit of our collective process, we at bluemouth inc. propose to write a collective dialogue sharing some of our thoughts and experiences in creating site-specific performance.

There are four issues that recur for us in discussing or creating site-specific work:

1   **Through the Fourth Wall (Lucy Simic)**

2   *The Living Space (Richard Windeyer)*

3   The Paradigmatic Shift (Stephen O'Connell)

4   Lost in Space (Sabrina Reeves)

What we have decided to do is to pass around these topics between us as in a game of telephone via e-mail, each of the four of us starting with a specific idea then, in turn, getting an opportunity to illuminate, mutate or transform each of the four ideas, accumulating our personal perspectives as they are passed along.

***

Through the Fourth Wall

How does an audience prepare for a performance situated in a living *site? Which expectations are met and which expectations are thwarted? What happens to the audience experience when* the spectator is asked to join the performer in the action? Does the self-consciousness that accompanies a diminished fourth wall augment or impede the potential for a deeper, richer experience? In site-specific performance, there is a disorientation that occurs for both audience and performer as they glide through **a kaleidoscope of suggestive images;** the result is never what **one expects.**

The sites that we choose always have an enormous impact on the audience's experience. What I find particularly interesting is the way the sites we choose affect

and transform **the relationship between the audience and performers. Our goal is to have the audience share the space with the performers, and we encourage them to move freely** *through the site.* **By directing their** movement *throughout the perform-ance, we* **are asking them** not only **to travel through the** *site, but to travel through the content of the piece as well.* **We invite them to enter** <u>into</u> **the images. Thus their expe-rience of the site becomes wonderfully entangled with their experience of the piece. In** *What the Thunder Said,* **audience members are picked for two teams to play a game of baseball. In** *American Standard,* **an audience member is** *lathered up and* **shaved in a barber's chair** *while a* **performer** *dressed as a* terrorist **delivers text to the** *surrounding* **audience.** *Wherever possible,* **we** *attempt to create* **intimacy with the audience by sharing the performance space with them.**

<u>With</u> *almost every project, we experience the unpredictable responses and behaviour of audiences. The ultimate reality of breaking through the "fourth wall" is that* you are made <u>immediately</u> aware <u>of the safety and anonymity this barrier is designed to pro-vide, not only for the spectator, but for the performer as well.</u> We, *as performers, may suddenly find ourselves considerably more vulnerable, stripped of the protected no-man's land that exists between* the fixed seating *and the stage in conventional theatre spaces.* **As the performer moves closer to the spectator, the wall gradually recedes and diminishes until finally either participant is capable of reaching through.** <u>An interesting question becomes: Has the wall been internalized? For if the wall were truly to vanish, what would happen then?</u> What would it be like *if the* viewer felt permis-sion to reach back <u>and affect the performer?</u> **Where would this lead us and how and where would it eventually end?**

Unfortunately, *the choice of performance site can* impede spontaneity by *establish***ing** *and maintain***ing** *levels of audience control automatically. In some performances,* **we've chosen venues that, although they were ideal for the piece, have forced us to drastically re-think our relationship to the audience. The boiler room used in** *The Memory of Bombs* **had a dangerously uneven floor, with metal braces sticking up out of concrete on one side and a dirt floor covered with potholes on the other. We had no choice but to seat the audience** *for the duration of the performance,* **particularly given the dim lighting and the aggressive physicality choreographed to spill out around and, at times, above the audience. In previous sites, we** *could afford to be* **less concerned about sightlines and acoustics and rely on the audience to move freely, as close or far from the action as they liked. With** *The Memory of Bombs,* **however, we found ourselves weighing the** *options—do we take* **full advantage of all** *areas* **in the boiler room** *and include the use of an underground tunnel winding through a series of decrepit rooms as part of the audience experience? Or do we eliminate* **the problems of bad sightlines, poor acoustics** *and injury by placing the audience in a* static **location within the space. We chose** *the latter* **and created seating along three walls, satisfying ourselves that each view had an ideal perspective of a part of the piece and at least 90% of the piece was visible from any of the angles.** *Instead of the* **audience moving freely through and around us, we moved around and through the audience. The choice of what to focus on and what to** *ignore remained with the audience.*

Another *primary* **intention in creating site-specific work, is to** draw from the viewers' *own personal* **histories or from their preconceived ideas of the site. We choose locations that are a functioning part of the city's landscape, locations people have walked by and wondered about before they came to the show and may continue to walk by long after the end of the run.**

When someone tells me, "I walked by the Gladstone Hotel and it reminded me of your piece" (referring to *LENZ*), it means **the work has become embedded in the** life memory **of that location and is integrated into the location's history. Although I may walk by a theatre and remember a show I've seen there, the theatre remains a theatre, fulfilling its function. Whereas a park, a porn theatre, an old hotel or a funeral parlour remains haunted by the works performed there.**

bluemouth inc. is a continuous process in development. *The four of us* **function** as *both creative* **directors and** *performers. As a collective,* **we have an** affinity **for creating performances that exist in close proximity to the audience. These are works** that are **guided by our own experiences as audience members.** We **strive to create** *experiences that we ourselves* **would love to have.** A primary focus of our creative process includes a rigorous and thorough examination of **the relationship between the audience and the performers. While creating and developing each new work, we keep returning to** *a central* **question:** "What would surprise, excite, inspire me as a spectator **at this point?" That question applied to the search for a venue has led us to some rich territory, with a new set of questions and much more to unearth.**

The Living Site

bluemouth inc. has developed performances in a funeral parlour, an abandoned boiler room, a city park, a run-down hotel and an old porn theatre. Each location is a living site—born, raised, adapted, renovated and reinvented by a steady succession of owners, proprietors and tenants struggling to make a sustainable living. Over time, each *site has become the centrepiece of a unique community and micro-culture. Attempting to integrate the* conceits and constructs *of a theatrical performance into this often requires* some fancy footwork. *To work harmoniously with the site requires* listening *and learning,* for *it is all too easy to step on each other's toes.*

BLUEMOUTH INC.'S EIGHT IMPORTANT DANCE STEPS

1   *Be certain that the person inhabiting the space is the owner, not just a tenant. Permission to use the space ultimately rests with the property owner. One time we simply assumed that a local barber owned the building containing his shop. When the actual landlord found out about our show, not only were we shut down, but the barber's own rental agreement was* jeopardized as well.

2   *bluemouth inc. always seems to approach the owner of a potential performance site in the wake of a film crew shooting a TV commercial or a rock video. Since film crews*

have big budgets and use them freely, the owner will *expect the same of you. Be clear with them what your financial limitations are from the start. Expect ambivalence or* complete *disinterest, but don't be discouraged. The owner may secretly welcome extra income but hesitate at the thought of allowing the public onto their property. Empathize with her or him. You may be trying to make innovative theatre, but the owner is simply trying to run a successful business. Can you demonstrate that your performances hold the promise of something they can use? Increased publicity? Free advertising? A new source of revenue?* While negotiating, maintain a positive attitude. If the situation seems dire, step back and reassess. Knowing what your limits are, ask yourself "How can I make this work?" *Surprisingly, when the hotel owner saw how much beer bluemouth audiences drank in his downstairs bar, our show became a "good thing" and he was decidedly more enthusiastic and generous with us.*

3   Know when you have spent *too much* time and resources going down a wrong path. Be prepared to walk away from a site *when* "no" simply means "no." *It can be a waste of time* trying to convince someone else of the value of your art. But if they say, "I don't know," consider it an open opportunity. Your ability to *clearly articulate* your artistic vision, *along with a willingness to compromise,* will determine the outcome of *your negotiation.*

4   *Once you have permission to use the space, maintaining good relations with the owner and the people inhabiting the space is crucial.* Occupants of the building may see your event as potentially disruptive. *Inform them of the performance dates, start/end times and exact locations well in advance.* Assure them *that no one's work or privacy will be disturbed.* Reassure them by inviting them to your work as your guest. Most people feel less threatened when they feel informed and involved in making decisions. *A sure sign of a healthy relationship with the owner and occupants is that they attend the performance, are interested in it and reveal themselves to be interesting, imaginative people in their own right.*

5   *Legally, audiences cannot be allowed into the site until it is declared by the city to be structurally safe or* "up to code." *This means*

   a)   *There is no danger of falling debris.*
   b)   *The building is not a potential fire trap.*
   c)   *Fire exits are reliable and clearly visible.*
   d)   *Any stairs used by the audience have regulation step dimensions and handrails.*
   e)   *Potentially hazardous areas are made inaccessible to audiences.*
   f)   *Washroom facilities are located in or adjacent to the site.*

   Consult with your city hall and fire department for details.

6   *If the site you crave is city property, you may require a special events permit. You may choose to employ "guerrilla theatre" tactics (perform without permission), but you are always at risk of being shut down. A special events permit enabled us to perform in a city park, use the city's power supply and install a* barnboard *shed for our*

audience. Be forewarned—permits take six to eight weeks to process and usually require some persistent voicemail prodding. The city will also require you to provide them with liability insurance (with the city named as the 3*rd party) and address* issues of noise level and public safety.

7   *A third-party liability insurance policy is absolutely* necessary, *especially if you expect to lead your audience through the site during the performance. This* will *protect your company* and audience **members** *should something unexpected happen. Some theatre companies will ask each audience member to sign a waiver before entering the site.* In theory, this *should protect you and your company against legal actions taken against you, in the event of an accident or injury.* In reality, *a signed waiver does not always hold up in court. bluemouth obtains its policies from an insurance agency specializing in outdoor theatre and sporting events.*

8   *Without reliable on-site security, lights, video projectors, audio gear and computers are at risk of damage or theft. Search out secure places to safely lock up your gear as part of your initial investigation of the site. If security is lacking, find a friend who does carpentry and get her or him to build you a lock box. Make sure the box is then secured to the site itself. These precautions will also help you to avoid poisoning— with suspicion or potentially false accusations—the relationship between you, the owner and the other occupants of the site.*

9   Never underestimate the importance of taking ownership and full responsibility of your relationship to a space. It can make the difference between a convincingly integrated performance and a performance that seems superficial or imposed.

The paradigmatic shift

The current **postmodern** paradigm is **a direct** result of *life in a heavily mediated* "information age." The shift from modern to postmodern has occurred just as fast as the shift from the first computer to the computer age. **The** reigning paradigm **in the theatre** of the early twentieth century was "realism" as **conceived** by playwrights like Ibsen and Zola. Darkened theatres, **the** proscenium arch, **a slice of life glimpsed through the fourth wall creating** a *mostly* two-dimensional experience. But has it seen its day? Replaced by ...? hyper-realism? Realism represented? Re-presented? Reality shows, globalization and worst of all: choice? Too much choice ... WAY too much choice.

Is mediation really the culprit or are we simply experiencing a backlash against the dominance of realism in theatre during the modern period? Does the state of all live performance reflect the political economy of our society, or should we talk only about theatre in this context? Is this same postmodern political economy in fact creating a deeper gap between theatre and the more avant-garde forms of performance? Is it possible that we are unconsciously experiencing a resurgence of romanticism amongst the avant-garde? **At least some of us are moving towards**

feeling and emotion versus structure and logic. Is it even possible to see the forest for the trees?

I suppose "performance" most accurately captures the feelings I have about my **experience of the world and, more importantly, the** *wide variety of possible methodologies* **appealed to my** creative process. **There are certain difficulties that come with working in a less clearly defined form. Some are mildly frustrating, as when** my aunt, **the painter,** still introduces me to her friends as her nephew "the dancer." **Then there are the more frustrating consequences, as when** the Arts Council thinks what we practise is too theatrical. Too conventional? Too accessible? Too narrative? *Too* be or not *too* be?

It is not like we consciously sit down before a rehearsal and decide to deconstruct the modernist paradigm. Our response is more intuitive. **It** reflect**s** a choice to steer away from certain conceits. **More accurately, we make a** choice **towards** creat**ing** work collectively, rather than **a reaction to the traditional hierarchy of play-wright–director–actor or choreographer–dancer or composer–musician.** There is a fluidity that is possible, a debate that keeps the work changing every day; it is hard to pinpoint any particular hierarchy, but that doesn't mean there isn't a dynamic we work within. **It's just that the structure itself is dynamic, constantly shifting and being put into question.**

Perhaps any movement away from the permanent building may be an indication of the structure's inability to contain the continued development of our craft. This does not necessarily imply any direct connection to the growth of site-specific works, but it does underline the limitations *that* the proscenium frame places on a contemporary vision of theatre. At the very least, it should suggest the advantage of incorporating more flexible spaces to house contemporary work.

It would appear from **this** vantage point that we have begun to witness a gradual retreat of modernism, but the battle is far from over. Our numbers are still small and the resistance is plagued with spies who would lead us to believe our differences are greater than our similarities. Theatre is slowly dying. It suffers from the terminal ill-ness of the classics and is in desperate need of originality to resuscitate itself. It does appear that a healthy resurgence of the avant-garde has begun to take root across urban centres in Canada and abroad. Perhaps the instability of current world politics has shaken the mortar from the foundation to allow enough light for experimental weeds to grow through the cracks. However, what I believe to be radical is far from fixed and falls somewhere vaguely to the left of centre on the continuum of performance—although my collaborators might disagree and they usually do.

Who is to say exactly why we are drawn toward certain practices and repelled by others? *As if* you could actually quantify any of the many choices which lead you down this page. We collectively create site-specific interdisciplinary performance. Don't worry—I have come to recognize the distant and glazed look that comes over people's eyes as that label rolls from my tongue. We work outside of the theatre simply because it is more exciting for us to create that way. For sure, I have a greater attraction to radical street performance than to parlour-**room** dramas. I feel our work, while drawing from **both** histories **(and various others)**, is a far cry from either one. Probably, what we do best is borrow from anyone or anything that inspires us, whether it is **pop culture,** circus clowns, **poets**, French experimental cinema or **contemporary** dance. The guiding rule is: If it serves the moment, than it stays in the piece. We don't prescribe any answers and I am pretty sure the only thing we can all agree upon at bluemouth is the non-existence of any universal truths. What we seek, as far as I can see, is an authentic experience, not unlike any other worthwhile theatrical experience. The most effective way for us to do this is to directly engage the audience. The best way we find to engage passive viewers is to get them on their feet and out of their seats. Here at bluemouth inc., we like to promote proper circulation because it helps keep people awake longer. *We want to shake you from your centre, weaken your defences. We want to leave you with a feeling you can't quite describe and which will follow you home and live in your fridge for days on end. We want to breathe in a single light with you, to celebrate this life that we're living, together. Right here. Right now. Just this place, this moment. No hiding and no commercials. Welcome. We've been expecting you!*

Lost in Space

The directive "Dress warmly and wear comfortable shoes" will never be issued for a play in a theatre. There is no need to consider the weather or environment when going to a dance piece (unless you are going to see Sens Productions in NYC or Dusk Dances in Toronto) or a comedy show or the opera. In fact, for many of these events you are expected to dress up, not down. Only for performance will you need to carefully consider where it is that you are going. **This play with expectation, the choice to invite an audience to experience** performance**, where they're asked to** expect **the** unexpected is **at the core of our belief: "Theatre has limits** but **performance is limit-less." As much as we put into question the formal aspects of theatre, dance, music and film by creating hybrid work, we also** want to challenge **the theatres and galleries that traditionally** like framed **performance by creating** bare-canvas site-specific work.**

One thing that is so exciting to us about site-specific performance is the possibility of re-awakening an audience to space. Our lives tend to be focused on what we *need* to do and the ordinary demands of our particular lives, such that we are rarely allowed to truly live in the moment, seeing rather than experiencing that which is directly around us. We spend the day listening to our own internal noise. Site-specific performance is not just another opportunity to tune out the world. It is the direct opposite. You need to be fully aware in the present moment—quite literally—or you might stumble on a rough patch of terrain or **miss an invitation to play base-ball.** I like to think that, as opposed to escapist entertainment, we are offering a way into awareness of the world around oneself. *Television, movies, radio and proscenium theatre encourage audiences to retain varying degrees of physical and emotional* *detachment during a performance. Our work attempts to envelop and at times even overwhelm audiences.*

From an artistic standpoint, space is one of the raw materials of creation, just as much as the text or movement or sound; in fact, if there is any sort of hierarchy in our method of creation, space would be the element that all others serve. I recently read a description of a noble class of nomadic ascetics in India whose entire existence was made up only of eating, sleeping and sacrificing to the gods. What spoke to me about this particular group was the fact that they would never sacrifice in a temple. The reason is described thus:

> A temple was unacceptable, because that would have meant using something ready-made, once and for all, whereas what you had to do was start from scratch, every day, transforming whatever clearing you found into a place of sacrifice, choosing one by one the positions for the fire and the altar, evoking the whole from an amorphous, mute, inert scene, until the Gods would come down and sit themselves on the thin grass mats that had been carefully unrolled for them.

> They lived without the comfort of crafted images. Not because they didn't trust them. On the contrary. A mental spring of images bubbles up unceasingly. But there was no need to copy them in stone. Rather they must be channeled by ritual. Bridled by hymns. Made to travel with the hymns, which are chariots. Every gesture unleashed more of them, like shadows. And if you tried to find where they came from, you arrived at something that "burns without wood in the waters." (Roberto Calasso)

I would be hard-pressed to come up with a more poetic description of what we are trying (in an ideal world) to do by creating site-specific work. For the ascetics, there were ten or fifteen elements from which to create infinite variations on the ritual. For us, there is text, movement, film, sound and all of **the accompaniments** to realize any possible combination of their use. Most importantly, like the ascetics, we trust each other and we trust in the magic that can be created by giving these elements a place to play.

I don't want to make it seem as though we are constantly co-mingling with the audience because this is definitely not the case. But we are not up on a stage isolated by a defined and culturally ingrained space known as "the fourth wall." Systematically breaking this down allows for a level of intimacy that may be the closest live performance has ever been able to come in competing with mediatized performance; we can truly create "the close-up" and place it next to "the wide shot" because physical proximity is one of the elements we have at our creative disposal.

When I think about it I often wonder, "Why isn't everybody doing this?" but I need only put on my producer's cap to answer that question. And then the statement becomes, "Why would anybody in their right mind do this?" You will never make a living doing site-specific performance: There is no infrastructure for producers to support site-specific performance; funding is limited (we often get the feedback that our proposals are "too ambitious"); audience capacity is limited; permits, fire-codes, liability insurance—and the list goes on. It is a challenge that you have to believe is worth **undertaking.**

It has always been the place of the avant-garde to disrupt the status quo and instigate change. Street performance, site-specific work, happenings—these will not replace theatre as we know it, nor do they intend to. But in a world of limitless choices crammed into an increasingly limited attention span, all live performance inevitably gets lumped under one heading when you are choosing something to do on a Saturday night. And just as reality TV seems to have pushed the one-hour drama off the TV waves, are the days of theatrical realism numbered as well? I don't have the answers, but I do know that when assessing my options on what sort of live event I will partake of, I would choose site-specific performance over conventional theatre any day of the week. What is ultimately reassuring is that we are certainly not the only ones who would choose this kind of experience as a form of weekend entertainment. Audiences are forming and growing and it is becoming clear to us that, more than ever before, there is a real hunger for new kinds of experience. This is what keeps us going.

(2006)

Beneath Bridges, Loading Docks and Fire Escapes: Theatre SKAM Tours *Billy Nothin'* and *Aerwacol*

by Amiel Gladstone

"Hi. My name is Amiel. I just wanted to come by and let you know we will be performing a show, a play actually ... Over there." And I point. A company of four or five actors can be seen, working the ground with rakes, unloading chairs from a van, and running a power cord from a nearby building.

The scruffy man is looking at me curiously.

"For how long?" he asks.

"The next two weeks or so," I tell him.

"All right. I think that'll be okay." And he returns to his makeshift lodgings with his compatriots, a small collection of people who have taken up residence here, amid the towers and support structures.

And, with that, I have breached the final bureaucratic hurdle of performing beneath the Burrard Bridge in Vancouver.

***

I was raised on a steady diet of outdoor theatre: The Caravan Farm in the Okanagan Valley, the San Francisco Mime Troupe and the Berkeley Shakespeare Festival in California. This was theatre that felt truly alive—unamplified sound; simple, if any, set pieces; and a palpable focus on actor, text and audience. I remember stories that were both personal and political, the incorporation of live music and a smart sense of humour. To this day, this seems to me to be the essence of theatre.

Vancouver Island is geographically and culturally isolated, with limited theatre opportunities. Theatre SKAM [1] began by performing in cafés and bars, venues that already hosted our peers—our desired audience. In the early years, we didn't limit ourselves to conventional theatres. In actual fact, they weren't really a viable choice—we didn't have any money. Instead of making them come to a traditional venue, which can feel stuffy and intimidating, we brought the theatre to our youthful audiences. We packed them into the tiny brick-walled Grace Bistro in Chinatown. A performance run took place on the dance floor of the Drawing Room, a nightclub filled with velvet couches, the audience sitting on stools and gulping back watered-down drinks. The

Belfry Theatre invited us to perform late nights, but not on stage—in the lobby. We took George F. Walker's *Zastrozzi* and performed a chilly back-alley version, the cast entering aboard a screeching 1977 Plymouth Volare. Our performance style matched our locations: unpretentious, riotous, with an emphasis on sharp topical writing and the relationship between ourselves and our adventurous audience. As the company grew, our locations remained unconventional: apartments, parking lots, parked cars, garages, loading docks, tents, galleries, courtyards, town squares and parks, and eventually even the occasional theatre.

In neighbouring Vancouver, other companies were forming that were also creating versions of this type of work. Radix, Electric Company, boca del lupo, and Neworld were part of the next wave, new ensembles that were taking it upon themselves to explore the inherent theatricality of the Lower Mainland, outside of traditional performance spaces. An inspiring landscape, a temperate climate and, perhaps, the residue of our hippie West Coast upbringings can all be traced as influential on this movement. It was when networking with these artists that I first heard the term "site-specific" and it helped to contextualize what we were all attempting to do. The moniker became a way for ourselves, as theatre artists, and for the media to easily explain what we were attempting. For myself, the sites wouldn't always come first in the process, but they were integral to the art.

Through this time, several details became apparent. The national theatre community rarely experiences work performed in Victoria—in fact, they rarely even hear about it. Up until recently, there was no CBC radio, and as it currently stands, there is no CBC TV station. *The Globe and Mail*, the country's national newspaper, seldom covers a Vancouver Island cultural event. If we were going to get noticed by our theatre-community peers and funders, if we were going to develop as artists through the sharing of work, if we were going to build larger audiences, SKAM was going to have to tour.

Touring for SKAM has become a peculiar endeavour. The company still has small budgets, so theatre production, especially on the road, has involved all kinds of methods of cost reduction. [2] We have crossed both Canada and the United States by Greyhound bus. [3] We don't have fancy light rigs, sound systems or comfortable seating. We scrounge up what we can, creating a particular aesthetic. We joined Fringe Festivals as a means of marketing our work. While the comfort level for our artists may have changed, the aesthetic for the work has remained the same. Find suitable spaces and exploit, as much as possible, the opportunities they provide.

Sean Dixon, our "playwright out of residence," was discovered through his play *District of Centuries*, which we performed in an outdoor courtyard behind a restaurant in downtown Victoria. [4] The following year, Sean wrote *Billy Nothin'*—which we built and performed in Victoria in this same courtyard—specifically with the SKAM ensemble in mind. Sean was performing at the Caravan Farm while we were rehearsing and performing, and it wasn't until we transferred the production to the Vancouver Fringe that he was able to see the work. The Victoria run had taught us a lot about the show, what the audience was responding to and what was making them scratch their heads—two people inhabiting one body, the imagination at work and jump-cuts from the West to New York City, all within a cowboy motif, punctuated by songs. It's a bizarre piece with a winning charm; yet it was taking some time to perfect.

In Victoria, the entire playing area was a raised platform in a downtown court-yard. In Vancouver, we used a loading dock behind Wonderbucks, a store on Commercial Drive. The box office was located in the store, which was used as a lobby of sorts. To define the playing area around back, we positioned the Volare, upon which our fiddler Daniel Lapp would sit and play, next to a stack of pallets for the stage, along with several dumpsters and the loading dock, with a door that could open and close. All of these elements became integral to the telling of the story. With Sean now with us, we clarified the text, sharpened the physical staging, and the Vancouver run was much more successful.

The second of Sean's plays to be premiered by the company was *Aerwacol*.[5] We built and premiered *Aerwacol* (about a group of disparate citizens who find them-selves riding the rails), in the Belfry's Studio,[6] travelled to Toronto, where we performed just off the train tracks of the West Don Lands,[7] and then back to the West Coast for the Vancouver Fringe, where we performed it beneath the Burrard Street Bridge.

I had been able to scout out the Vancouver site, while Sean worked on finding something in Toronto. The subject matter of the play demanded some reference to trains in its locale. Sean scouted out a Toronto site and sent me snapshots so I could get an idea of the place. Looking at the photos, I had no idea how we would stage it. It looked like one big open space. It looked ugly and cold.

The run indoors to open the show in Victoria was successful. Sean was also in the cast, so he was present the entire time to make changes to the still-evolving text. As we were in a proper black box, we had strict control over all elements, specifically lights, sound and weather. We treated the theatre as a site-specific location, exploiting all doors as possible exits—in fact, for his character's final exit, Sean went into the control booth. I felt the Victoria run was a successful start—in fact, that production was a gelling moment for the company. We were in good shape to hit the road.

With little money, we had to find a way to transport the show, the most substan-tial object being a three-quarter-scale railway jigger. Designer Ian Rye had created a railway handcart, complete with pump action and large inflatable casters so that it could move easily across the uneven concrete in Toronto and Vancouver. Greyhound Bus Lines had a sale. We were young enough to think about taking the bus for seventy-two hours, and Matthew Payne, SKAM founding member, actor and produc-tion manager, researched the exact dimensions of Greyhound's luggage allowance. When we arrived at the bus depot with three enormous cardboard boxes, which contained the specially designed collapsible jigger, along with costumes, instruments and hand props, the attendants initially refused to allow our "luggage" to be shipped. They relented once we showed them that the dimensions were just within the stated allowance. The boxes were so large that they couldn't put them under the bus with us, so our show elements travelled separately.[8]

My first visit to the site wasn't as bad as I'd been imagining. On the site in the West Don Lands, there was an area in a corner of this vast concrete expanse that had possibilities, including the remains of a covered loading dock. We spent four days preparing. Much of this involved digging to create a trap door, which was necessary for one entrance, and re-blocking. On the Greyhound bus east, I had had a new idea for the ending. Somewhere in Saskatchewan, Sean and I had a script meeting, in which we developed a new "split-screen" ending in which we were able to tie up several parts of the story at once. We integrated this idea with thoughts of how to negotiate the trains that were running behind the playing area. During the time when we would be performing, an average of three GO commuter trains would whiz by. The only way to deal with them was to acknowledge them. The rule for the actors was to wave to the engineers, unless it felt completely inappropriate within the context of the scene. I remember, in rehearsals, dramaturge Brian Quirt had joined us for a look-see and a freight train lumbered by. On and on and on. For a full five minutes. We all lived in fear that another massive freight train would interrupt the show during the two-week run.

We built into our box office projections the possibility that we might lose some shows to rain. And yet, the onset of rain can provide a tension and a strong need to tell the story. Both the opening and closing nights of *Aerwacol* in Toronto had rain, and we were forced to move the entire audience, chairs and all, beneath the long narrow roof of a nearby loading dock. The cast went ahead anyway—all my staging discarded as needed—and told the story the best they knew how, with their voices and bodies, no props or real blocking. At one point, Camille Stubel, an ensemble member who earlier had looked at me with complete disbelief when I suggested we were going to proceed with the performance, weather be damned, frolicked in the puddles. She had discovered a perfect way to portray the cathartic epiphany of her character Kimpy. To this day, director Chris Abraham, who was at that performance, says that he couldn't imagine the play any other way—he refused to come on a clear night.

The Vancouver run was less successful artistically. We secured the use of the space beneath the Burrard Bridge, jumping through what proved to be many bureaucratic hoops. [...] We were able to mould the space into a usable playing area, and the nearby Molson Brewery gave us permission to use some of its electrical power to run lighting, as it was dark under the bridge. The bridge did provide shelter from the rain; the challenge was the ongoing drone from the overheard traffic and the dreary Vancouver weather. The show still stood up, but we couldn't duplicate the experience that audiences in Victoria and Toronto had had.

A few years later, we decided to revisit *Billy Nothin'* and bring it to Toronto. Sean sent photos of a site, the parking lot behind Honest Ed's. Once again I had no idea how it was going to work, but it was the only real possibility available to us. That year's Toronto Fringe and SummerWorks Festivals featured at least two other site-specific shows. Seventeenth Floor Performance, in the basement of a record store, and bluemouth, performing in an old porn theatre, were within a block of the site.

The Honest Ed's loading dock needed some work. We requested that the enormous dumpster be reconfigured for the run, and the store had it moved. We brought in as many pallets as we could find for different levels, and Matthew made a stage out of an old fence that we salvaged. We utilized the fire escapes, as high as was safe. Sean and I went back to the text once again, further clarifications were made and the run was successful, with long lines in front of Honest Ed's along Bloor Street.

A discovery from years of utilizing unusual venues: You can create your own rules and the audiences will learn from you and respect them.[9] You can create a sacred space by setting up the box office away from the performance area, holding the audience there until just before show time and then letting them pour in. It's also nice to have set up approximately the same number of chairs as there are audience members.[10] This sacred space for performing, as well as the walk from "box office" to "lobby" to "house," was employed in all our venues.

I find now that, when I walk through an urban centre, I often look at places— whether a quiet alley, loading docks or a secluded city park—and think, "We could do a show there." When I go back to working in conventional theatres now I look at them differently. I have a much greater appreciation for control over the elements, for the nuances that are possible, but also I look at them more in the way I do with unusual venues: What is available in this room? Where are the exits? What could be a playing area? How can we exploit the inherent theatricality of this space to tell the story? This flexibility is key to our methods of working, enabling productions to be placed in various locations and even moved as necessary within that location.

In his review of the Vancouver version of *Aerwacol*, Colin Thomas of the *Georgia Straight* complained that I didn't sufficiently use the full depth of field available to me under the bridge. He wanted action to be placed further upstage, beneath the great columns supporting the bridge. I agree with the criticism. I would have liked that too, but there were people living there.

(2006)

Notes

1   Founded with three fellow theatre artists, Sarah Donald, Karen Turner, and Matthew Payne. The impetus for the company was creating work for ourselves and other like-minded performers in Victoria. For our first show, we needed a company name, and so we used an acronym of our first names: S, K, A, and M. Calling ourselves "skam artists" fed into our creative sensibilities.

[2] SKAM's 2005 operating budget was \$94,000. This included presentations at the Belfry Theatre, the University of Victoria and Atelier du Rhin, in Colmar, France, along with three self-productions. The principal expenditure is artist fees.

[3] The bus driver in Ontario came back and threatened to throw us off because he could "smell the dope."

[4] La Papa Hot Potato, which was a new restaurant with no established clientele. This made it easier for us to convince them to allow us to perform there. La Papa Hot Potato went bankrupt, perhaps for obvious reasons, and by the time we returned to this courtyard to premiere *Billy Nothin'*, we had to negotiate with Foster's Eatery and the Victoria Eye Care Centre. Foster's has also since gone under; the Eye Care Centre is still there.

[5] Originally written prior to *Billy Nothin'*, *Aerwacol* was first discussed while we were performing at the Vancouver Fringe. We held a reading of the work with the *Billy* cast, most of whom went on to originate roles.

[6] *Aerwacol* was first performed indoors, for several reasons. I felt that, as it was a new play with some challenges, it made sense for us to work within the focused environment of a theatre. It would need to work as a script, without the advantages that the compelling Toronto and Vancouver environments would provide. In some ways, the indoor production remains my favourite.

[7] The site is currently the new home for the Soulpepper complex. We like to think of ourselves as trailblazers.

[8] They arrived separately too. It was a full tense day after we'd arrived when they showed up in Toronto.

[9] See Sean Dixon's "Things I learned from Theatre SKAM" in this volume.

[10] This isn't without some logistical problems:

> **Stage and General Manager Jennifer Swan:** (*folding up chairs*) Remind me again why we are taking the chairs away?
> **Me:** (*folding up chairs*) Because we want people to feel like they are at the right party. They will feel like that if there are the right number of chairs. Even if there are only thirty of them.
> **Jennifer:** But it's so much work, just before the show.
> **Me:** That's how we do things.

"This is not a conventional piece so all bets are off": Why the bluemouth inc. Collective Delights in our Disorientation

by Keren Zaiontz

As a teenager in the Toronto suburbs my sympathy for sidewalks was unshared, even singular in its predilection. I was part of a landscape that had been scrubbed clean of passersby. The passage between entries and exits—from house to car to store to car—was the only sign that there was still life on Earth. To the unhabituated, those unfamiliar with the featureless terrain, the suburban citizen must have appeared as if she were permanently caught in the act of fleeing. The scurry to and from the mini-van resembled the anxiety of vacating the scene of a crime.

Fleeing the sidewalks is far from what Michel de Certeau imagines when he discusses the emancipatory act of the pedestrian in *The Practice of Everyday Life*. De Certeau examines acts, or tactics, that most philosophers have, until recently, rejected as merely functional: walking, cooking and talking. In the course of mining these daily activities for their creative traces, de Certeau overturns the established vision of the modern subject as a figure straitjacketed into what Michel Foucault calls a self-disciplined operator—a subject that regulates her behaviour through the surveillance of others. In this worldview, norms are not thrust upon the person but internalized through the disciplinary gaze of the other.

De Certeau questions the capacity of vision (or surveillance) to consume the subject into a self-disciplined operator. He inspects tactics—elusive acts that evade visual terrains, and, in the process, pulls our attention to that "vast reservoir of alternate developments" in which self-individuation leaves its traces (de Certeau qtd. in Reynolds and Fitzpatrick 66). De Certeau cites walking in the city as a tactical operation that escapes legibility: "Walking affirms, suspects, tries out, transgresses, respects, etc., the trajectories it 'speaks.' All the modalities sing a part in this chorus, changing from step to step [...] which vary according to the time, the path taken and the walker. These enunciatory operations are of an unlimited diversity. They therefore cannot be reduced to their graphic [visual] trail" (de Certeau 99). Tactics are by nature inventive, non-localizable procedures that temporally invade "proper" places—an upscale neighbourhood, or sites of government, corporations, schools and other institutions. De Certeau privileges tactics because they have the potential to permeate and reorganize the proper.

It is at ground level, on the streets, that the tactic most visibly, or, rather, *invisibly* "insinuates" itself (de Certeau 93). The city walker, in particular, is so entangled in her surroundings that she can not easily rise above her actions and disinterestedly observe her route through alleys and avenues. If she were able to watch herself walk through the city, her distanced scrutiny would fail to capture the transitory sensation of passing by, the impulse that motivates a sudden detour and all those other "stubborn procedures," which de Certeau says "elude discipline without being outside the field in which it is exercised" (96). Every footstep, every "cutting across" can be said to repotentialize a proper place.

Unlike the city walker, my pedestrianism in North Toronto assumed the visibility of a landing strip—that is, completely visible. Seen traversing the suburban bush from miles away, a walker can rarely evade the surveillance of her neighbours. The failure to dodge the scopic is best instanced in the Filipina nannies and pasty-skinned teenagers—too poor to own a car, too young to drive—who huddle around windswept bus stops and empty parking lots. Landlocked by endless concrete, grey fields and rows of palatial homes, these walkers are sealed in the double position of being background and foreground, monument and detail, skyscraper (or, more accurately, big box store) and passerby. In this instance, ambulation does not reorganize the all-consuming governance of panoptic fields; rather, it stratifies the walker into a lanky, flatfooted spectacle that moves to a slower clock than those slick doorways on wheels.

De Certeau's tactics and his well-known delineation between space and place are poor fits for suburban surroundings: space is a set of non-localizable possibilities that, constantly in motion, favour movement over stability; place restricts itself to a definable number of choices so that it may assume the authority of a locale (117). In the suburbs, proper place seems to assert itself *everywhere*—even vast fields are colonized by housing developers that display billboards of happy couples with smiles so expressionless one wonders if their frontal lobes have been removed. No outskirt seems immune to the homogenous proper that duplicates itself across regions (think malls and pre-fab homes), and, in its viral-like course, wipes out a key characteristic of place: the local. In such generic surroundings, tactical incursions can only falter since, in de Certeau's words, a tactic "does not have a place" but "depends on time—it is always on the watch for opportunities that must be seized 'on the wing'" (xix). If tactics permeate and reorganize local places through deliberately non-localizable means, then how can they emancipate places, such as the suburbs, that are designed to resist locality?

The endangered tactic plays a curious—even vital—role in contemporary site-specific performance. Many practitioners who work outside playhouses often choose vacant landscapes such as warehouses, stripped office spaces and rundown shops to stage their shows. In both scenographic and dramaturgical terms, these artists deal first-hand with the issue of the citizen-consumer who has been compressed into a generic landscape. The compact relationship that certain site-specific companies stage between background and foreground, person and place, *I* and *here*, runs counter to the very basis of performance, which usually depends on distinct and stable notions of time, place and subject. Keir Elam, in *The Semiotics of Theatre and Drama*, explains that drama is founded on spatial and temporal indicators known as deictics: "[T]he drama consists first and foremost in this, an *I* addressing a *you here* and *now*" (139, emphasis in original). [1] Similarly, de Certeau draws on indexical markers when he observes that "the walker constitutes, in relation to his position, both a near and a far, a *here* and a *there*" (99, emphasis in original). Elam and de Certeau use linguistic enunciation as the basis of their analysis. But rather than examine subjects through the contingencies of stages and streets, they model the conditions of performers and pedestrians after linguistic models.

In contemporary environmental performance, indexes such as *here* and *there, you* and *I* are immediate concerns that encompass bodies and sites as well as language. Deictics are constantly being negotiated, collapsed and folded into one another as performers navigate fickle locales and flexible actor-audience relations. Toronto- and New York City-based interdisciplinary collective, bluemouth inc., exemplifies how *here* and *there* are subject to constant configuration. In the brief case studies that follow, I examine two remounts by bluemouth inc., *American Standard* and *What the Thunder Said*. These remounts demonstrate how whole scenes, movement pieces, lighting and spectator-performer interaction, designed around the specifics of a particular site, undergo a deliberate *dis*orientation—a deictic free-for-all—that, as a result of setting the production in a new space, revitalizes the potentialities in a performance piece.

Because the bluemouth collective stages its work in the spirit of art installations, spectators move through the performance site as episodes unfold around rather than directly in front of them. The pliant relationship between performer and spectator speaks directly to the concept of "lived space," which Rebecca Schneider, by way of Edward Soja, explains is "an always *mobile* negotiation between monumental, emblematic structures and their intimate or microspatial engagements" (Schneider 3, emphasis in original). In proscenium arch theatre, lived space is a tightly controlled replay of tradition: the audience sits and witnesses the show rather than invents a relationship to the play in the moment of performance. The dominance of the cultural monument (or play) is reinforced through the patron who institutionalizes the work of art through the act of spectatorship. The seating in proscenium arch playhouses further underscores a non-negotiable arrangement: as a static and inflexible mass, the audience is itself physically monumental since it subsumes individual detail.

bluemouth's work deliberately attempts to contravene the traditional spectator-stage divide and forge a lived space. In the article, "Please Dress Warmly and Wear Sensible Shoes," core member, Lucy Simic writes:

> With almost every project, we experience the unpredictable responses and behaviour of audiences. The ultimate reality of breaking through the "fourth wall" is that you are made immediately aware of the safety and anonymity this barrier is designed to provide, not only for the spectator, but the performer as well. We, as performers, may suddenly find ourselves considerably more vulnerable, stripped of the protected conventional theatre spaces. As the performer moves closer to the

spectator, the wall gradually recedes and diminishes until finally either participant is capable of reaching through (bluemouth 17).

In both *American Standard* and *What the Thunder Said*, the audience arrangement lends itself toward the tactical play—or "unpredictable responses"—that Simic describes. The audience in *American Standard*, for example, sits in the round and so affects the conditions of how the site functions in performance. Performers speak their lines to audience members, move in between and under their seats and call upon people to directly participate. In *What the Thunder Said*, the monument (or audience) must disperse and scatter through the site if it is to get a "good view," hear a performer, or keep up with the mobile nature of the show. bluemouth's flexible reception practices simultaneously exhilarate and panic spectators who, without the regular markers of performance, become painfully shy, clump together—forcing performers to work around an immobile mass—or, alternatively, move swiftly out of the way or risk getting caught in the middle of a scene or piece of choreography.

The semi-immobile state of bluemouth audiences recalls the image of the land-locked suburban walker who, seen from miles away, becomes an object rather than a subject entangled in her environs. Audiences do not transform into tacticians but continue to rehearse a disciplined (in the Foucauldian sense) reception that is governed by the visibility of the performance. Of course, the disciplined spectatorship of site-specific theatre is clearly different than proscenium arch productions—the earlier quote by Simic attests to the spectators' unparalleled proximity to the actor and performance environment. Yet Simic's emphasis on the performer—the performer is "vulnerable," "stripped," "moves closer" and "reach[es] through"—reveals that, more often than not, it is the actor who engages in tactical procedures and the spectator who *aids* in the operation rather than engages in the act herself. [2]

American Standard [3]

The spinning red and white pole outside Pat's Barber Shop on D'Arcy Street in Toronto carries all the promise of a "clean cut"—flat-top, military cut or shave with a straight-edge razor—fast and cheap. Inside Pat's shop, there is more talcum powder than oxygen, and the *mise en scène*, consisting of yellowed walls, worn chairs and a hat rack, appears like a deteriorating illusion nesting among city hospitals, university buildings and trendy restaurants. It is precisely this incongruous setting of small-town coiffeur and modernist architecture that first attracted bluemouth to mount their March 2005 production, *American Standard*, in Pat's Barber Shop. Unfortunately, the shop's landlord did not share the collective's enthusiasm for turning a men's grooming business into a performance site and abruptly denied them the use of the store one week before the production was scheduled to open. "It's not uncommon for us to lose a space at the last minute," says core member and composer, Richard Windeyer (Personal interview). Fortunately, Zero Gravity Circus, an east-end movie theatre turned circus rehearsal hall, was made available to the collective, and spectators were bused from the original D'Arcy Street location to a simulated version of Pat's

Barber Shop that consisted of a lone barber chair, multimedia and some masking tape.

Busing spectators to peripheral or residual locales throughout the city is a staple of bluemouth productions.[4] It enables the transport of audiences to non-conventional performance sites, and, in the process, makes the city part of the event. In the 2003 Summerworks production of *What the Thunder Said*, blindfolds were laid out on the seats of the bus so that spectators could willingly incur a feeling of disorientation — deliberately lose their way through the city. The means to disorient oneself—wheels rather than walks—recalls a largely suburban method of transport that lifts spectators out of the realm of tactical operations.

In *American Standard*, associate member Kevin Rees gave an informal disclaimer about the audience's transport to Zero Gravity Circus, while wobbling up and down the aisle of the moving bus: "I've been designated to explain to you that this bus trip we are on is not some sort of wacky, 'Is this part of the show?' type thing" (bluemouth, *American Standard* 1). Powdered in the ghostly white makeup and black eyeliner that marked the faces of the entire ensemble, Rees maintained that the east-end pilgrimage to Zero Gravity Circus was a purely logistical decision: "It is practical. It is an example of creative problem solving" (*American Standard* 1). More than a guide to the practical, the transporting of spectators reveals a site-specific dramaturgy that desires to be part of the motions of city life.

It would have been simple enough for spectators to make their way to Zero Gravity on their own, but the collective could not resist the urge to show the audience the link between the original location and the Zero Gravity site. The troupe's self-conscious linking of the two locales is similar to the role that de Certeau attributes to the pedestrian who, "in relation to his position, creates a near and a far, a *here* and a *there*" (99, emphasis in original). Like the improvised and repeated routes of the walker, the bluemouth collective fashioned a concept of "city" when they created a spatial relationship between Pat's Barber Shop and the east-end circus hall. When the audience boards the bus, they act as mobile onlookers that facilitate rather than directly produce the tactical play between the two locales. They assume a double position that makes them witnesses to and objects of the action. But the link between locales is not confined to the bus ride. This link makes its way into the performance event when the production's intended *here*, the barbershop, is transposed onto the space of the last-minute *there*, the circus hall. bluemouth reconstructed the chamber-like proximity of Pat's shop in the cavernous warehouse of Zero Gravity, where more traditional markers of performance, such as audience seating and lighting, stood in for the implicit spatial proximity of the barbershop.

American Standard is composed of a series of monologues by seven figures, or what the collective refers to as "American archetypes": Poet, Preacher, Tourist, Politician, Soldier, Immigrant and Terrorist. Archetypes in *American Standard* are connected through the same spatial event (the show) rather than plot. Organized through a spatial order, the performance acts as a frame through which a heterogeneous flood—a sensorium of ideas, images, sounds, bodies and spaces—can emerge into a polyvalent concept of America. The production grafts the logic of the streetscape onto the performance and reflects the motion of the street through a diverse mix of disciplines, conventions, spaces and bodies that operates in relative relationship to one another. But beneath the contemporary metropolis lurks a suburban condition that has infiltrated contemporary cityscapes and is most visible in bluemouth's use of audience reception. As the actors strive against the increasing homogeneity that marks the neoliberal city through theatrical tactics such as archetypes and bus rides, the audience continues to reflect a suburban condition through a docile spectatorship.

Originally intended for no more than a handful of spectators, the March 2005 production of *American Standard* expanded to include more than 20 spectators per show. Chairs were laid out along the perimeter of the performance space and resembled customers waiting for a cut and shave. This layout culminated in the show's final scene, when the performer who played the Preacher archetype shaved a spectator. The panoptic quality of the seating arrangement allowed audience members to sit in full view of one another and study each other's reactions as fully as those of the performers. The arrangement of the audience evoked a suburban legibility that compressed the spectator into an object and subject of attention.

The troupe conceived of a dramaturgy that enabled them to import one scenic locale, the D'Arcy and McCaul barbershop, to another, the Greenwood and Gerrard rehearsal hall, by thinking in terms of a "*Dogville*-style event." Core and founding member, Stephen O'Connell, explains: "The choice was either to recreate Pat's Shop or find another barbershop. [...] [W]e figured that it would be easier to recreate the piece since there was only a week left. We were left with either cancelling the show or doing a kind of *Dogville*-style event" (Personal interview). Lars von Triers' experimental film, *Dogville*, is set on a bare soundstage and uses chalk markings on the floor and a select number of props and set pieces to represent the homes and streets of a mountain town. *American Standard* lifted the *Dogville* conceit and taped the streets D'Arcy and McCaul on the floor of the circus hall. However, tape markers and linguistic utterances were only part of a larger range of signifiers used to represent the spaces of the production. Music, movement and pieces of the set—such as a barber chair positioned in the centre of the performance space, and a wall-sized screen that projected black-and-white images of Pat's Shop, country roads and nondescript cities in sepia—became part of the characteristic collision of conventions that make up bluemouth events.

The collection of archetypes in *American Standard*, six of which are performed by Stephen O'Connell, can be compared to the kitsch shops in Chinatown that sell everything from religious candles to bullets. Assembled in a freewheeling theatrical bazaar, the archetypes as iconic kitsch reflect the simultaneity of postmodern city space, which is governed by multiple perspectives and non-hierarchical organization (Olalquiaga 65).[5] It is an emancipatory experience of the city that the performers embody and the spectators facilitate and witness. Like shifting landscapes, the archetypes *pass by* the spectators when they dance, rant and, in some scenes, hang above the performance space. Normally, the act of passing by belongs to the walker, who, always in motion, moves past the landscape and constitutes the city through a *near* and *far*. However, once the audience is inside the playhouse, be it on the bus or in the circus hall, bluemouth localizes the walker-turned-spectator in a seat, creates a near and far and, through a series of gestures (such as clashing images, bodies, narratives), constructs commentaries on city and nation.

Because the archetypes are staged through a series of monologues, the audience views them in relationship to one another. Additionally, the relational position of the archetypes is produced through the performers' bodies, audience interaction and the sonic and visual aspects of the show. Connected through the contiguities of mimetic space rather than plot, the seven figures operate through a synchronic (simultaneous) rather than diachronic (cause and effect) representation of events. Simultaneity enables the archetypes to interrogate their universal status by staging a multiplicity of perspectives that would otherwise be subsumed by a gradual, evolutionary development of events across time. The Terrorist, for example, does not enter the performance space but hangs immediately outside it from what appears to be a noose. Projected on the back of a newspaper held by an audience member, the Terrorist stands in close spatial proximity to his simulation, which he controls through a live feed. The projection instantiates the Terrorist in two places at once and defamiliarizes his presence through the duplication of his body. When simultaneity occurs within the archetypes' bodies, it resembles a physical montage. The archetypes' materiality (bodies) becomes a site of multiple *heres* and *theres* as it juxtaposes physical movements so that oppositional gestures prevail over archetypal unity. For instance, Preacher, Politician and Tourist move through the performance space with bent knees, which makes them appear as if they were continually falling. On the verge of collapse, the archetypes must repeatedly prop themselves up—an attempt to convince themselves and the audience of a seamless indestructibility.

Along with character-driven movement, *American Standard* deconstructs the archetypes' authority when they apply repetition to verbal clichés, discordant sound and song, audience interaction and choreography. The Preacher, for example, says to the audience, "Repeat after me: 'One race. One nation. One blood'" (*American Standard* 3). The antiphonal response of the audience highlights the reductive and racist theme of the preacher's call. In another instance, the Soldier archetype folds his jacket like a military flag and sings a nationalistic song about Ireland. An electronic recording of his voice—fractured, cut-up and dissonant—reverberates half-phrases and sings along with him. Later on, in a movement-based vignette, the Politician archetype performs a piece of choreography with a silent woman (Lucy Simic) who enters the barbershop wearing a crinoline gown. Unable to repeat their movement phrases, both characters gradually break down and collapse on the floor. Their collapse points toward Heidi Gilpin's suggestion that contemporary movement performance demonstrates a self-conscious "failure to control experience through repetition" (110).

In the final moments of the show, when the Preacher returns drenched in sweat and bruised from moving aggressively on the concrete floor, he has all the archetypes inscribed on his body. No longer is he God's smooth-talking messenger; his hand shakes as he is handed a razor to shave an audience member: "n ... n ... nnnnn ... n ... nnn. yes, it is true. tru ... truly wonderful. isn't it? iiiit is good nnnews. iiiit is the good ... iiiit is the goo ... good news" (*American Standard* 13). The Preacher's message is no longer simply a New Testament calling card, but a comment particular to the production's construction of a theatrical and performative reality that has drawn on the excess of repetition. The replay of letters and words reveals the incapacity of the archetypes to hold all its referents. Having stepped into the subjectivity of each figure, the Preacher's repetition now carries the entire production's set of associations, commentaries and memories. Like urbanites, whom de Certeau describes as being "criss-crossed by the city" (101) as they make their way from one site to another, bluemouth's O'Connell (the actor, not simply the Preacher archetype) is equally subject to, or criss-crossed by, the archetypes, whose totality he punctures through repetition.

What the Thunder Said

Multi-coloured wires stick out of walls like dead tree branches. Exposed pipes traverse the room pumping their limitless supply of white noise into defunct ventilators mummified in grey insulation. More precarious than the ceiling is the floor. It is concrete but offers no stability. Anyone who claims to occupy the room has yet to breathe in its incendiary combination of dust and air. To move through the room is not to fill it but be defined by it. Dancing in its corners, projecting images off its walls and transmitting choric dirges across its boomy interior is the bluemouth collective. Their July and August 2006 production of *What the Thunder Said* was staged in a stripped office space in the old AT&T headquarters at 6th and Canal streets in lower Manhattan.

First produced in 2003, in Toronto, *Thunder* was remounted that fall as the final part of the company's trilogy, *Something About a River*—a work that had been in development for more than two years.[6] The trilogy (over five hours long) transported spectators by bus to three different sites—XXX Porn Theatre, the Bates and Dodds funeral home and Trinity Bellwoods Park—traversing a section of the city's buried Garrison Creek.[7] In the New York City production, *Thunder* appeared in Sitelines, a performance series funded by the Lower Manhattan Cultural Council (LMCC), and staged as part of the River to River Festival—a multidisciplinary festival that took place in locations throughout Manhattan.[8]

Like *American Standard*, *Thunder* is populated with archetypes but, in this instance, a nuclear family: Mother, Father, Daughter, Brother, Uncle and Second Cousin. Monologues and scenes are spoken in the absence of family members, who, through the short-sightedness of those closest to them, disappear, drown or fall ill. For example, the Daughter (Lucy Simic) speaks of a husband whose "suspicions" possess him to the point that his wife vanishes into a pile of dust. The Mother (Sabrina Reeves) replays a "terrible dream" in which her son drowns. In one section, the Daughter and Mother join the Neighbour (Ciara Adams) to gossip in an imperceptible code about Aunt Mary's withdrawal from the world: "As her brothers and sisters filled her backyard with their wives, children and husbands I noticed her smile changing into an empty blank look" (*Thunder* 9). The family converges as a unit in two sections: the baseball scene, which involves a game of softball with the audience and later on, in one of the final episodes, a dance piece performed by the entire collective. [9] Characters are rarely roles that subsume the actor but a means to interact with ideas, emotions and spectators. The transpersonal figures Mother, Father or Daughter are far from convincing illusions but points of encounter between the performers and the roles they play.

Just as in *American Standard*, *Thunder* renegotiates *here* and *there* to fit the demands of the new site. In lower Manhattan, the dormant energies of the Garrison Creek could not be drawn on, or referenced, with the same immediacy as in Toronto. bluemouth rewrote scenes to include descriptions of surrounding intersections and several rehearsals were spent experimenting with choreography that acknowledged the site's physical proximity to the former World Trade Center. The opening scene, in particular, was stripped to its basic contingencies. As if starting from scratch, the collective asked themselves: How do we welcome the audience? Introduce the show? Introduce the site?

These questions sparked creative answers that, over the course of the rehearsal process, played with spatial and temporal markers. bluemouth built a room the size of a service elevator and installed it directly in front of the entrance. The audience was brought into the constructed room at the start of each show, which made it appear as if the tiny space was the site of the performance. Following the opening lines, performed by Second Cousin (Greg Shamie), the collective immediately dismantled the room to reveal performers dancing around pillars. The Neighbour accompanied the dancers with a fluid song, whose lyrics ask: "Where do I belong?" The collective then used the dismantled wall surfaces to project images such as a stretch of desert road. At this point, the audience was as exposed as the performance site, and clumped against a wall, taking safety in their immobile status. The audience's fixity replays the suburban experience of nannies and adolescents who huddle around bus stops while cars zoom by. As observable entities, the audience was locked in the double position of being a spectacle—such as participants in a softball game—and an embedded detail—for example, performers regularly directed lines to audience members.

Stephen O'Connell describes how bluemouth played with audience arrangements in *Thunder* as a way to revitalize the potential in the show. In the following quote, O'Connell discusses what motivated the collective to reconsider the play's opening rather than simply restage it. The passage is worth repeating in its entirety:

> We felt like there needed to be a transition in the piece from the lobby [in the AT&T building] with its overwhelming golden Art Deco decor before entering into the raw space of the site. We also thought the

opening gesture [scene] needed to reflect the ideas of the piece while marrying those ideas with the location we were given by the LMCC. We played around with what we thought would be the expectations of a person when you open one of those doors. We wanted to play upon that expectation and subvert it at the same time. The notion of what lies beneath or behind the social veneer is obviously a motif in all of our work. The opening gesture also seems to have taken on a greater importance in most of our work. It is important and useful to the collective to somehow disorient the audience at the top of the show in order to prepare them for an experience that right off the bat says, "This is not a conventional piece so all bets are off." I think the room, like the bus in *Something about a River* and the maze through the streets of the *Memory of Bombs* succeed in accomplishing this same disorientation (O'Connell e-mail).

O'Connell describes bluemouth's surprise method as an active "disorientation." The opening scene in *Thunder* makes each moment more slippery than the next rather than establish relationships, plot and place. From the start, it filters out the consistencies implicit in how the *here* and *now* are constituted in a dramatic performance. The site is revealed in stages so that space and place are continually being reconstituted from one minute to the next.

In the pejoratively termed "Gimp scene," spatial and temporal indicators compress as *I, you, here* and *there* are overturned. Two tramps (performed by O'Connell and Shamie) pick several audience members from the crowd and have them hop, roll or piggyback into a line. In the 2006 production, once audience members had hopped into place, they frequently scurried back to the safety of the audience only to have the tramps solicit them to return to the line. The performers broke the spectators' habituated desire to see rather than be seen. The tramps had the spectators become "parts" of a table which involved audience members arching their backs and lying on each other's thighs. It was a test of endurance and skill—a "magic trick" orchestrated by the gimps—but also an "expansion of a body's repertory of responses," to borrow Brian Massumi's words regarding potential (100). [10] The audience has been folded into a spectatorship that simultaneously reinscribes their role as docile facilitator and expands what is possible in the moment of performance. What emerges in both *What the Thunder Said* and *American Standard* is a dramaturgy that enables remounts in the spirit of adaptations rather than reruns.

To examine bluemouth's work through the lens of a compressed landscape that bends the spectator into subject and object, background and foreground, monument and detail, is to reconceive of audience reception in site-specific performance as a construct. Lived space—the ambulatory exchange between the monumental and the microspatial—underpins this reconsideration of environmental spectatorship as a tightly managed interplay of compressions, reversals and deliberate disorientation of audiences and the spaces they occupy. This ambulatory exchange between edifice and detail challenges the rusty binary between environmental and proscenium arch theatre—site-based work is unregulated, while conventional theatre imposes constraints on its audiences—and does not hold true in productions like *American Standard* and *What the Thunder Said*, which take into account a visible and responsive audience throughout the entire play. To quote Lucy Simic: "Our goal is to have the audience share the space with the performers, and we encourage them to move freely through the site. By directing their *movement* throughout the performance, we are asking them *not only* to travel through the site, but to travel through the content of the piece as well (bluemouth, "Dress" 16–17, emphasis in original). Although Simic states that a spectator may "move freely through the site," the mobility of the audience must be directed through most of the performance if the bluemouth collective is to create a spatial link between neighbourhoods, play baseball in a warehouse or transform audience members into a table.

It is no longer useful to discuss site-specific performance in terms of a libratory or unfettered stage experience. It should be noted that few if any of the scenarios in bluemouth productions are improvised or spontaneous. (Can we attribute this badge of non-restraint to a hangover from the 1960s and 70s, when an artificial communitarianism was attached to environmental productions like *Dionysus in 69* and *Paradise Now*?) [11] The application of de Certeau to site-specific performance, specifically, the use of tactics as creative acts freely taken-up by spectators and performers alike, needs to be refocused on how audiences facilitate the actor's dramatization of tactical operations. The dynamic between the actor and the audience mirrors the tension between the de Certeauian city walker and the Foucauldian citizen: the former strives to self-individuate everyday practices through tactics that elude visibility, and the latter recognizes her collective condition every time she repeats a disciplined operation. That this conflict enters the realm of representation, specifically through shows that model themselves after the postmodern city, uncovers that tactics are endangered act in cities as well as suburbs. Neoliberal policies, bound to the footsteps of the city walker, and the non-hierarchical metropolis that she traverses, are transforming cities in "flagship destinations" (Hannigan 51)—entertainment districts, sports domes, concert stadiums—that cater to suburban visitors in the name of economically vibrant downtowns. Peter Eisenger writes that, "city regimes now devote enormous energies and resources […] to the task of making cities […] 'places to play'" (316–17). Eisenger's use of the word "play" is useful because it speaks to the bluemouth spectator who re-enacts a suburban docility in urban environs. And yet, the spectator's role as tactical midwife reveals that "play" is not a stable term and the line between de Certeau and Foucault far from clear cut. That bluemouth requires its audiences to assist in its tactical liberation shows that creative and critical spaces can only be cultivated through collective support. Walking alone, one can only travel so far.

(2007)

Notes

Sincere thanks to Ciara Adams, Elijah Brown, Erin Klee, Alexander Lane, Kevin Rees, Greg Shamie and to the core members of bluemouth for their openness and generosity: Stephen O'Connell, Lucy Simic, Sabrina Reeves and Richard Windeyer. I am grateful to Natalie Alvarez, David Fancy, James Gladstone and Andrew Houston for their insights and edits.

1   The use of the word "indicator" and, later, "indexical," draws on American linguist, Charles Peirce, and his three-pronged semiotic model: icon, index and symbol. See Hawkes 127.

2   I am indebted to Natalie Alvarez and David Fancy's observation that audiences in site-specific performance are subject to disciplined reception practices that are obscured often by the proximity to the theatrical event.

3   This excerpt is a revised version of an article about *American Standard*, originally published in *Canadian Theatre Review*'s site-specific issue (Houston and Nanni).

4   Forced Entertainment has also used a bus for their show, *Nights in this City*, first produced in Sheffield and later remounted in Rotterdam. See Etchell. A Canadian version of *Nights* was staged in Lloydminster, Saskatchewan (see Houston).

5   My treatment of American archetypes as theatrical kitsch is influenced by Celeste Olalquiaga's assertion, in *Megalopolis*, that kitsch is synonymous with the post-modern condition: "[I]n its chaotic juxtaposition of images and times, contempo-rary urban culture is comparable to an altarlike reality, where the logic of organization is anything but homogenous, visual saturation is obligatory, and the personal is lived as a pastiche of fragmented images from pop culture" (42).

6   The summer 2006 remount of *What the Thunder Said* included core members Stephen O'Connell, Sabrina Reeves, Lucy Simic and Richard Windeyer. Associate members included Ciara Adams, Elijah Brown, Alexander Lane and Greg Shamie. The original production included associate members Ciara Adams, Chad Dembski, Kevin Rees and Robert Tremblay.

7   For more information about the show see bluemouth inc., "River."

8   The Lower Manhattan's Cultural Council website describes the summer 2006 Sitelines Festival in detail.

9   Richard Windeyer operated the music and film projections throughout the show.

10 In *A User's Guide to Capitalism and Schizophrenia: Deviations from Deleuze and Guattari*, Brian Massumi explains that encounter suspends habit, or stimulus-response circuits: it is a "momentary stall instead of an automatic response" (99). Following this suspension, the subject then "spring[s] into a new synthetic mode of operation" and invents something new (99).

¹¹ A genealogy of how tactical procedures are dramatized—from Dada anti-art evenings such as Cabaret Voltaire, happenings in the 1950s, environmental productions staged by the Performance Group and Living Theatre, in the 1960s, to contemporary site-specific companies like bluemouth—would uncover how audiences have been directed to aid in tactical liberation within the context of avant garde performance.

Works Cited

Alvarez, Natalie and David Fancy. Conversation with author, St. Catherines, Ontario, 20 January 2007.

bluemouth inc. Presents (Lucy Simic, Richard Windeyer, Stephen O'Connell, Sabrina Reeves). *American Standard.* Collective Creation. Zero Gravity Warehouse 2005. Toronto, Ontario. Stephen O'Connell, Kevin Rees, Sabrina Reeves, Lucy Simic, Richard Windeyer. Unpublished performance text, 2001. Revised 2005.

———. "Please Dress Warmly and Wear Sensible Shoes." *Canadian Theatre Review* 126 (Spring 2006): 16–22.

———. "River." bluemouthinc.com/projects/rivertrilogy.html.

———. *What the Thunder Said.* Collective Creation. Summerworks Festival 2003. Toronto, Ontario. Ciara Adams, Chad Dembski, Stephen O'Connell, Kevin Rees, Lucy Simic, Robert Tremblay, Sabrina Reeves, Richard Windeyer. River to River Festival. Sitelines Festival 2006. New York City, New York. Ciara Adams, Elijah Brown, Alexander Lane, Stephen O'Connell, Greg Shamie, Lucy Simic, Sabrina Reeves, Richard Windeyer.

de Certeau, Michel. *The Practice of Everyday Life.* Trans. Steven F. Rendall. Berkeley: U of California P, 1988.

Elam, Keir. *Semiotics of Theatre and Drama.* London: Methuen, 1980.

Eisenger, Peter. "The Politics of Bread and Circuses: Building the City for the Visitor Class." *Urban Affairs Review* 35. 3 (2000): 316–33.

Etchells, Tim. *Certain Fragments,* London: Routledge, 1999.

Gilpin, Heidi. "Lifelessness in Movement, or How Do the Dead Move? Tracing Displacement and Disappearance for Movement Performance." *Corporealities: Dancing, Knowledge, Culture, and Power.* Ed. Susan Leigh Foster. New York: Routledge, 1996.

Hannigan, John. *Fantasy City: Pleasure and Profit in the Postmodern Metropolis.* London: Routledge, 1998.

Hawkes, Terence. *Structuralism and Semiotics.* Berkeley: U of California P, 1977.

Houston, Andrew. "*Nights In This City*: Mapping the Sublime in Lloydminster…By Bus, by Night." *Canadian Theatre Review* 103 (2000): 38–41.

Houston, Andrew and Laura Nanni, ed. *Canadian Theatre Review* 126: Site Specific Theatre (2006).

Lower Manhattan Cultural Council. "Sitelines." lmcc.net/art/programs/2006.8sitelines/index.html.

Massumi, Brian. *A User's Guide to Capitalism and Schizophrenia: Deviations from Deleuze and Guattari.* Cambridge: MIT Press, 1992.

O'Connell, Stephen. E-mail to the author. 31 October 2006.

———. Personal interview. 1 May 2005.

Olalquiaga, Celeste. *Megalopolis.* Minneapolis: U of Minnesota P, 1992.

Reynolds, Bryan and Joseph Fitzpatrick. "The Transversality of Michel de Certeau: Foucault's Panoptic Discourse and the Cartographic Impulse." *Diacritics.* 29.3 (1999): 63–80.

Schneider, Rebecca. "Patricidal Memory and the Passerby." *Scholar and Feminist Online* 2.1 (2003): http://www.barnard.edu/sfonline/ps/schneide.htm.

Windeyer, Richard. Personal interview. 2 March 2005.

Suggested Further Reading

Avila, Elaine. "Lieutenant Nun." *Canadian Theatre Review* 121 (2005): 56–74.

Bachelard, Gaston. *The Poetics of Space.* New York: Orion, 1964.

Barton, Bruce. "Through a *Lenz* Darkly: bluemouth inc.'s S(t)imulated Schizophrenia." *Canadian Theatre Review* 127 (2006): 54–59.

Bennett, Susan. *Theatre Audiences: a Theory of Production and Reception.* London: Routledge, 1990.

Berger, John. *Ways of Seeing.* Harmondsworth: Penguin, 1972.

bluemouth inc. "Lenz." *Canadian Theatre Review* 127 (2006): 60–70.

Bourriaud, Nicolas. *Relational Aesthetics.* Trans. Simon Pleasance and Fronza Woods. Paris: Les presses du reel, 2002.

Brookes, Chris. *A Public Nuisance: A History of the Mummers Troupe.* St. John's: Institute of Social and Economic Research, Memorial University of Newfoundland, 1988.

Buck-Morss, Susan. "The Flâneur, the Sandwichman and the Whore: The Politics of Loitering." *New German Critique* 39 (1986): 98–140.

Canadian Theatre Review 126. Special Issue, *Site Specific Theatre.* Ed. Andrew Houston and Laura Nanni (2006).

Carlson, Marvin. *Places of Performance. The Semiotics of Theatre Architecture.* Ithaca and London: Cornell UP, 1989.

Chaudhuri, Una. *Staging Place. The Geography of Modern Drama.* Ann Arbor: U of Michigan P, 1995.

Counsell, Colin and Laurie Wolf. *Performance Analysis: An Introductory Coursebook.* London: Routledge, 2001. 170–76

Cousin, Geraldine. "Exploring Theatre at Play. The Making of the Theatrical Event. " *New Theatre Quarterly* 12 (47) (1996): 229–36.

Cresswell, Tim. *In Place/Out of Place: Geography, Ideology and Transgression.* Minneapolis: U of Minnesota P, 1996

de Certeau, Michel. *The Practice of Everyday Life.* Trans. Steven F. Rendall. Berkeley: U of California P, 1984.

Deleuze, Gilles and Felix Guattari. *A Thousand Plateaus*. London: Continuum, 1987.

Dempsey, Shawna and Lorri Millan. *Lesbian National Parks and Services Field Guide to North America: Flora, Fauna and Survival Skills*. Toronto: Pedlar, 2002.

Etchells, Tim. *Certain Fragments*, London: Routledge, 1999.

Etchells, Tim, Hugo Glendinning and Forced Entertainment. *Void Spaces*, Sheffield: Site Gallery, 2000.

Forced Entertainment. "A Decade of Forced Entertainment." *Performance Research*, 1.1 (1996): 73–88.

Foucault, Michel. "Of Other Spaces." Trans. Jay Miskowiec. *Diacritics* 16.1 (1986): 22–27.

Gorman, Sarah. "Wandering and Wondering: Following Janet Cardiff's Missing Voice." *Performance Research* 8:1 (2003): 83–93.

Grosz, Elizabeth. *Architecture from the Outside*. Cambridge, Mass: MIT Press, 2001.

Harvie, Jen. "Being Her: Presence, Absence, and Performance in the Art of Janet Cardiff and Tracey Emin." *Auto/Biography and Identity: Women, Theatre and Performance*. Ed. Maggie B. Gale and Viv Gardner. Manchester: Manchester UP, 2004. 194–213.

Houston, Andrew. "*Nights In This City*: Mapping the Sublime in Lloydminster…By Bus, by Night." *Canadian Theatre Review* 103 (2000): 38–41.

Kaye, Nick. *Postmodernism and Performance*. London: Macmillan, 1994.

———. *Art into Theatre. Performance Interviews and Documents*. Singapore: Harwood, 1996.

———. "Site/Intermedia." *Performance Research* 1.1 (1996): 63–69.

———. *Site-Specific Art. Performance, Place, and Documentation*. London: Routledge, 2000.

Knowles, Ric. *Reading the Material Theatre*. Cambridge: Cambridge UP, 2004.

Kobialka, Michal. *A Journey Through Other Spaces. Essays and Manifestos 1944–1990. Tadeusz Kantor*. Berkeley and London: U of California P, 1993.

Kwon, Miwon. "One Place After Another. Notes on Site-Specificity." *October* 80 (1997): 85–110.

———. *One Place After Another. Site-specific Art and Locational Identity*. Cambridge, Mass.: M.I.T. Press, 2002.

Lacy, Suzanne, ed. *Mapping the Terrain: New Genre Public Art*. Seattle: Bay, 1995.

Lane, Jill. "Reverend Billy: Preaching, Protest, and Postindustrial flânerie." *Performance Studies Reader*. Ed. Henry Bial. London: Routledge, 2004.

Lefebvre, Henri. "Social Space." *The Production of Space*. Oxford: Blackwell, 1991. 68–168.

Leigh Foster, Susan. "Walking and Other Choreographic Tactics: Danced Inventions of Theatricality and Performativity." *SubStance: A Review of Theory and Literary Criticism*, 31. 2-3 (2002): 125–46.

MacAuley, Gay. *Space in Performance. Making Meaning in the Theatre*. Ann Arbor: U of Michigan P, 1999.

Mackenzie, Jon. 'Theatre/Archaeology (review)' *Theatre Journal* 54.2 (2002): 332–33.

Marcus, Greil. "The Long Walk of the Situationist International." *Guy Debord and the Situationist International*. Ed. Tom McDonough. Cambridge: MIT Press, 2002.

Modern Drama 46:4. Special Issue, *Space and the Geography of Performance*. Ed. Joanne Tompkins. (2003).

Nora, Pierre, ed. *Les lieux de mémoire*. Paris: Gallimard, 1984.

O'Donnell, Darren. "Social Acupuncture." *Social Acupuncture*. Toronto: Coach House (2006). 10–97.

Pearson, Mike. "The Dream in the Desert." *Performance Research* 1.1 (1996): 5–15.

────── and Michael Shanks. *Theatre/Archaeology*. London: Routledge, 2001.

Performance Research 2.2 (1997).

────── 3.2 (1998).

────── 6.1 (2001).

────── 6.3 (2001).

Phillips, Andrea. "A Path is Always Between Two Points." *Performance Research* 2.3 (1997): 9–16.

Pile, Steve and Nigel Thrift. "Mapping the Subject." *Mapping the Subject: Geographies of Cultural Transformation*. Ed. Steve Pile and Nigel Thrift. London: Routledge, 1995. 13–51.

Pollock, Della, ed. *Exceptional Spaces: Essays in Performance and History*. Chapel Hill: U of North Carolina P, 1998.

Read, Alan. *Theatre and Everyday Life. An Ethics of Performance*. London: Routledge, 1993.

────── , ed. *Architecturally Speaking: Practices of Art, Architecture and the Everyday*. London: Routledge, 2000.

Royle, Nicholas. *Literature, Criticism and Theory*, Harlow: Longman, 2004.

Schafer, Murray R. *Patria: The Complete Cycle*. Toronto: Coach House, 2002.

Schechner, Richard. *Environmental Theater*. New York: Applause, 1994 [1973].

Schneider, Rebecca. "Patricidal Memory and the Passerby." *Scholar and Feminist Online* 2.1 (2003). http://www.barnard.edu/sfonline/ps/schneide.htm. Sept. 16, 2006.

––––––. "Performance Remains." *Performance Research* 6.2 (2001): 1–8.

Schweitzer, Marlis. "Staging *Lieutenant Nun*: Theatre SKAM's Military 'Re-enactment' at Macaulay Point." *Canadian Theatre Review* 121 (2005): 46–55.

Shanks, Michael (2002), "Creating an Archaeology of Performance." www.roehampton.ac.uk/artshum/arts/performance/ARCHAEOLOGY/TowardsArchaeology.html. April 11, 2005.

Soja, Edward. *Third Space: Journeys to Los Angeles and Other Real-and-Imagined Places*. Oxford: Blackwell, 1986.

Suvin, Darko. "Approach to Topoanalysis and to the Paradigmatics of Dramaturgic Space." *Poetics Today* 8.2 (1987): 311–34.

Taylor, Diana. *The Archive and The Repertoire: Performing Cultural Memory in The Americas*. Durham: Duke UP, 2003.

Turner, Cathy. "Palimpsest or Potential Space? Finding a vocabulary for site-specific performance." *New Theatre Quarterly* 20.4 (2004): 373–90.

Vergara, Camilo. *American Ruins*. New York: Monacelli, 1999.

Vidler, Anthony. *Warped Space: Art, Architecture, and Anxiety in Modern Culture*. Cambridge, Mass: MIT Press, 2000.

Wilkie, Fiona. "Mapping the Terrain. A Survey of Site-Specific Performance in Britain." *New Theatre Quarterly* 18.2 (2000): 140–60.

Notes on Contributors

bluemouth inc. is four artists trained in various disciplines, brought together by a common vision of sharing their training and forging a new language. Its goal is to reach beyond the boundaries of conventional performance practice to create site-specific interdisciplinary art that leads audiences and artists alike into new forms of play. bluemouth inc. is especially committed to furthering the growth of interdisciplinary art in Canada and the United States. As a not-for-profit performance collective, bluemouth inc. continues to explore formal issues related to site-specific work: compositional counterpoint between the properties of film, movement, sound design and spoken word; a temporal installation integrated within a challenging setting; and an ongoing adjustment of the relationship of the performance to the spectator (http://www.bluemouthinc.com).

Chris Brookes, founder of the Mummers Troupe, is currently a radio and television documentary-maker living in St. John's. He is a recipient of the Order of Canada, and his radio work won the 2006 Peabody Award.

David Burgess is a graduate of the B.F.A. program in Theatre (performance) from York University and the M.F.A. program in Drama (directing) from the University of Alberta. He is a teacher and writer living in Damascus, Ontario.

Shawna Dempsey and **Lorri Millan** have been collaborating full-time in a variety of media since 1989. They articulate their feminist and lesbian identity through the use of humour in their performance art, video, film, and bookworks. They have created a variety of characters that cleverly disrupt and challenge conventional representations of women, and their interventions in public spaces are as engaging as their stage work. Shawna and Lorri tour extensively, performing their work locally and internationally. Winnipeg is their chosen home.

Sean Dixon was best known in the 1990s for a play called *The Painting*, about a priapic man. He's best known in the Oughts for *Billy Nothin'*, about a cowboy in crisis. His latest is *The Gift of the Coat* and a novel called *The Girls Who Saw Everything*.

Alan Filewod is a Professor of Theatre Studies at the University of Guelph. His research fields are Canadian theatre cultures, political intervention theatre and subjunctive authenticity roleplay. He is the author of *Collective Encounters: Documentary Theatre in English Canada* (1987); *Performing Canada: The Nation Enacted in the Imagined Theatre* (2002); and, with David Watt, *Workers' Playtime: Theatre and Labour since 1970* (2001).

Jennifer Fisher is a founding member of the curatorial collaborative DisplayCult, which produced the exhibitions "CounterPoses" (1998), "Vital Signs" (2000), "Museopathy" (2001), and "Linda Montano: 14 Years of Living Art" (2002) among other projects. She is the editor of *Technologies of Intuition* (2006) and her essays have appeared in anthologies such as *The Senses in Performance* (2007) and *Image and Inscription* (2006), and such journals as *n.paradoxa* and *Public*. Currently, she is Assistant Professor of Contemporary Art and Curatorial Studies at York University.

Amiel Gladstone is the current Artistic Producer and a founding member of Victoria's Theatre SKAM. He directed much of the company's work over the first eleven years. As a playwright, his plays include *Hippies and Bolsheviks*, *The Wedding Pool*, and *The Black Box*. He divides his time between Victoria, Vancouver, the Caravan Farm and on tour.

Andrew Houston is a Views & Reviews Editor for the *Canadian Theatre Review* and a faculty member of the Department of Drama, Speech Communication and Digital Arts at the University of Waterloo. He is an Associate Artistic Director of Knowhere Productions, an interdisciplinary, site-specific performance company based in Regina, Saskatchewan.

Nigel Hunt is a writer, director and TV producer. He works for CBC TV. He was the founding Editor of *Theatrum: a theatre magazine*.

Kathleen Irwin is an Associate Professor of Scenography at the University of Regina. Her scenographic practice investigates places of memory and, through community-based collaboration, she creates events designed to refocus attention on defunct urban and industrial sites towards their cultural reuse and redevelopment.

Ric Knowles is a Professor of Theatre Studies at the University of Guelph and editor of the journals *Canadian Theatre Review* and (from 1999–2005) *Modern Drama*. He is author of *The Theatre of Form and the Production of Meaning*, *Shakespeare and Canada*; *Reading the Material Theatre*, and co-author (with the Cultural Memory Group) of *Remembering Women Murdered by Men*. He is editor of *Theatre in Atlantic Canada*, *Judith Thompson*, and *The Masks of Judith Thompson*, and co-editor (with Joanne Tompkins and W. B. Worthen) of *Modern Drama: Defining the Field* and (with Monique Mojica) of *Staging Coyote's Dream: An Anthology of First Nations Theatre in English*.

Kyo Maclear is an independent writer and editor based in Toronto. Her first book, *Beclouded Visions: Hiroshima-Nagasaki and the Art of Witness* (published by the State University of New York Press, 1999), addresses questions of historical memory and witnessing in twentieth century art. Her work has been published in several art and culture magazines, including *Toronto Life*, *Brick*, *Mix*, *Fuse* and *This Magazine*.

Steven O'Connell has a BFA in Modern Dance from Rutgers University and an MFA in Interdisciplinary Art from Simon Fraser University. From 1990 to 1997, he was Co-Artistic Director of Radix Theatre of Vancouver, a site-specific interdisciplinary performance collective. His collaborations include experimental films that have been screened at the Vancouver International Film Festival, the American Dance Festival, and the Moving Pictures Festival in Toronto. He is also a Co-Curator of FREE FALL and a Co-Artistic Director of bluemouth inc.

Richard Plant Long-time theatre scholar; Professor Emeritus, Queen's University (Kingston) and Graduate Centre for Study of Drama, University of Toronto, where he continues to teach Canadian theatre history and criticism. Honorary Fellow, Catherine Parr Traill College, Trent University. Honorary Life Member, Association for Canadian Theatre Research/Association de la recherche théâtrale au Canada. As well as being an intrepid cyclist, kayaker, and money-losing farmer, he recently appeared on the stage in productions by St James Players, the Lyric Stage, and Peterborough Theatre Guild, and has a role in 4th Line Theatre's forthcoming *Beautiful Lady, Tell Me.*

Sabrina Reeves graduated from Carnegie-Mellon University with a BFA in Drama. Upon graduation, she moved to New York, where she worked as an actor in film and theatre from 1990 to 1997 (some credits: *Big Night, The Misanthrope, My Children! My Africa!, Soul Food*). In 1997, she moved to Montreal, where she co-founded bluemouth inc. with Lucy Simic. Sabrina is also a professional photographer/videographer who contributed to the WarChild documentary: *Musicians in the War Zone* and directed the David Usher video *My Way Out.*

Natalie Rewa is the author of *Scenography in Canada: Selected Designers* (University of Toronto Press, 2004). She was an editor of *Canadian Theatre Review* from 1987 to 1995. She has published on design in *Canadian Theatre Review, Australasian Drama Studies* and *Tessera.* Her current research focuses on Michael Levine's production design for opera. She is Professor of Drama at Queen's University in Kingston. She is the co-curator of the Canadian exhibit for the Prague Quadrennial 2007.

Lucy Simic's particular area of interest is in the integration of text and movement. She has been creating performance pieces for close to ten years; in Vancouver as Co-Artistic Director of Radix Theatre; in Montreal as an independent artist, where she co-founded bluemouth inc. before moving to Toronto; in London, England, in collaboration with Woodenhead Works and Sirius Productions; and most recently, in New York. She has taught movement for actors and holds a degree in French, Dance and Mathematics from Simon Fraser University and an MFA in Playwriting from York University.

Andrew Templeton is a Vancouver-based writer and playwright who has had plays produced in both Canada and the UK, including *Portia, My Love* and *Howard Johnson Commits Suicide.* His latest play, *This Mortal Flesh* is scheduled for production in Vancouver during the 2007–2008 season.

Rachael Van Fossen is the Founding Artistic Director of Common Weal (1992–1999), a company acknowledged as a Canadian leader in community-engaged arts practices. In her four years as Artistic Director of Black Theatre Workshop (2001–2005) she successfully integrated community arts programming into the life of this Montreal professional theatre company. Rachael currently teaches as part-time faculty in the Theatre and Development specialization at Concordia University, a program for which she helped to develop the curriculum, and is completing an MFA in Interdisciplinary Arts at Goddard College in Vermont. In 2007 she is the Creative Director of a Teesri Duniya Theatre international exchange project in Theatre for Human Rights.

Kathryn Walter is a visual artist who uses a variety of media to consider the interface between visual art and social space. *Private Investigators: Masquerade and Public Space* is Kathryn's curatorial debut. This project continues her research on ways that artists access, interact with and disrupt public space. She has diversified her practice to include teaching and curating with an interest in working with others to build culture and local histories. She is currently living and working in Toronto.

Hildegard Westerkamp is an internationally recognized soundscape composer. She lectures on topics of listening, environmental sound and acoustic ecology, and she conducts soundscape workshops internationally. By focusing the ears' attention to details in the acoustic environment, her compositional work draws attention to the act of listening itself and to the inner, hidden spaces of the environment we inhabit. She is currently on the board of the World Forum for Acoustic Ecology and is a founding editor of the journal *Soundscape*. For more details see her website http://www.sfu.ca/~westerka.

Richard Windeyer (BMus, MFA) creates music, sound and visuals for experimental theatre, radio, film and integrated media projects. When not working with bluemouth inc., he collaborates with laptop trio FINGER and the Open Ears Music Festival and takes on the occasional solo project. His work has been heard across Canada, Europe, the UK and on the Internet.

Keren Zaiontz is a Ph.D. candidate at the Graduate Centre for Study of Drama, University of Toronto. In winter 2005, she conducted primary research on site-specific collective, bluemouth inc. Her current research focus is on how theatre companies use site-specific practices (in process or production) to enable performance of social agency and expand and reconfigure city-dweller identities.